S0-AHN-391

The Lorette Wilmot Library
and Media Center
Nazareth College of Rochester

DEMCO

Composers of North America

Series Editors: John Beckwith, William C. Loring, Jr.,
Margery M. Lowens, Martha Furman Schleifer

Series Note

This series, Composers of North America, is designed to focus attention on the development of art music and folk music from colonial times to the present. Few of our composers had their works performed frequently enough during their lifetimes to establish them in the standard repertoire of soloists, chamber groups, orchestras, or choruses. Their compositions, therefore, even when published, have often suffered undeserved neglect.

Each volume begins with the life and works of a given composer, placing that person in the context of the musical world of the period and providing comments by contemporary critics, and noting those compositions that today's listeners might enjoy. Each volume includes a catalog of the composer's works with publication details and locations of unpublished works.

The series will have served its purpose if it draws attention to the large body of work that has so long been treated with benign neglect. The editors firmly believe that a number of these compositions are worthy of being regularly performed today. They hope these works will be considered for performance by planners and conductors of concert programs and that performers will add some of these works to their repertoires.

John Beckwith, William C. Loring,
Margery M. Lowens, Martha Schleifer
Series Editors

Chou Wen-Chung

New York, 1982, portrait, after election to American Academy of Arts and Letters. Photo by Pach Bros., NY

Chou Wen-Chung

*The Life and Work of a Contemporary
Chinese-Born American Composer*

Peter M. Chang

Composers of North America, No. 25

THE SCARECROW PRESS, INC.
Lanham, Maryland • Toronto • Oxford
2006

DISCARDED
LORETTE WILMOT LIBRARY
NAZARETH COLLEGE

SCARECROW PRESS, INC.

Published in the United States of America
by Scarecrow Press, Inc.
A wholly owned subsidary of
The Rowman & Littlefield Publishing Group, Inc.
4501 Forbes Boulevard, Suite 200, Lanham, Maryland 20706
www.scarecrowpress.com

PO Box 317
Oxford
OX2 9RU, UK

Copyright © 2006 by Peter M. Chang

All rights reserved. No part of this publication may be reproduced, stored in a
retrieval system, or transmitted in any form or by any means, electronic, mechanical,
photocopying, recording, or otherwise, without the prior permission of the publisher.

British Library Cataloguing in Publication Information Available

Library of Congress Cataloging-in-Publication Data

Chang, Peter M.
   Chou Wen-Chung : the life and work of a contemporary Chinese-born American
composer / Peter M. Chang.
      p. cm. — (Composers of North America)
   Includes bibliographical references and index.
   ISBN-13: 978-0-8108-5296-9 (hardcover : alk. paper)
   ISBN-10: 0-8108-5296-9
   1. Chou, Wen-Chung, 1923—Criticism and interpretation. I. Title. II. Series.

ML410.C5416C43 2006
780'.92—dc22

2005022758

♾™ The paper used in this publication meets the minimum requirements of
American National Standard for Information Sciences—Permanence of Paper for
Printed Library Materials, ANSI/NISO Z39.48-1992.
Manufactured in the United States of America.

780.92
Cho
Cha

Contents

~

Illustrations

Examples

Figures

CHAPTER ONE

~

Prologue

Let the different traditions intermingle to bring forth a new mainstream that will integrate all musical concepts and practices into a vast expanse of musical currents. But let us also make sure that each individual culture will preserve its own uniqueness, its own poetry.—Chou Wen-Chung

Chou Wen-Chung's Position in Contemporary American Music

One of the hallmarks of twentieth-century music is the exploration and inclusion of non-Western compositional resources. With its beginning in Europe, this trend became markedly noticeable in America in the mid-twentieth century. Quite a few American avant-garde composers have tried to integrate Eastern elements in their works either by direct borrowing of melodic material or philosophical concepts. As a whole, these composers have challenged the American musical community to recognize cultural differences by finding the artistic values in this approach. A twentieth-century innovator, Chou Wen-Chung has not only answered this challenge with his intellectual depth and artistic quality in his moderate oeuvre of over thirty works, but also established himself as a champion of musical synthesis. His compositional approach has been especially influential to a generation of promising young composers in Asia and America.[1]

Chou came to America from China in 1946 to pursue his musical studies and spent the next several decades teaching, working, and advancing modern concepts in contemporary compositions. Drawing upon his rich Chinese cultural heritage while advancing the Varèsean experimental tradition, he has been responsible for the musical development in America and earned recognition as one of the prominent postwar-generation American composers.

In 1992, Brian Morton pointed out that "it is difficult to overestimate Chou Wen-Chung's importance," and his work "is of considerable significance in the slow rapprochement of Western and Eastern music in the second half of the twentieth century."[2] Glenn Waltkins, in his book *Soundings: Music in the Twentieth Century*, made a remark that Chou Wen-Chung was the first Chinese composer who, "with a Western audience in mind, attempted to put his native musical culture to account."[3] For the past several decades, composers, music critics, and scholars have appraised Chou's compositional approach, which is a successful example of fusing Varèsean ideas of sound as moving masses and organic matter and concepts of serialism and traditional Chinese ideas. Chou is also the first Chinese composer to be recognized in the West.[4] In assessing Chou's contribution to contemporary music in the West, music historians have different emphases. Wiley Hitchcock, for example, sees that Chou's contribution lies in promoting awareness of the organic nature of sound. Thus, Chou was among "many present-day American composers [who] are building a whole new musical aesthetic on an assumption of the potential vitality—in a literal sense—of sounds themselves."[5] Charles Hamm classifies Chou as an American avant-garde who is "an articulate spokesman for the incorporation of non-Western techniques into the compositions of American composers."[6] Chou's personal style is seen as a solution to the problem of musical fusion between Western and non-Western elements.

In the preface of their book *Contemporary Composers on Contemporary Music*, Elliot Schwartz and Barney Childs (1978) praise Chou's compositional approach as offering "a unique and fresh viewpoint"[7] in reference to the effort to fuse Eastern and Western musical languages by European and American composers.

More important, however, is the impact of Chou's approach to musical fusion of Western and Chinese sources on East Asian composers of the late 1970s and early 1980s. With success introducing traditional Chinese music in contemporary Western idiom for the West, Chou began to communicate with Chinese and other Asian composers about trends and techniques in contemporary Western music. His influence on post-Mao era compositions in China became a forceful current representing the need for liberalization and artistic freedom in the political, economic, and social reforms in the 1980s. His activities in initiating composers' forums, cultural exchanges, and in publishing articles on East-West musical confluence have promoted an observable growth of contemporary Asian works. This growth signifies Asian composers' increased consciousness in sharing compositional resources with their Western colleagues and in seeing a closer musical tie between the East and West.

Elements in Chou's Compositional Style

The Essence of Chinese Aesthetics in the Process of Cultivating Ya

In his book *The Way of the Pipa*, John Myers (1992) accurately identifies the concept of recurrence in Chinese aesthetics and points out that in Chinese fine arts, there is no revolutionary replacement of the older style or school by a new one. Instead, refinement and renewal of existing material has been the norm.[8] Specifically, using "preferred" subjects such as mountain peaks with flowing water, specific varieties of figures in painting such as gnarled pines and craggy rocks, and stock melodies in music have become quite common.

Another important aspect in Chinese aesthetics related to reaching the Confucian ideal of ya is the high value of an individual's versatility to cultivate several different subjects simultaneously. To compare the subjects and contents required by both Confucian tradition of the classical period (sixth century BC) and the intellectual tradition of the early Six Dynasties (third century AD), Kenneth Dewoskin wrote, "The superior men of classical times were masters of the six arts—the rites, music, archery, riding, writing, computation. The aesthetics of the early Six Dynasties were masters of the *qin*, poets, painters, calligraphers, and conversationalists."[9]

During the Ming period (1368–1644), the concept of ya was seen as the refinement of pleasure through the fusion of beauty, comfort, and lofty ideas. The literati or *wenren* cultivated leisurely enjoyment and abstract contemplation.[10] Therefore, a man with limited resources in arts or with only specialized knowledge in a given subject is viewed as merely an artisan, not a true gentleman scholar or *wenren*, in Chou's words.

These aesthetic views, together with Taoist sentiment, all found their way in Chou's expression and as underlying principles in Chou's creative composing. In a sense, on his way to cultivating ya, partly during his childhood in China and partly during his study in the United States, Chou learned a great deal about developing musical synthesis through Chinese classical poetry, music, calligraphy, painting, and concepts in Western contemporary music.

Influences of Varèse and Webern

Chou's handling of harmonic materials in his works during the 1950s was quartal harmony plus ornamental dissonance. Such an approach gave way to the verticalization of intervallic patterns of seconds and thirds in *Cursive* (1964), *Metaphors* (1961), and ultimately, *Pien* (1966), *Yun* (1969), *Echoes from the Gorge* (1989), and *Windswept Peaks* (1990). Unlike his teacher, Varèse, Chou hardly ever ventured into electronic medium. The Varèsean legacy for Chou was the conception of musical sound, not only as a media for artistic expression but also as a physical phenomenon that goes beyond cultural boundaries, thus redefining music as the combination of art and science. Chou succinctly summarizes what he learned from Varèse thus: "To think of sound as 'living' and musical space as 'open' was all that he [Varèse] taught."[11] Ultimately, the most important contribution Chou made in mediating Chinese and Western cultures through fusion was his discovery of conceptual compatibility in his reinterpretation of Varèsean concepts of sound in Chinese terms, which provided the basis for a set of Chinese aesthetics.

Chou's interest in Webern's sparse textural layout in spatial design allowed him to associate such a laconic style with the Chinese classical ink brush painting style, in which the expression is rendered by the most effective, yet most economic means.[12] In contrast to Western oil or water paintings, the Chinese style of each brush stroke, though often conventionalized, such as bamboo leaves, flowers, fish, or birds, marks the personal stock-in-trade of the artist.[13]

Chou reinterprets Webern's use of rests as the emphasis on blank spaces in Chinese ink brush painting and the individual tone as a living matter of Varèsean sound in Chinese terms. Chou's reliance on interpreting contemporary Western techniques in Chinese terms built up his inner strength and authority and expanded his inner resources in Chinese terms, as seen in explanatory notes for each of his compositions. Chou's emblem of ethnicity is built not merely on the use of Chinese melodic material, Chinese titles, and evocation in Chinese poetic images, but also on his confidence with Western techniques and his ability to use this technique to express Chinese aesthetic views toward the above matters.

Chou's Stylistic Development

The fusion of Chinese and Western elements in creating an organic synthesis is the unifying factor in Chou's style. Technically, a pattern of development can be detected in Chou's works. Direct borrowing of Chinese melodies, which were recycled in his works up to 1957 and even as late as 1965, was replaced by the concept of "composing with intervallic patterns," which has been essential to Western serial music. The results of such a concept can be seen in works of the 1960s and up to the 1990s. Yet, both were overshadowed by the Chinese emphasis on timbre, especially in *qin* music. The poetic association of Chinese programmatic titles and evoked imageries are basically retained but with modifications in the direction of abstraction, that is, reverberation in nature and transformation. The flexible and prosodic characters of the phrase structure and mood changes in Chou's early works, such as *Landscapes* (1949), *All in the Spring Wind* (1952–1953), and *And the Fallen Petals* (1954), approximate such characters in Chinese poetry. The interest in the approximation of Chinese instrument sounds by means of Western instruments is evident in *Willows Are New* (1957) and *Yu ko* (1965), a learning process in which Chou experimented with the Chinese concepts of control, articulation, and the resulting textural and structural formation appears to be transformed and deepened in Chou's later works. However, as the result of the emphases on structural fluidity and the interrelationships between texture, timbre, and horizontal motion, the additive rhythmic features and fluidity of tempo and form that appeared as early as Chou's two masterpieces, *All in the Spring Wind* and *And the Fallen Petals*, are brought back in the works of the 1960s, 1980s, and 1990s with increased sophistication. On his quest for a true understanding of musical resources, Chinese as well as Western, Chou never stopped probing, questioning, and analyzing, even those resources he already knew.

External Factors Contributing to Chou's Success in the West

"Theoretical Composition"

The increased interest in non-Western musical sources among academic composers of the 1990s in the United States, though partly due to the influence of Colin McPhee, Lou Harrison, Harry Partch, Henry Cowell, Alan Hovhaness, and John Cage, is the result of acculturation of Western composers as well as non-Western composers. Western fascination with exotic or non-Western music goes back to late eighteenth and nineteenth centuries when artists and their public alike were very much under the spell of romantic ethos of the time. Instead of pure musical interest, attention was increasingly paid to the thoughts behind the composition. In fact, a composition had become a facade and ideological statement of its creator. Thus, in order to grasp its essence, the audience had to know the composer's thoughts and intentions, which were given as program notes. This tradition has been revived, especially after World War II. Not only is a composition attached with a program, but detailed technical direction for the performers are specified. The gap between academic composers and general audiences widened because of audiences' unfamiliarity with the vocabulary of contemporary music. Composers, especially of the postwar generation, including Chou, felt the need to minimize the consequence of such a gap by revealing these "theories" on which their compositions were built. In observing this tendency, Benjamin Boretz and Edward T. Cone have characterized the fad as "an age of theoretical composition."[14]

The issue was not the concerns of composers for the adequacy of their "theoretical explanations" for their compositional approaches but their ideological positions behind their theories. After emerging from silence during the post–World War I years, Varèse used his alliance with physics to define music as crystallized human intelligence in sound, and he described sound as a moving mass. Chou inherited from Varèse the notion that composing is a process of unfolding composers' ideological concepts, whether it is the emphasis on elevating timbre or the argument that a musical composition is analogous to the ink flow in a Chinese calligraphy.

Explorations in Using Non-Western Material for Contemporary Works

Concurrent with "theoretical composition," however, was the need for musical material as well as inspiration from non-European sources. Studying non-Western music has been a fad among the postwar academic composers. Pierre Boulez, as part of the trend, voiced the basic concerns of the postwar generation of Western composers and their need for new resources.[15] Although Hollywood produced many war movies with oriental-flavored scores during World War II, no serious attention was given to writing contemporary Western works with Chinese material after the war. There had been a dearth in authentic Chinese work, which would please the Western audience in the meantime, and the renewed interest in Chinese arts lasted only briefly during the early 1950s. With his understanding of Western taste and shrewd choice of Chinese material in launching his first work, *Landscapes* (1949, premiered in 1953), Chou anticipated and captured Western fascination with classical Chinese arts, painting, and poetry, although music was not as well appreciated as the other Chinese arts.

Connections with Influential Persons and Organizations

In promoting Chou's music, Nicolas Slonimsky played an important role. Slonimsky encouraged Chou to deepen his understanding not only in Chinese music but also in other art forms. This emphasis prevented Chou from falling into the trap of the trite pseudo-oriental approach in which superficial imposition of Western harmony on Chinese melody was a distinct feature. From Slonimsky, Chou learned that in order to preserve and ensure the survival of an ancient art, he had to make himself a carrier, an insider, and a voice of this tradition in the modern world. Chou's association with several important organizations also helped him disseminate his works and advance his career, including the American Composers' Alliance, Composers' Recording Company, and C. F. Peters Publishing Company. Through the *American Composers' Alliance Bulletin*, the newsletter of the organization, Slonimsky introduced Chou's life and works. This work promoted awareness of and interest in Chou's approach among his colleagues and the interested public.

Colin McPhee was another important person who helped Chou to advance his career. In their first meeting in 1949, shortly after Chou's arrival in New York, McPhee recommended that Chou study with Varèse instead of Cowell and that he contact Stokowski for performing his music.[16] An exponent of contemporary music, Stokowski had already become interested in East-West musical fusions in the early 1950s.[17]

Even before the war in the 1930s, there had been organizations actively promoting new music and international exchange between Western and non-Western cultures. The New York–based Polyhymnia was such an example on whose technical and advisory board Colin McPhee had served.[18] Lazare Saminsky, a Russian-American composer and conductor, was an advocator of fusing oriental and Western traditions. Such a tendency was not only seen in his own music, which fuses Hebrew and western European elements, but also in his writings: "This new and triumphant cortege of the musical East, augurates [sic] a real return to our common racial spring, heralds a reunion of the musical creeds, a tonal merging of the Orient and the Occident."[19] Such an enthusiasm for exotics did not cool off; it had been rekindled by contact with Southeast Asian countries during World War II and persisted well after the war.

After hearing Chou's *Landscapes*, performed by the Chicago Symphony Orchestra with Fritz Reiner conducting, Alexander Tcherepen strongly encouraged Chou to talk to Walter Hinrichsen, who was the publisher of C. F. Peters. Hinrichsen became especially interested in Chou's works and began publish Chou's scores after 1959. In the late 1950s, Composers' Recording Company had issued an album containing one of Chou's works, *Landscapes* (1949).[20] Another album containing four of Chou's works was released in 1970, again by CRI.[21] Articles on the performance of Chou's music began to appear in American newspapers in the mid-1950s. During this time Chou received two commissions from Robert Whitney of Louisville Orchestra. Fritz

Reiner of Chicago Symphony and Stokowski helped inform the public about Chou's ideas for fusing Chinese aesthetics and certain musical elements with contemporary techniques. The dissemination of Chou's style and works worldwide was expedited by performances of his works by prestigious American, European, and Japanese orchestras such as the New York Philharmonic Orchestra (*Petals* 1961), Philadelphia Orchestra (*Petals* 1960), Chicago Symphony Orchestra (*Landscapes* 1959), San Francisco Symphony (*Landscapes* 1953), Berlin Philharmonic Orchestra (*Petals* 1960), Japan Philharmonic Orchestra (*Petals* 1959), *Orchestre Nationale*, Paris (*Petals* 1963), and two European tours (1960, 1963). By the early 1960s, Chou's cross-cultural approach to composition and his position as an original creative artist among contemporary Western composers was widely recognized and firmly established. Chou was seen not only as a successful representative of East-West musical fusion but also as the initiator of a new strand of exoticism.[22]

Notes

1. Chen Yi (b. 1953), Zhou Long (b. 1953), Bright Sheng (b. 1955), and Tan Dun (b. 1957) are among many of Chou's successful students actively teaching and composing in the United States.

2. Brian Morton and Pamela Collins, eds., *Contemporary Composers* (Chicago: St. James Press, 1992), 181.

3. Glenn Waltkins, *Soundings: Music in the Twentieth Century* (New York: Schirmer Books, 1988), 33.

4. Eric Salzman, *Twentieth Century Music: An Introduction*, 2nd ed. (Englewood Cliffs, N.J.: Prentice-Hall, 1974), 165. There are numerous similar acclaims in published and unpublished materials.

5. Wiley Hitchcock, *Music in the United States: A Historical Introduction*, 2nd ed. (Englewood Cliffs, N.J.: Prentice-Hall, 1974), 274.

6. Charles Hamm, *Music in the New World* (New York: W. W. Norton, 1983), 612.

7. Elliot Schwartz and Barney Childs, eds., *Contemporary Composers on Contemporary Music* (New York: Da Capo Press, 1978), 308.

8. John Myers, *The Way of the Pipa* (Kent, Ohio: Kent State University Press, 1992), 35.

9. Kenneth Dewoskin, *Song for One or Two: Music and Concept of Art in Early China*, Michigan Papers in Chinese Studies No. 42 (Ann Arbor, Mich.: Center for Chinese Studies, University of Michigan, 1982), 158.

10. Robert Hans Van Gulik, *The Lore of the Chinese Lute* (Tokyo: Sophia University, 1968), 166–67.

11. Wen-Chung Chou, "Varèse: A Sketch of the Man and His Music," *Musical Quarterly* 52, no. 2 (1966): 168.

12. For comments on Chou's "pointalistic" style, see Harold Schoenberg's review of the October 8, 1955 Louisville concert, *New York Times*, October 10, 1955.

13. For more discussion on Chinese ink brush painting style, see Li-Pu Wu's *Zhong Guo Guo Hua Lun [The Chinese Classical Painting Styles]* (Beijing: Beijing University Press, 1985).

14. Benjamin Boretz and Edward T. Cone, eds., *Perspectives on Contemporary Music Theory* (New York: Norton, 1972), vii.

15. Pierre Boulez, "Dire, Jouer, Chanter," in *La Musique et ses Problèmes Contemporains 1953–1963* (Paris: n.p., 1963), 317; quoted by János Kárpáti, in "Non-European Influence on Occidental Music (A Historical Survey)," *The World of Music* 22, no. 2 (1990): 20–35.

16. Carol Oja, *Colin McPhee: A Composer in Two Worlds* (Washington, D.C.: Smithsonian Institution Press, 1990), 202.

17. Oliver Daniel, *Stokowski: A Counterpoint of View* (New York: Dodd, Mead & Co., 1982), 659.

18. Other forces promoting new music in New York during the 1930s were International Composers' Guild, the League of Composers, Pan-American Association for Composers (founded by Henry Cowell in 1931), and the Cos Cob Press for publishing scores of new works, and so forth.

19. Lazare Saminsky, *Music of Our Day: Essentials and Prophecies* (New York: Thomas Y. Crowell Co., 1932), 81–83.

20. The album is cataloged as CRI-122, which also included works by Irwin Fischer and Robert Nagel. According to Chou, his *And the Fallen Petals* was released on Columbia Records soon after its premiere with Louisville Orchestra in 1955.

21. Arthur Cohn, "Very Special: The Music of Chou Wen-Chung," *American Record Guide* 36 (September–August 1969–1970): 886–87.

22. Ross Parmenter, "Stokowski Conducts Contemporary Works," *New York Times*, December 4, 1958; Edward Downes, "Work by Chinese Has Its Premiere," *New York Times*, February 4, 1957; and Lester Trimble, "Composers, Conductors," *New York Herald Tribune*, January 25, 1954.

CHAPTER TWO

⌒

A Biographic Sketch of Chou Wen-Chung

The Chou Family (1890s–1927)

Chou Wen-Chung was born on July 28,[1] 1923, in Chefoo or Yantai (a port city on the northern coast of Shandong province), China, to an extraordinary intellectual family whose members are the heirs of Chou Dun-Yi (1017–1073 AD), the most important philosopher of the Song Dynasty (960–1279 AD). Chou Dun-Yi was the founder of the so-called neo-Confucianism, which synthesized the elements of Taoist (especially *I-Ching*), Buddhist doctrines, and Confucian ethics with metaphysics that had become the dominant mode of thought in China for nearly 1,000 years. The Chou family had been in Wocuo Bu (near Changzhou, Jiangsu province) for generations, ever since the philosopher had settled in the Changzhou area. According to the 1879 revised edition of the 1642 Chou family genealogical record (Changzhou branch), Chou's family line is linked without a gap to Chou Dun-Yi.[2] However, beyond Chou Dun-Yi, the 1642 edition had traced the history of the Chou family back to the youngest son of King Ping (eighth century BC) of the Chou Dynasty. Chou's family had three sons; Chou was the second youngest in addition to two younger sisters. Besides the Chou clan, the other largest clan in the area included the Wu families.

One thing that motivated Chinese families to educate their sons was the idea of acquiring governmental positions and wealth through obtaining academic titles at the civil-service examination.[3] Even to qualify for the exam, a promising scholar must spend years at a school or with a private tutor to

11

solidly master all the Chinese history, classical philosophy, literature and poetry, and to demonstrate attainment in these areas by completing treatises and composing poetic essays[4] in a matter of hours. With a deep intellectual family tradition, Chou's grandfather, Chou Xue-Qiao (1870–1910),[5] born in Changzhou, surpassed many aspiring young men of his generation and did not have to take the local civil-service exam since he was recommended, based on his superior scholastic aptitude, as a *Bing Gung Sheng*, the scholarly title for the highest degree candidate to study at the Imperial Academy in Beijing.[6] At the time of graduation, the candidate could either take the *Jin Shi* exam, the highest level civil-service exam held at Beijing for more prominent government jobs, or directly accept a government job offer. Chou Xue-Qiao was resentful of the Manchus and neither took the exam nor became an official. Instead, he remained mostly in his community, performing various services to the local residents, often acting as an elder and an adjuster to settle disputes. In his eyes, the late Manchu government had grown increasingly impotent and rampantly corrupt, while the country had suffered humiliating military defeat by the Western powers. With Western military and diplomatic pressure, the Manchu government made considerable concessions in allowing the Western powers to lease Hong Kong, Macau, and other port cities and territories. The country was virtually bankrupt for paying heavy indemnities to the Western nations. More disturbing was the fact that between mid-September 1894 and early January 1895, the Chinese Navy was completely destroyed by the Japanese in less than four months in two decisive battles; the major event that followed was a feeding frenzy to divide China into "spheres of interest" by Japan, Germany, Russia, France, and England.

Chou Xue-Qiao was shaken by these facts, which sharply contradicted the traditional Chinese belief that Chinese culture was superior to those of the foreigners. Lamenting on China's weakness, he worked on a novel, *Cang Sang Ji* [Lamenting the End of Time] on which he spent many years. While the novel exposed the rotten foundations of the late Ming Dynasty (1368–1644), it was, in fact, an indirect condemnation of the era. An open criticism of the Manchu government would have resulted in death by decapitation. Chou Xue-Qiao completed 116 chapters and planned to write four more, but was unable to finish them before his death. The novel was published as a series in a literary journal in the city of Tianjin, but the manuscript was lost.

Still, the Chinese intellectuals were compelled to find answers for the apparent contradictions.[7] They enthusiastically debated cultural reform issues by comparing Chinese and Western cultures and then moved on to political actions. With the support of the reform-minded emperor, Guang Xu (1871–1908), the reformers had begun to establish governmental administrations to promote industrialization; to adopt Western school system; to trim government bureaucracy; to abolish *Ba Gu Wen*, or archaic writing style, in everyday communication; and to encourage freedom of press and association. These men saw the future of China in the adaptation of Western science and technology and, to a lesser degree, Western-style democracy, and Chou Xue-Qiao was sympathetic to these ideas, in addition to being a friend of Kang Yu-Wei, the mentor of the leading reformers. Unfortunately, the so-called "Hundred Days of Reform" (from June to September 1898) came to an abrupt end with a bloody suppression by the infamous Empress Dowager (1835–1908) who orchestrated a coup d'état to oust the emperor and ordered the executions, by decapitation, of six leading reformers. While being hunted down, Kang Yu-Wei decided, unlike his protégés who wanted to become martyrs, to run for his life and got help from the foreigners to hide in a boat and escape to Japan.

For modernizing a country by adapting Western culture, Japan was looked upon by the reformers not only as a successful model to emulate but also as a major source of information. To inform the public, the reformers such as Kang You-Wei and Huang Zun-Xian and many others wrote books about Japan's success. According to Chou, his grandfather's reading sources on Western culture probably came from Japan.[8] Fascinated by the Western ideals, Chou's grandfather wrote yet another book to introduce Western civilization to Chinese readers. He also published a large number of Lin Qing-Nan's translations of classic Western literary books in the classical Chinese language, which opened a window for Chou to see the West. Chou's grandfather studied Western history seriously and published two volumes of the *Outlines of the History of the West* in 1902.[9] He was not only known for his knowledge in Western studies but also for his knowledge of medical science. He established the Chinese Association of Medical Science, the first medical society in China, and the *Journal on Medical Science*, which began in 1904 in Shanghai and was widely distributed to sixteen provinces and cities as well as to Hong Kong and Japan. He published 154 volumes with various monthly and quarterly editions.[10] Chou Xue-Qiao was invited to become the provost of the Shan Xi Medical College. He resigned in 1908 and lived in Beijing before returning to Shanghai. He died in 1910.[11] Chou Xue-Qiao was among the very first to advocate the synthesis of Western and Chinese medical sciences. He used to say,

> For medical treatment, I would advocate the use of Western equipment. For prescriptions, I would advocate the use of Chinese traditional prescriptions. Whenever there is an emergency, where Chinese medicine does not serve the purpose, Western medicine should be used.[12]

He also financially sponsored one of his students, Ding Fu-Bao, who became a renowned physician in China, to study Western medicine. Now, historical circumstances afforded Chou Xue-Qiao an opportunity to experience his own tradition with a new Western perspective, and he became an advocate of a cultural synthesis that would combine the best of both cultures.

Chou's father, Chou Miao or Chou Zhong-Jie (1891–1987), was brought up when China was contiguously experiencing a period of extreme political instability and violent cultural clash, a period during which the nation was struggling to modernize itself while trying to preserve its cultural heritage. The frustration with China's subservient international position developed into an inferior complex in the Chinese psyche, appropriately termed *chung yang*, or having a blind faith in things from the West; there were sustained debates as to whether the traditional Chinese way of life had degenerated, and the only way to rejuvenate Confucian China was to reform Chinese society completely with scientific Western ideas.[13] At the age of twenty, influenced by his father and because of his beliefs in reform, Chou Miao participated in the 1911 revolution, which was to overthrow the Manchu or Qing Dynasty (1644–1911) and establish a new republic.[14]

The very essence of a republic inevitably conflicted with the deep-rooted Confucian literary and philosophical ideals for the Chinese society. Between 1915 and 1919, there was a new literary movement to promote Western-style science, democracy, and a nontraditional literary style, while denouncing the Confucian ethics as shackles to prevent China from becoming a modern nation. The call for the real cultural and literary revolution came on May 4, 1919, on the heel of the Paris Conference, convened three months earlier, when China's demand to recover foreigner-controlled territories was ignored. The Chinese were humiliated yet again. More than 3,000 Chinese students and teachers staged demonstrations and forums to protest against imperialism and their government's compromise in this matter. The May-fourth movement signified the awakening of Chinese intellectuals and youth who were to become the driving force in this revolution, promoting Western science, liberalism, and modernism. The May-fourth movement had made a decisive impact on dragging China out of isolation and imposing modern ideas on Chinese society.

As the second generation of the new intelligentsia, Chou Miao was versed in Chinese poetry and classics while also interested in Western science, particularly in medicine. Still a teenager, he assisted his father with lectures and publications for his father's Medical Society in which he was a member. He graduated at the top of his class at Longmen Shuyuan in Suzhou, a city just east of Changzhou. Longmen Shuyuan was a famous traditional Chinese academy, which would be equivalent to a college, before China's adoption of the modern education system.[15] Following graduation, he spent several years working as a teacher and served as the headmaster of the Longmen Elementary School where he taught various subjects including music. In addition to his knowledge of Chinese classical literature and poetry, he was also interested in astrology, fortune–telling, and physiognomy and mastered the principles of another Chinese classic, the I-Ching, or the Book of Changes.[16] An eloquent speaker, he became known as "iron-mouthed Chou" among his friends. Chou later recalled that he regretted the fact that, as a child he did not benefit from his father's deep knowledge of the I-Ching.

After the Revolution, he studied economics in Beijing and then secured jobs in the government[17] in Taiyuan (Shan Xi province) and later Qingdao and Yantai (Shandong province), where Chou was born. At Yantai, he was responsible for setting up custom offices at the ports, an area that was controlled by Westerners, especially the British several decades earlier. He was also in charge of several custom offices as well as the Overseas Chinese Affairs Offices in Shandong Province. When his family left Yantai for Qingdao in 1927, Chou was only four years old. Qingdao or Tsingtao, a seaport city, is only about one hundred miles southwest of Yantai. Under an unequal treaty with Germany, the city was leased to the Germans for many years and has been known for its resort beaches and hilly scenic sites, besides its famous beer. In Qingdao, Chou's father was a leading figure in the city and was an important member of a board for overseeing operations of the two important railroads: the Beijing-Nanjing line and Beijing-Wuhan line. In Qingdao, the family lived in a traditional Chinese courtyard house with servants' quarters. Chou could still remember this place with two of his boyhood experiences with music. One afternoon, he was playing outside the house and heard music coming out of the servants' quarters. He followed the sound and saw servants enjoying themselves by singing and playing the bamboo flute while eating peanuts and drinking alcohol, which was made from sorghum. A woman was singing to her male friends' flute accompaniment. The sound of the flute and smell of the alcohol left a lasting impression. Another experience was that although cars were still rare during this time in China, his father had one. He remembers that the pedals inside the car moving up and down were very much like those of the harmonium, and he had opportunities to go to his family friend's house to play the instrument. Playing with the pedals, which could change the sound from loud to soft and vise versa fascinated him.

As a young child, Chou was familiar with famous Western fairy tales, since his father often bought the Chinese translations of these books for him from business trips to Shanghai and other big cities.

Domestic Turmoil and Travel (1927–1937)

More traveling to the south immediately followed the family's departure from Qingdao. Between 1929 and 1933 the family was in Hankou, an industrial city in Hubei province, and between 1932 and 1937 in Nanjing, the capital of the republic in the Jiangsu province and the political and cultural center of the country. The two cities are separated by the Yangtze River with Nanjing on the south bank and Hankou on the north, west of Nanjing. In the city of Hankou, there was an enclave on the riverfront with business offices and shops rented by Westerners. Through frequent visits, Chou had an opportunity to glimpse the Western way of life. And it was also in this commercial district, during the winter break, that Chou and his elder brother bought a child-sized violin. The boys were fascinated by it. They initially thought that it was a toy and later realized that it was a real instrument. While in Hankou, Chou's eldest brother first took some violin lessons and then became Chou's teacher.

Concentrated violin study did not come about until the Chou family moved to Nanjing, where Chou attended the Jinling Junior Middle School (equivalent of eighth grade), the training school for the famous Jinling Women's College, which was founded and operated by American missionaries. The curriculum included Chinese history and literature, archaic Chinese language, as well as courses of Western civilization and modern sciences taught in English. At school, Chou and his two brothers studied Western instruments. His eldest brother, Wen-Tsing, played violin; his other brother, Wen-Ho, who was two years older than him, played flute and trumpet in the school band and the school's Chinese orchestra. Chou studied violin and *erhu* (a two-stringed Chinese fiddle) and tried to emulate his second brother by dabbling in the harmonica, mandolin, *xiao* (a vertical Chinese flute), and the musical saw.

A curious youth, Chou often marveled at the wonders of nature. He would lie on the lawn and gaze at the clouds to see how they intermingle and transform. His father caught him once and scolded him for being lazy. This was unfair because he was experiencing the artistic inspiration for Chinese painters and calligraphers, he later realized. In 1937, the Chou family moved again from Nanjing to Shanghai when the Sino-Japanese War broke out. On August 13, 1937, with 300,000 troops, the Japanese army forcefully attacked Shanghai and marched into the city in early November.[18] Exactly four months later, the Japanese army captured Nanjing and massacred nearly 300,000 residents and prisoners of war, known as the infamous "Nanjing Massacre."

In Shanghai, the family lived in the international settlement zones, which were relatively safer than other parts of the city since they were leased to Western diplomats and businessmen. However, as a result of the Japanese biological warfare, Chou and his two brothers contracted typhoid fever. Wen-Ho, Chou's second older brother for whom he had the fondest memories, died. Chou had a severe case but survived, and his younger brother also survived with only a mild case. During this time, the family often traveled between the estate in Changzhou and Shanghai. For years, the Chou family had been patrons for the maintenance of Qingliang Si, a local temple in Changzhou area. Chou still remembers part of his childhood spent in Changzhou, especially at the temple attending his grandmother's funeral at which the chanting, the sound of the processional percussion band, the vivid colors of the monks' robes, and the flowers on the wreath in front of the coffin impressed him.

By 1937, when the Chou family arrived in Shanghai, the cultural life of the city was already cosmopolitan in its outlook after nearly a century of transforming the indigenous culture due to Western impact. Shanghai was known both in the East and the West as the "paradise of the adventurers," and it had attracted a large number of foreign immigrants. Except for a few Asian countries like India, Japan, and the Philippines, these foreigners came mainly from Europe and America across a wide social spectrum from adventurous capitalists and business men to policemen, ordinary workers, and musicians who came from Italy, Austria, Germany, and Russia. White Russians had left their country before and during the revolution two decades ago. There were also European Jewish musicians. Many came to Shanghai to avoid the Nazi persecution shortly after Hitler became the chancellor of Germany, and many came while the war was imminent. Chou remembers the scene vividly: "Shanghai then was full of refugee musicians from Europe as well as white Russians and Italians, and as a result, the music making was highly advanced, diverse, and of superior quality."[19]

Western music, whether it is jazz, popular songs, or classical, became more accessible to the music-loving citizens than ever before. The taste for Western music had become an emblem for cultural sophistication and prestige to be cultivated among the college students and the members of the middle and upper classes.

Musical organizations and institutions played an important role for nurturing the musical life of the city. There were foreign resident, amateur theatrical groups, church choirs, choral societies, and the Shanghai Conservatory's chorus.[20] R. B. Hurry, who, during the 1920s, was the music director of a British church in Shanghai, reported that a traveling Russian opera group had toured Shanghai and performed eighteen different operas such as *Carmen, Aida, Tosca, The Barber of Seville, Faust, Madame Butterfly, Rigoletto, Boris Godounov*, and so forth, in a month.[21]

Shanghai maintained a professional Western orchestra, called the Shanghai Gongbuju Orchestra, or Shanghai Municipal Orchestra, transformed from a wind ensemble in 1881 by the administration of the international settlement for the purpose of entertaining its residents. The administration was a foreign residents, self-governing body. Its board members were mostly British. Since 1919, Mario Paci (1878–1946), the Italian pianist and conductor of the Shanghai Gongbuju Orchestra, had traveled to Italy, Germany, Austria, and Russia to recruit musicians. By 1927, the orchestra had only one Chinese musician (the violinist, Tan Shu-Zhen), but not until 1935 were Zhang Zhen-Fu and other four provisional Chinese musicians accepted.[22] The artistic quality and performing level of the orchestra was high, and it had earned an international reputation as "number one in the Far East." Between the 1920s and 1930s Shanghai hosted an array of world-renowned musicians such as violinists, Fritz Kreisler, Jascha Heifitz, Josef Szigeti, Efrem Zimbalist, Jacques Thibaud, and Mischa Elman; cellists, Gregor Piatigorsky and Emanuel Feuerman; pianists, Arthur Rubinstein, Alexander Tcherepnine, Leopold Godowsky, and Lili Kraus; and vocalists, Feodor Chaliapin, Mabel Garrison, Amelita Galli-Gurci, and John McCormack; and so forth.[23] Among these, several performed with the orchestra.

Other than regular weekend concerts, the orchestra also offered outdoor, special, and children's concerts. Although works of Chinese composers such as Huang Zi and Sha Mei were occasionally included in the programs, such occasions were rare.[24] The orchestra's repertoire included primarily eighteenth- and nineteenth-century works. However, some twentieth-century works such as Debussy's *Prelude to the Afternoon of a Faun* and *Nocturnes*, Stravinsky's *Firebird Suite*, and Ravel's *Le Tombeau de Couperin* and *Mother Goose Suite* were also performed.[25] Chou recalls that, in Shanghai, he heard live performances of the works by Stravinsky, Bloch, Ravel, and other contemporary Western composers, and he still remembers the mourning of the death of Ravel shortly after arriving in Shanghai.

A major impetus for musicians in Shanghai to get acquainted with masterpieces of twentieth-century Western composers came from the activities of the Russian composer, Alexander Tcherepnine, who arrived in Shanghai in 1934 and gave lectures at the Shanghai Conservatory, encouraging Chinese composers to break away from mixing Chinese melody with nineteenth-century Western harmony by studying the works of contemporary composers such as Debussy, Stravinsky, and Schoenberg.[26]

Chou began to take violin lessons from Chen You-Xin[27] and then from Xu Wei-Ling.[28] Both Chen and Xu were members of the Shanghai Municipal Orchestra. Chou also took theory lessons, including modal harmony, form, and orchestration, from an Italian cellist (also a member of the Shanghai Municipal Orchestra) soon after his family arrived in Shanghai. Chou's brother studied violin with Wittenberg, a former concertmaster under Richard Strauss. Chou's father was generous in spending money on records and sheet music, and Chou's collection of records by famous violinists grew. Chou became increasingly serious about studying music and learning to play the violin. He also experienced an urge to compose by recreating the acoustic effects of a food vender's song as the vendor approached and passed the window late at night when Chou was preparing for an exam. He later recalls that this aural experience was important because it allowed him to hear changes in pitch, tempo, and dynamics. By now, the Chou family had grown to include seven children, all of whom were studying Western musical instruments. The family also found a new event, family chamber music recitals, for which Chou arranged some of Mozart's vocal scores for one of his sisters who was playing in a piano trio.

Chou entered high school when he arrived at Shanghai and graduated in the spring of 1941. Meanwhile, as a part-time music student, he also enrolled at Shanghai Yinyue Guan, or the Shanghai Music School, which was founded by Ding Shande and Chen Yu-Xin—professors at the National Shanghai Conservatory—since the conservatory itself was taken over by the puppet government set up by the Japanese.[29] Although Chou already spent more time practicing the violin than schoolwork, he was still dissatisfied with his progress in music. He contemplated seeking the best musical instruction abroad, either in Europe or America. This idea met with his father's disapproval as impractical daydreaming and a waste of time. His father's opposition to the idea of pursuing music in college was again brought up when he was about to graduate from high school and trying to select a subject of study for college. Although Chou's mother, Fu Shou-Xian (1895–1986), was sympathetic to her son's needs, she tried to convince her son that for him playing music could only be a hobby, not a profession, since, traditionally, professional musicians were looked down on as social outcasts. Like most Chinese intellectuals of his generation, Chou's father had faith in Western science, and he was quite patriotic. He believed that, now, China was being invaded again, encouraging his son to study science and technology as the only way to help the country, especially during the war with Japan. Chou followed his father's advice; he did not choose music. Instead, he decided to study architecture. He later regretted this decision. According to Chou, the only person who believed that he could excel in music was his family friend, Mrs. Zhu Jin-Nong, wife of the vice minister of education. After graduating from high school, Chou entered the civil engineering/architecture department at St. John's University in the fall of 1941. Chou chose St. John's because it was the only college in Shanghai that offered engineering with an architecture component. Chou thought architecture was a compromise between art and engineering due to the influence of British art and social critic John Ruskin (1819–1900), who considered architecture "frozen music."

With the escalation of the war, even the International Settlement Zone in Shanghai was no longer safe. The Japanese troops had encircled the Zone and were about to occupy it. The smell of the war began to permeate in the Zone, and the war suddenly became very real. On November 14, 1941, the U.S. government finally pulled out their marines from Peking, Tianjin, and Shanghai and advised the U.S. nationals to leave Shanghai.[30] In December, almost immediately after the bombing of Pearl Harbor, Chou personally witnessed the Japanese army march into the international settlement zone. It was time to leave Shanghai.

Escalation of the War and Journey to the Southwest (1941–1945)

The Chou family was already separated before the international settlement zone in Shanghai fell to the conquerors. His father, a high government official, left the city and traveled with the retreating government. His eldest brother was on his way to the United States to study at MIT in Boston. Left behind were Chou and his mother with his younger siblings. Chou wanted to help his mother but couldn't bear the fact of living under Japanese occupation. As his mother heard the news that the Japanese were planning to round up teenagers to work for the Japanese army, she urged Chou to leave.

Chou traveled with a group of young people led by the father of Zhang Wenjin (the Chinese ambassador to the United States in the 1980s). The group went southward on an armed junk taking off from the Zhoushan Islands and sailed along the coast to the port of Sanmen (Zhejiang Province, between Ningbo and Wenzhou). The trip was dangerous. The junk the group was on had evaded the enemy warships, repelled a pirate ship, and navigated through a typhoon. From Sanmen, Chou traveled westward and then southwestward to Leiyang (Hunan Province, between Hengyang and Chenzhou), about 500 kilometers. Because of the high elevation and rugged terrain, most of the journey was on foot. There was a close encounter with Japanese soldiers who were dispatched especially to capture the group. One night, Chou was with his group hiding in a small inn. Everyone was scared when news came that Japanese soldiers were searching for them in the vicinity, and everyone started to run by climbing over the backyard wall, which was connected to a restaurant next door. In the restaurant, there was a raucous wedding party that provided a cover for Chou and his group. Chou later found that several women in the other room of the same inn were raped, and men were taken away and shot. Behind the enemy lines, Chou walked and hitchhiked all the way to Leiyang, where he met with his father who, as a high administrator, had been there for some time. He finally reached Guilin (about 100 kilometers southwest of Leiyang) in early 1942.

Guilin, a small city, was known for its scenic surroundings and for tourism. During wartime, Guilin accommodated waves of refugees, many government offices, and schools from the coastal and other Japanese-occupied regions. The famous U.S. "Flying Tiger" squadron was once stationed in Guilin. Unlike Shanghai, the bucolic tranquility seemed detached from the cruel reality of the war, which was going on in most of the central and eastern parts of the country.

In Guilin, Chou entered Guangxi (Kwang Si) University as an engineering student. The university was situated in a rundown garden, which used to be the villa of an imperial governor, just outside of Guilin. As realized in his routine practice of the violin, Chou's love of music sustained his energy, despite his busy studying schedule. He practiced on the tops of hills and nailed the music to trees for music stands. In addition to practicing the violin, Chou discovered that in the university library there was a large collection of donated books in Western languages, mostly in English, which occupied the whole floor, on various subjects including some of his favorites: history, literature, music, culture, and architecture. He often immersed himself in that library reading and learning about Western culture. His reading of Goethe's works inspired him to compose melodies for them. He later recalled that he was not satisfied with these compositions. Chou also spent much of his time reading Chinese poetry and attempted writing Chinese poetry, but his works often received harsh criticism from his father.

To find an escape from his situation during the war, Chou sought solace in the beauty of nature. Despite intermittent bombings and the sound of gunshots, he would sit on the railing of a little bridge at sunset, watching for the changing colors of the tree leaves in the reflections of the brook. All this seemed surreal to him since witnessing a Japanese bomber shot down by two American Flying Tigers fighters. He cheered and ran to the wreckage only to be shocked to see the totally charred body of a Japanese airman still holding a machine gun.

Because of the advancement of the Japanese troops to the south, Guilin was no longer a safe haven; Chou left Guilin in 1944 and went to Chungqing (Chung King).[31] Chungqing was in west central China, in a valley surrounded by mountains. It was the wartime capital of the nationalist government.[32] Because of the Japanese occupation in the international settlement zone in Shanghai, some faculty members and students of the Shanghai Conservatory of Music had moved to Qingmu Guan, a suburb of Chungqing[33] to join the newly formed conservatory, which was sponsored by the nationalist government. Between 1944 and 1945, Chou attended the National Chungqing University. Although, during most of his two years in Chungqing, Chou was not involved in music or with the conservatory, toward the end of his stay he was able to study violin with Wang Renyi,[34] the conductor of the national orchestra in Chungqing. Chou graduated in 1945 with a BS in civil engineering. After graduation, Chou decided to study architecture in America. He applied to Yale University through his eldest brother in Boston and was accepted. He left Chungqing on a steamboat to Shanghai. Traveling downstream on the Yangtze River, his boat passed the Three Gorges, and he could see corpses still floating in the river. On the way, he stopped at three war-torn cities: Hankou, Jujiang (Jiangxi Province), and Nanjing. He saw that Hankou, where he bought his first violin, was completely flattened.[35] From Shanghai, he bid goodbye to China and left for America.

Boston and the Road to Music (1946–1954)

Chou arrived at Yale in August 1946 on a five-year architecture scholarship. Now, both the war and the constant moving for safety were over. Chou was far away from his parents, and he saw an opportunity to follow his desire to pursue music, the idea that seemed less patriotic for his parents during the war. Chou's qualms about switching from architecture to music intensified. Agonizing over an important choice in life, Chou felt that he was a "dying man." He first tried to change majors. But when he asked Bruce Simonds, the dean of the School of Music, for advice, the dean suggested that he stay in architecture but take some music appreciation classes instead. He was disappointed with the suggestion and then went to see the dean of the Architecture School, hoping for approval and encouragement. The dean did not advise him to give up his scholarship and to major in music either, since it was a little late to decline the offer because school had already started. Chou later reflected:

> In fact, I felt that I was really taking a chance. I agonized for years before I finally gave up the opportunity of becoming an architect all because of a rather

stupid faith in myself. . . . Whenever someone asks whether he or she should be a composer, I usually say, do you feel that you would rather die without being a composer? Otherwise, I wouldn't.[36]

After a week, Chou left New Haven for Boston where his eldest brother was teaching at MIT and taking violin lessons from Reasoner at the New England Conservatory. At this time, his brother was managing Chou's allowance from their parents, who were still supporting their sons. Chou was totally surprised when his brother reported that their father had granted his wish. He was happy and realized that his father really understood his feelings.

Shortly after his arrival in Boston, Chou auditioned for admission to the New England Conservatory and was accepted to major in violin performance. After a semester, he changed his major to composition with a second major in viola (studying with Joseph Pasquale, the principal violist of the Boston Symphony Orchestra). He also studied chamber music with Wolf Wolfinson, the founder and first violinist of the Mendelssohn Quartet, and a faculty member at the Longy School. For composition, he studied with Carl McKinley, who was a student of Nadia Boulanger and a strict traditional harmony and counterpoint teacher. Chou remembered him as always saying "later!" when he deliberately deviated from tonal centers, and McKinley only encouraged him to add Chinese flavor to counterpoint exercises.

In his first year at the conservatory, Chou studied music history with Warren Storey Smith, a well-known critic for the *Boston Herald*, who first introduced Varèse's music to Chou. Chou later confessed, however, that at that time he thought Varèse's music sounded like a pig being slaughtered, a sound he used to hear when he was a little boy in China; the sound had stuck in his mind and he could not comprehend why Varèse composed like that. The second year, Chou took a contemporary music survey course from Nicolas Slonimsky, who was teaching part time at the conservatory. In Slonimsky's class, Chou heard Varèse's music for a second time. He was impressed with Slonimsky, and asked to be accepted as a private composition student. Slonimsky soon discovered Chou's aptitude in composition. He wrote:

> It was immediately evident that the complexity of contemporary theories presented no difficulties to him [Chou]. Perhaps his training in exact sciences helped him in this respect. But above all, he knew what he wanted to do in musical composition.[37]

Slonimsky played an important role in Chou's career because he was the first person to ask Chou whether he knew much about Chinese music and to suggest that Chou develop his compositional style with both Chinese and Western materials. During Chou's second year at the conservatory, there had been some enthusiasm for Hindemith's works. Before Chou left Yale, he had tried to see Hindemith to explore the possibility of studying with him, but was told that Hindemith had gone back to Switzerland shortly after the war. Chou's first work, *Scenes from Tibet*, a rondo for viola and cello, was composed with this possibility in mind. In the spring of 1947, Chou performed it with himself on the viola at the conservatory and later sent the score to Hindemith as a follow-up. Hindemith responded by saying, "you have the ability to compose," quite a complimentary remark that was exceptional, according to a former student of Hindemith who confided to Chou. Having studied many of Hindemith's scores, his theory, and the two books on the craft of composition, Chou lost interest in studying with him. Chou commented that he found Hindemith's theory arbitrary and Hindemith's music uninspiring.[38]

While in Shanghai, Chou only heard the works of a few Western contemporary composers such as Stravinsky, Piston, and Bloch. During his three and half years of study at the New England Conservatory, he was able to attend live performances of contemporary music. At Harvard University, he heard the premiere of Schoenberg's *String Trio*, opus 45 (1946), and in New York, he attended the premiere of Stravinsky's 1948 *Mass*. In New York, again, he heard a live performance of Varèse's works. In fact, he sat just a few rows behind Varèse.[39]

In his Boston years, Chou accomplished a great deal in terms of mastering composition techniques and acquiring familiarity with quite a few major contemporary works. He also read writings of Alexander Helmholtz and Ferruccio Busoni. But because he had not developed his own consistent way of processing the musical material, he had difficulty in determining what to do with them.

While in Boston, Chou continuously received financial support from his family in China, but because of the establishment of the People's Republic in October 1949, this support eventually ended. Chou left Boston and followed his brother who had moved to New York.

New York and Varèse (1949–1954)

When Chou arrived in New York, he did not know where and with whom he would be studying. However, he learned from the newspaper that Bohuslav Martinu was teaching at Mannes School of Music and at Princeton University as a guest lecturer. Chou asked Martinu for lessons, and Martinu agreed. According to Chou, Martinu was more interested in composing than teaching. At that time, Chou did not devote himself entirely to the study of modern composition techniques. What he studied, however, was much of Bach's *The Well-Tempered Clavier*. Chou's creative urge often impelled him to experiment with synthesizing counterpoint exercises with Chinese subjects. On one occasion, Chou showed his Chinese-flavored fugues to Martinu, who started to read them on the piano and suddenly stopped after a few measures. He looked at Chou and simply uttered one word: "why?" Chou could not answer. Such an embarrassment disturbed him profoundly and made him realize that substituting pentatonic for heptatonic modes in fugue, which had been developed in the heptatonic and triadic tradition, was like putting Chinese words into Bach's mouth. Fugue was Bach's natural language, but not his. This incongruity was the direct result of his pragmatic way of finding simplistic and effective solutions for combining materials from two different cultures very much like many Chinese composers did in the 1920s and 1930s. Chou believed that this was one of the greatest lessons he ever had because, beginning with the word "why," he had to satisfy his own questions before moving on.

Thus, Chou began to take Slonimsky's suggestion to study traditional Chinese music seriously and started to study the sources and playing techniques of the Chinese *qin* (a seven-stringed zither) music. Chou changed his attitude to studying Chinese music from the mere interest in looking for quick and shocking results in compositions to seek genuine understanding of the cultural values. Chou studied not only Chinese music but also tried to extract aesthetic values from Chinese poetry, painting, calligraphy, and Zhuang Zi's Taoist philosophy. Chou's first successful work, *Landscapes*, composed in 1949 in New York, reflects his own conviction in the aesthetic ideals of Chinese visual and poetic arts and signals the initial stage of his personal and compositional style and development.

After Martinu, Varèse became Chou's second and most important teacher in New York. Chou studied with him for five years, and because the two shared certain aesthetic views that are derivative of visual and literary arts other than music, they remained lifelong friends.

Chou met Varèse through Colin McPhee, who recommended that Chou ask Varèse to take him as a student. Chou recalls the situation:

A childhood friend of mine, Lin Pei-Fen, who is now living here in Rhinebeck, the wife of Meyer Kupferman—at that time, she was a dancer—called me one day. We had known each other as young kids (we used to fight for the jumpseat in the car!). Well, she called me because she was supposed to take a composer to Chinatown to hear Cantonese opera. She was sick and asked if I would do it, and the composer turned out to be Colin McPhee. He asked me what I was doing in New York and I said that I'd just arrived and was looking for a teacher. He was great; he spent time talking about the various people and why I shouldn't study with them (at that time, everybody from the Orient would automatically go to Henry Cowell first). Suddenly, he said, "I've got the person for you!" It was Varèse. But then he warned me to be aware of the differences in cultural background. Varèse had his temperament, which was right for him, but if I were to imitate him, I would be lost. His only hesitation was that Varèse was such an overwhelming personality.[40]

McPhee himself had studied with Varèse in the late 1920s and had rented a room in Varèse's house. For finding an orchestra to perform his works, McPhee also advised Chou to approach Stokowski, who had an interest in promoting contemporary works. Yet, according to Slonimsky:

He [Chou] did not have to fight for recognition, which came to him, so to say, on a silver platter. Leopold Stokowski, with his discriminating taste for the unusual and the exotic, performed Chou's Landscapes in 1953.[41]

Five years later on December 3, 1958, again, Stokowski premiered Chou's To A Wayfarer (1958) together with McPhee's Balinese-influenced Nocturne (1958) at the Metropolitan Museum of Art. Chou admired McPhee's Tabuh-Tabuhan, for it was one of the most distinguished scores of that nature, using the Western orchestra to express the music of another culture.[42]

On Chou's behalf, McPhee wrote Varèse a short letter, and Chou visited Varèse in his home at 188 Sullivan Street in Greenwich Village, where Chou now lives. Chou's first impression of Varèse was good. His anxiety was eased about being criticized by Varèse for Landscapes, his first major composition, which had plain pentatonic modes, simple forms, and straightforward rhythmic structure. Instead of being critical, Varèse encouraged him and accepted him as a student. Chou asked him about the tuition. Varèse only told Chou about his own studies with Debussy and Busoni, who never charged him. Varèse did not expect Chou to pay, but told Chou that he expected him to pass on his legacy in future.[43]

Chou became Varèse's student in 1949. This master-pupil relationship was a version of apprenticeships practiced in China that Chou knew. Routinely, Chou saw Varèse several times a week. The master would give him lessons or take him places. Chou copied music and ran errands for his teacher. Often Varèse cooked for Chou, and Chou did the driving for his teacher. The two would go together to concerts, gallery openings, parties, and cafés in the village. Varèse constantly had visitors of artist friends such as Carl Ruggles (composer), Thomas Bouchard (photographer and filmmaker), and Meyer Schapiro (art historian). A prentice to the household, Chou was also close to Varèse's wife, Louise, whose literary interest in translating poems by Baudelaire and Rimbaud inspired Chou to work on his translations of Chinese poems. From 1949 to Varèse's death in 1965, Chou gradually imparted his teacher's way of thinking and way of teaching, first as his pupil then as his close friend.

Chou's lessons with Varèse were exhausting yet enlightening, for Chou learned much from Varèse not by imitation, which was forbidden, but by defending his motivations and the logic behind his selection of certain techniques. In other words, Varèse taught him how to formulate an idea and turn it into a master plan that establishes logical connections for the very technical details by relating everything to the central idea.

As usual, Chou often received harsh criticism from Varèse and was forced to debate and argue with him. Varèse wanted Chou to find his own way. Chou remembers:

> He [Varèse] would immediately sit down and become glued to your music. He would literally attack you all the time. "Why do you do this? Why this . . . ? that . . . ?" He would point out that this cannot work and so on, and he would always say, "And don't say 'yes' out of politeness." He was always attacking you and he would back you into a corner; he wanted you to argue with him and debate him and it was very, very exhausting. He wouldn't let you go! He said, "you wrote it, you are responsible for it; you have to tell me why you think it would work. What are you trying to say, anyway?"[44]

Varèse rarely talked about his own music with Chou, nor did he comment on whether it was appropriate for Chou to analyze his music. However, in the following statement, Chou recalls that by working as Varèse's copyist, he learned a great deal:

> I also learned much about him and his music by copying a lot for him. But this was a very complex process in his case. For one thing, his music would be all over the room. By the piano, on the floor . . . all over. He would give me snatches of *Deserts*, which were like pieces of a puzzle to be assembled as a score. Usually, they were written on irregular pieces of paper on which he would draw his own staff lines—even on the inside of an envelope that he had unfolded carefully. He would still be composing while I copied and he did not go to the piano. So I think that they are separate processes—planning, trying on the piano, and working things out at the desk. He was acutely aware of what was going on in his work.[45]

During the early 1950s, many composers in New York became interested in Webern. Chou was no exception. According to Chou, in New York in 1951, there were several Webern scores, opus 5, 6, 10, 11, and a couple more, available at the 58th street library, and he studied these scores avidly. Varèse also admired Webern. Initially, he was polite toward Chou for a few months because he heard that Chou was drawn into serialism. His criticism of Chou's style-imitation finally emerged when Chou showed his Webern-inspired piece to him. He told Chou, "Wen-Chung, you want to be a composer: then you have to have courage; you have to be willing to burn your music. Sometimes you have to piss on it. . . . Piss now! And he walked away."[46] When Chou completed his *Seven Poems of T'ang Dynasty* (1951–1952) for tenor, seven wind instruments, piano, and percussion, Chou knew this piece did not sound Chinese as the title suggested, and he did not have the courage to show it to Varèse directly. Instead, he left the score on Varèse's piano and made an excuse to go to bathroom. To his surprise, Varèse's comment on this piece was complimentary because the idea was original. Chou translated the seven Chinese poems used in this piece from French with Louise Varèse's editing, and Chou later dedicated the piece to her.

Chou eventually realized that he had benefited from studying with Varèse by learning to be independent and finally abandoned the lure of the practical idea of taking a fashionable technique and working it into something new. He now understood that being an artist, he had to resist influences of others and be responsible for his own actions. Chou became critical and astute and grasped unspoken principles in Varèse's teaching. As mentioned before, Varèse rarely told Chou what to do to fix a problem when he disliked Chou's chords or other things. Varèse often played these chords on the piano by rearranging the notes in the same chord and took them to different registers. All was guided by his discriminate hearing. Chou was to pass this teaching style to his own student years later. Varèse detested the idea of learning quick tricks, and Chou remembered an anecdote:

George Gershwin wanted to study with him [Varèse] before studying with Ravel. Gershwin said to Varèse, "I heard that you are a wizard with orchestra. I want to learn some tricks from you." Varèse replied, "Tricks! I have none. Get out of here!"[47]

Chou and Varèse maintained a good relationship, and, according to Chou, there was a spiritual bond between them. The two had similar interests in viewing the sculptural and geometrical aspects of music and in classical literature. Yet they rarely made statements such as "I believe this or that" in front of each other. Varèse seldom made corrections in Chou's works. Instead, he would inspire Chou by suggesting workable plans and then scratching it immediately. Chou understood Varèse well. He recognized the fact that the common mistake in viewing Varèse as a radical experimentalist due to his irreverence to tradition was simply not true, and, deep at heart, Varèse was well grounded in the music of the medieval, renaissance, and early baroque periods.[48] Much of Varèse's musical material has emotional, mystic, and symbolic content deeply rooted in the past but reinterpreted with his own view of the modern age. Varèse's understanding of early music impressed Chou when he heard him rehearsing the Greater New York Chorus with Monteverdi's works. Chou worked as Varèse's secretary to the chorus.

From Varèse, Chou learned a great deal about how artists should look at their tradition critically, absorbing the essence and transforming it to reflect new concepts. "Instead of following the rules of any system or method and even if it happens to be of my own devising, I have always preferred to rely on my instincts as a composer and a sense of logic as conditioned by my esthetic convictions," Chou reflected.[49]

Relearning and Interpreting
One's Own Tradition (1954–1959)

For Chou, upon his graduation from Columbia University in 1954, there was the lure of finding a college teaching job. Professor Luening strongly opposed it. The idea was that Chou had the potential to further develop and perfect his techniques and to explore his unique cultural heritage as a composer, and Columbia might buy him back. Columbia eventually did in 1964.

With the help of Professor Otto Luening, Chou secured a research grant from the Rockefeller Foundation to study traditional Chinese music and drama. Between 1955 and 1957, as the director of this research project, Chou began to devote himself again to the study of the literature, notation, historical background, and playing techniques of *qin* music. His early training in reading classical Chinese helped him tremendously because he had to use original sources (after finding superficial writings on Chinese music by some Western writers). For these two years, Chou concentrated not only on the study of Chinese music history but also on Chinese painting, calligraphy, poetry, and philosophy; he was able to discover the principle for the process of artistic creation, a common denominator in the traditional Chinese arts. It is the means and the act of creating, not the end result that governs artistic creation. He tried understanding what traditional Chinese art and music meant to him rather than looking for quick solutions for the next piece and trying to imitate the sound of traditional Chinese music. His new understanding of the basic components of culture, such as aesthetic values, triggered perceptive questions like whether Chinese melody on the piano would sound "right" to someone who has heard traditional Chinese music.

With the research grant, Chou traveled and spent hours in libraries where he could find collections of scores of traditional Chinese music and books on Chinese music and culture. His friends also helped him by giving him their own collections of scores and recordings of classical Chinese music, such as the recording of monk Putuo Shan performance of Buddhist music and *qin* music performed by Zha Fu-Xi, a legendary *qin* master. As a necessity, Chou taught himself to read the Chinese *qin* notation by studying some of the most significant editions of the Ming Dynasty with extensive introductory chapters on technique and aesthetics. The complexity of this notation or tablature, which indicated hand positions on the instrument and instructions on articulations of the string, modifying the pitch, vibrato, and glissando all in one character, impressed him tremendously. The system's precision, spontaneity, and emotional content reflect a high degree of sophistication of his native culture. He remarked:

> Ch'in [*qin*] notation, for example, had such an influence on my own work—makes you realize that hundreds of years ago, someone already systematized the way sound can be controlled, played, and communicated through this notation. This was already total organization of sound, long before any attempt to try that in European music. And this is a more musical approach; it tells you how to use vibrato and even how to change from one vibrato to another.[50]

Chou was obviously more interested in learning about the lore of the instrument, such as aesthetics and its application through notation and the performing renditions in actual sound, than merely teaching himself to play the instrument. While living in the United States, Chou never had the opportunity to study with the greatest *qin* master, Guan Ping-Hu, who died just before Chou was able to return to China in 1972. However, Chou was fortunate to meet and spend time with Zha Fu-Xi in China.

To widen understanding of his own tradition and for a comparative view, Chou studied and compared the Indian raga, Indonesian gamelan music, Korean and Japanese court music, and the Chinese *yayue* (or ceremonial) music and discovered that among these, there is a shared structural and aesthetic principle. For example, layered construction as a prominent structural feature and its association with register and rhythmic activity is common in music from these cultures. A junior faculty member at Columbia, Chou was not only teaching composition but also involved in the curriculum development for the ethnomusicology program. The program offered non-Western music classes for composers and theorists and invited guest lecturers. Shinichi Yuize, Chou's friend from Japan and a student of Henry Cowell, taught a course of *koto* music. As there were not enough students in the class, Chou and Nicholas England (one of the founders of the ethnomusicology program at Columbia) sat in to make the class more vibrant. His study of the *koto*, a derivation of the Chinese zither *Zheng* with movable bridges, gave him new insights into the aesthetic principles of the Chinese *qin* music.

A major issue in Chinese music history was the so-called "microtonal temperament," which had occupied the minds of Chinese music scholars for over 2,000 years. The search for perfect ratio in pitches such as the *huangzhong* pitch, or yellow bell, was motivated by political, astrological, mathematical, and pure theoretical interests. There was an overt disparity between the theory of twelve chromatic tones and seven-tone scales and the practice of five-tone scales. In fact, many pitches and scale tones existing in theory were never used in practice. Chou studied the system, and came to the conclusion that this discrepancy allows composers to not be obligated to use all the existing pitches in their works. Still, today, many of the so-called "folk tunes" contain vestiges of the *Yayue*, or elegant court music, a conglomerate genre from different regions of China that, depending on regional practices, could be pentatonic or heptatonic and had been practiced outside of the court by commoners for centuries. Such a practice has invariably included, in the pentatonic mode, an interval of minor second, which appears as an upper neighbor note in Western terms or an ornament in Chinese terms. Chou thought this added minor second gave Chinese music a hexatonic flavor. But on the whole, he was more interested in the use of sliding tones or microtones produced by plucking while pulling or pushing the strings of the *qin*.

To create a musical work with these new concepts, an emphasis on pitch inflection must be included. However, there has to be a balance between pitch and timbre. In other words, pitch is not more important than timbre. Timbre is defined as the quality of the sound that carries cultural identity. For Chou, however, pitch and timbre are subjugated under the guiding principle of the work or, in Chou's words, the philosophy of the work. This explains the gap between the Asian composer and his non-Asian-sounding works. Chou commented:

> Even though, without my name printed on them, people might not realize that they were written by a Chinese person. It doesn't matter! But without the Chinese tradition, I couldn't have written them and for me, that's the point.[51]

His understanding of the philosophical underpinnings of his tradition and his acceptance of Varèsean concept of sound as a living object provided a basis for his next works.

Chou's study and research of his culture and music proved to be extremely beneficial for developing his personal approach to musical synthesis.[52] While trying to learn and interpret the meaning of *qin* music and other traditional Chinese musical genres, Chou also began to formulate how to use this resource to develop his own style. Chou's study of Western music history with Paul Henry Lang and Eric Hertzmann, an Austrian Beethoven scholar and medievalist at Columbia University, lent him yet another comparative perspective in his research. Chou wrote his first musicological term paper on Bach's adaptation of the Vivaldi material as illustrated by his concerto for four harpsichords, from which Chou learned a great deal about recreating an orchestral work from a model and a detailed comparison. In his student days at Columbia, Chou also read many of Jacques Barzun's books on Western cultural history, and through Varèse, he became a friend of Barzun. Barzun, an eminent scholar and biographer of Berlioz, had served as dean and provost at Columbia University and had profoundly influenced Chou's understanding of Western intellectual and music history.

From his teacher Otto Luening and his works at the Studio, Chou learned a great deal about electronic music. Also, between 1952 and 1953, during his student years at the Columbia University, ethnomusicology was beginning to be recognized in the United States, especially at Columbia.[53] Willard Rhodes, professor of conducting and composition, became an advocate of the discipline. Rhodes himself studied American Indian music and encouraged Chou to study not only Chinese music but also the music of other cultures, such as the Japanese *koto* music to broaden his cross-cultural views.

Chou completed *All in the Spring Wind* as his thesis project and submitted it to Columbia University at the time of his graduation in 1954. This work was later premiered and recorded by the Louisville Orchestra under Robert Whitney on December 7, 1961, and the work became one of Chou's most performed masterpieces. A commission followed his graduation, a "triolet for Orchestra" or *And the Fallen Petals* (1954) by the Louisville Orchestra. The work was premiered in Louisville on February 9, 1955, again by Robert Whitney.

Chou has not talked much about how he was influenced by Varèse to identify principles of traditional arts and music as a solid foundation for his stylistic development; however, it is clear that Varèse's concern over single tones or sound as living matters and his belief that innovative ideas during this century have more outlets in visual arts than in music had much impact on Chou's formulation of ideas. Chou was appointed research associate and composer-in-residence at the University of Illinois from 1958 to 1959 and composed and premiered his *Soliloquy of a Bhiksuni* (1958) for solo trumpet and orchestra there. He became a naturalized American citizen in 1958.

While at Urbana, Chou heard the work of Toshiro Mayuzumi, the first Japanese composer to gain international recognition, over the campus radio. It was Mayuzumi's "Niravan Symphony." Chou immediately wrote him a letter, not knowing that Mayuzumi was also trying to contact him after hearing a recording of *And the Fallen Petals* in Japan. A year later, the two finally met. According to Chou, it was a memorable meeting; the wariness caused by the hostility of the war melted away through a shared vision of music, and Mayuzumi offered an apology for the war atrocities committed by the Japanese army after they shook hands. They felt relieved and free to support each other. As a result, Mayuzumi arranged to have Chou's work performed by the NHK symphony. In return, Chou convinced his publisher, Walter Hinrichsen of C. F. Peters, to publish Mayuzumi's work.[54]

Compositional Maturity and Recognitions (1960s)

In 1960, Toru Takemitsu visited Chou in New York, and the two exchanged ideas concerning aesthetics and discussed their particular compositional developments. They also talked about their responses to the current cultural environment, which was characterized by the "cross-currents from both the East and the West," as Chou observed.[55]

In the 1960s, after experience with Chinese arts and drama and subsequent experimentation with Chinese aesthetic principles in several of his works of the late 1950s, Chou began to feel that he had a better command both in shaping a piece from a single idea and in expanding this single concept to every controlling detail of the piece. Chou was pleased with his progress: "I was on the top of the world artistically and was ready to write my masterpiece."[56] His works of the 1960s, such as *Metaphors* (1960–1961), *Cursive* (1964), *The Dark and the Light* (1964), *Pien* (1966), and *Yun* (1969), show mastery in terms of treating instrumental timbre, texture, and form. During this time, he was employed as a music lecturer at Brooklyn College (1961–1962) and Hunter College (1963–1964), adjunct theory and composition teacher at Horace Mann School (1962–1966), and assistant professor and professor at Columbia University (1964–1991). In 1960, he joined the American Composers Alliance, an organization that was instrumental in informing its members of their colleagues' new works and activities. An exclusive coverage of Chou by Nicolas Slonimsky appeared in the 1961 issue of the Alliance's bulletin, and a catalogue of his works appeared in the 1969 issue. In his 1961 article, Slonimsky pointed out that Chou's approach to West-East musical fusion had moved away from forcing Chinese melody into the mode of Western harmony through approaches that had not been tried before. And Chou had established himself with success in fusing two seemingly incompatible musical materials. Slonimsky wrote:

> When pentatonic melodies of the Orient are harmonized in this conventional manner, the incompatibility between the melody and the harmonic setting is such that the very essence of Oriental melody is destroyed. Even more difficult is the representation of microtonal intervals peculiar to some countries of the Orient. . . . Chou Wen-Chung is possibly the first Chinese composer who has attempted to translate authentic oriental melo-rhythms into the terms of modern Western music. . . . He poses the problem of conciliation between melodic pentatonicism and dissonance.[57]

Also in the late 1950s and early 1960s, Chou's works began to gain recognition in some European countries through an extended European tour. His works were also performed in Japan. His *Suite for Harp and Wind Quintet* (1951) was presented at the International Society for Contemporary Music–American Composers Alliance concert of American chamber music conducted by Francis Travis in Copenhagen on September 26, 1956. His *Two Miniatures from T'ang Dynasty* (1957) was performed in Lugano (Switzerland) in 1961 in Podio concerts also led by Travis. As part of the Fourth of July celebration abroad, his *Metaphors* (1960–1961) was performed in London on July 4, 1961, by the American Wind Symphony Orchestra conducted by Robert Austin Bourdreau. *Seven Poems of T'ang Dynasty* (1951–1952) was performed in Darmstadt as part of the *Internationale Ferienkurse für Neue Musik Kammerkonzert* on September 2, 1961, by *Kranichsteiner Kammerensemble*. In 1962, *Landscapes* (1949) had three performances in France: May 7 in Marseille, May 16 in Lille, and May 24 in Nice with the Orchestra Radio Marseille conducted by Pierre Pagliano. Other European performances of the 1962 work include two performances in July in Copenhagen and one on August 25 in Oslo.

Chou's *And the Fallen Petals* (1954) was first performed in Europe on March 25, 1958, with Francis Travis conducting the Hamburg Radio Orchestra. The work received its first Asian premiere outside of China in 1959. It was performed in Tokyo under the baton of Akeo Watanabe with the Japan Philharmonic Symphony Orchestra on November 10, 1959. During the first week of June 1960, John Bitter conducted the Berlin Philharmonic Orchestra, presenting this work to German audiences in Berlin and Bielefeld.

The work received positive reviews from half a dozen newspapers. This same work was premiered two years later on November 15 and 18, 1962, in Goeteborg, Sweden, led by Sten Frykberg with the Goeteborg Orchestra and a year later in Paris on March 22, 1963, by the *Orchestre Nationale*.

The 1960s was propitious for Chou in that he received awards with Russell Smith and Vladimir Ussachevsky from the American Academy of Arts and Letters in 1963.[58] He was elected a board member of the American Composers Alliance in 1963, a position he retained until 1976. Chou also saw releases of the first album of recordings of his works, *Pien, Yu ko, Cursive*, and *Willows Are New*. In his personal life, Chou and Yi-An Chang, a pianist who performed and recorded *Willows Are New*, were engaged in 1962, and the wedding took place on June 23, 1962.[59] Yi-An Chang came to the United States shortly before the bombing of Pearl Harbor at the age of thirteen, and as a seventeen-year-old soloist, she performed with the Los Angeles Philharmonic under Leopold Stokowski at the Hollywood Bowl. She later studied with Olga Samaroff, Stokowski's first wife, at the Juilliard School in New York, and at the time of her marriage, she was the chair of the music department at Abbott Academy in Andover, Massachusetts. The Chous had their first son in 1965 and a second son shortly thereafter.

In 1969, as chairman of the composition department at Columbia University, Chou succeeded Otto Luening to further develop the doctoral program, which was established less than a year earlier. With his own learning experience as a model, Chou developed potential in many of his young and talented students who also became his friends. He learned a great deal from his students. For him, teaching was extremely satisfying, especially when many of his students became successful composers and teachers themselves. As an administrator, Chou spent much of his time setting up program policies and solving problems resulting from fund shortage, bureaucratic delays, and academic politics. Although these responsibilities seem to contradict the mindset of a creative artist, Chou managed to expand his knowledge of issues in other arts such as poetry and filmmaking and to know those visual artists who were part-time teachers at Columbia. He later became associate dean and vice dean for academic affairs of the School of Arts in 1975 and 1976 respectively. He was also busy serving as chairman of the editorial board for the journal, *Asian Music*.

Still a student at Columbia in the fall of 1952, Chou met Jose Maceda, a fellow student from the Philippines. Already an accomplished pianist, Maceda was working on his musicology degree. After completing his degree at Columbia and his Ph.D. in ethnomusicology from UCLA, he returned to Manila to teach at the University of the Philippines and became a well-respected musician and prominent scholar of indigenous Filipino music. Chou admired

Maceda's efforts in research and preservation of the native tradition and kept close contact with him.

In this context, Chou attended an international music conference in Manila in 1966. He had extensive discussions on the musical confluence between Asian and Western composers' contributions to the world's musical development with Maceda and other composers such as Lucrecia Kaislag and Hsu Tsang-houei, a student of André Jolivet. The outcome of this conference was the founding of the Asian Composers League to promote contemporary Asian compositions.[60]

During the 1960s Chou's musical development reached a new height. Chou worked on ideas of control, in terms of pitch, form, rhythm, and organizational principles, in isolation; actually, concurrent musical events, trends, and other composers' experimentations were also having an impact on his thinking. Chou mentioned earlier that he was attracted to Webern's works, which he studied, trying to apply some of Webern's principles in his exercises. Webern's isolation of a single event such as pitch, which is packaged as a distinct sound with recognizable features, and his condensation of form encouraged Chou to think of pitch and form in a new way and relate this new view to Chinese artistic and musical principles such as "sound as a living being," the spontaneity in calligraphy, and laconic conception in poetry and ink brush painting. During the 1960s, Asian culture seemed to be a rich source for materials and ideas in the West. There was interest in exploring a wide variety of sonic sources, especially timbre, which was to gain equal footing as pitch, rhythm, and form, and on the concept of control and the philosophical underpinnings of either the composition itself or the process of composing. Eastern influences were strongly felt not only in the works of Olivier Messiaen, John Cage, Henry Cowell, Colin McPhee, and Harry Partch but also in those of Steve Reich, who studied Indonesian Gamelan and African drumming; Philip Glass, who worked with Ravi Shankar; La Monte Young, who studied Kirana style of Indian singing with Pundit Pran Nath; and Jean-Claude Eloy, whose *Equivalence for 18 Players* (1963) creates images of the Far East, Japan, and Tibet. Stockhausen's *Telemusik* (1966) even incorporated recordings from temple ceremonies in Japan, Vietnamese highlander music, and Balinese music. Unlike Western composers, who were interested in oriental material, two Asian composers residing in Europe, Toru Takemitsu (Japanese) and Isang Yun (Korean), went in the opposite direction: instead of presenting their Asian traits in a straightforward manner, these men presented works with oriental impressions but with no intention of imitating oriental sound either by thematic material or orchestration.[61]

Meanwhile, Chou was intrigued by avant-garde current involving diverse sources and styles that were exerting profound influence on American musical life, including electronic music being produced at the Columbia-Princeton Center, postwar serialism, minimalism, and multimedia, and the expansion of composition departments in universities. Academic institutions became instrumental in accommodating avant-garde composers, sustaining their livelihood, and disseminating their ideas.

Chou wrote seven works during the 1960s. These works show different compositional approaches in terms of form, pitch and rhythmic organizations, and combinations of certain instruments. Unlike his works of the 1950s, except for the similar instrumentation in *Metaphors* (1960–1961), *Riding the Wind* (1964), *Pien* (1966), and *Yun* (1969), there was very little overlapping in Chou's works. To achieve this, Chou toiled at each piece trying not to repeat certain procedures. Chou believes that not until the end of the 1960s and the beginning of the 1970s did he begin to formulate a systematic composition method, which was based on the principles of enharmonic equivalence, centricity, and ordering of Western posttonal music, especially of serial music and the reflective principle of the Chinese *I-Ching*.[62]

Chou's method rests on the aggregations of intervallic patterns; the ordering of a group of intervals is arranged according to ascending and descending orders or, in Chou's words, "variable modes." This is a crab principle (except that the ordering of descending retrograde is not the same as ascending ones). Chou first experimented with this theory or principle in *Metaphors*,[63] and later applied it in 1960s works such as *Cursive* (1963), *Pien* (1966), and *Yun* (1969) and his new works such as *Echoes From the Gorge* (1989) and string quartet *Clouds* (1996).

With *Cursive*, Chou experimented with fluidity of musical form, rhythm, and direction of the movement of voices. These were comparable to the flow of ink in Chinese calligraphy, as the title suggests. In *Yu ko* (1965), Chou tried to use nine Western instruments to recreate the timbre of the Chinese *qin*.

Chou consolidated his systematic compositional method in *Pien* (1966) in which the eight triagrams of the *I-Ching* provided a model for him to elaborate on the concept of constant change within a seemingly static state. *Yun* (1969) was the last work Chou completed in the 1960s. The work forebodes a decade of preoccupation with administrative duties mainly at Columbia University, especially after succeeding Otto Luening to develop the newly founded doctoral program in musical composition in 1969. After *Yun*, Chou became silent.

An Active Promoter of Cultural Exchange (1970s–present)

Chou's teacher and friend Edgard Varèse died on November 6, 1965. Apart from publishing commemorative articles on Varèse, Chou also spent a considerable amount of time on completing Varèse's unfinished work, *Nocturnal*, and on editing new editions of Varèse's *Ameriqus* (1972), *Intergrals* (1980), and *Octandre* (1980), experiencing pressure from Louise Varèse. He subsequently became the executor of the Varèse legacy and handled matters concerning Varèse's musical works such as recordings and publications. He was deeply involved in legal procedures concerning Varèse's publisher Franco Colombo, who was a kind of mafioso type and not always honest.[64] To commemorate the centennial of Varèse's birthday, he organized a series of concerts and events in 1983. He also oversaw the new release of recordings of Varèse's works in 1998. Recently, he has been promoting Varèse's works among major symphony orchestras in America.

Partly as a result of his study in Chinese aesthetics through traditional music and arts and partly because of his contact with Asian composition students and his deanship at Columbia University during the 1970s, Chou began to express his views on what Asian cultures and composers could offer for the enrichment of musical experience for both Eastern and Western audiences. On this subject, he published articles and gave talks at the 1974 world composers' forum *Musicultura* in the Netherlands, the UNESCO International Music Symposium in 1966 in the Philippines, the Asian Composers Conference and Festival in 1988 in Hong Kong, the Korean National Academy of the Arts in 1977 in Seoul, the sixth Asian Composers' League Conference and Festival in 1979 also in Seoul, Pacific Composers Conference in summer 1990 in Japan, and more recently, at the Hong Kong Millennium Congress in January 2000. Chou believes that the 1966 Manila symposium was the starting point for thinking that Asian composers' activities could become a historic force in contemporary musical development.

Chou kept personal contact with several prominent Asian composers such as Toru Takemitsu, Joji Yuasa, and Isang Yun to keep his composition style in a non-Western perspective, though Chou did not share aesthetics with these composers. Chou heard Yun's early works from recordings by German companies, and he used one of them as an example in his lectures. Chou never imagined he would get involved in helping Yun's release from a South Korean prison in 1966. Two years earlier, Yun was kidnapped in Berlin by a South Korean secret agent and sentenced to life imprisonment in his home country on charges of "antigovernment" activities. Chou joined Elliott Carter on a radio program to publicly criticize the incident and jointly signed a letter to the White House urging the U.S. government to act diplomatically for Yun's release. Through this incident, Chou's awareness of the societal repression on political, cultural, and artistic fronts made him more appreciative of the artistic freedom in the United States, although there is pressure from commercialism. He became more sympathetic to artists under totalitarian regimes, including his native China.

During the 1970s, Chou planned to work on two pieces, a Cello Concerto (completed in 1992) for a young artist Paul Tobias and *Echoes from the Gorge* (completed in 1989), while he was the resident composer of the Koussevisky composer's studio at Tanglewood. The cello concerto was commissioned by the New York State Council on the Arts in 1970. Because of his involvement in various administrative services, he would only be able to return and complete these works twenty years later. Between 1970 and 1975, Chou was the president of Composers' Recording Inc., which was on the verge of bankruptcy at the time. Chou was shocked by the unsympathetic societal attitude toward such a unique and important artistic organization for American and contemporary music. Chou and his fellow composers, recording professionals, and business and lawyer friends worked very hard to save the troubled company, and their efforts paid off. They eradicated the company's debt and restructured it as a nonprofit corporation. Chou felt he had learned a lesson about the meaning of culture in terms of commerce, human relations, and politics in a society.

In 1983 Carlotta Reiner, widow of the famed conductor Friz Reiner, died bequeathing funds ($1.2 million) and memorabilia in the form of an archive and an endowed professorship of musical composition, for two decades, at the newly created Friz Reiner Center for Contemporary Music at Columbia University. Chou was named as the first recipient of the endowment and was responsible for setting up the contemporary music center.[65] The center became instrumental in promoting and sponsoring performances of contemporary compositions at Columbia University and in New York. One of Chou's lasting contributions to Columbia was the transformation of the old electronic music center into the present computer music center in the early 1980s.

Since 1972, after U.S. President Nixon's visit to China, the communication between the United States and China resumed after over twenty years of isolation. From the late 1960s Chou had traveled to Asia frequently, and around 1966, the United States lifted travel restrictions to China. Encouraged by his colleagues, Chou tried to return to China. He applied and received his passport, without restrictions to visit China. This was the first time in seventeen years such a passport was issued. He tried hard to obtain a visa for several months; however, his efforts failed since the Chinese cultural revolution had just begun. He had to wait for yet another six years.

In December of 1972, after spending twenty-six years in the States, Chou was finally able to return to China, and he was also the first composer from the West to visit China. Chou responded quickly to the need for cultural exchange between both countries. Unfortunately, his proposal for establishing an arts exchange program at the time did not materialize. China was still embroiled in power struggles of the cultural revolution. However, in 1977, on his second trip to China, Chou was able to make a verbal agreement with leading Chinese artists and scholars, such as painter Wu Zuo-Ren and musicologist Yang Yin-Liu, on a nongovernmental basis. A year later, in October 1978, Chou founded the Center for U.S.-China Arts Exchange at Columbia University, the agency for promoting cultural understanding of both cultures. Under the sponsorship of the center, prominent American artists and citizens such as Isaac Stern, Arthur Miller, Schuyler Chapin, and Martin Segal visited China to stimulate interest in musical, dramatic, and visual arts. Many Chinese musicians, painters, sculptors, and quite a few young Chinese composers were able to visit the United States, particularly to participate in musical events and acquire necessary training. In 1973, Chou served on the National Committee on U.S.-China Relations, and from 1981 on, he served on the mayor's subcommittee of the New York-Beijing Friendship City Committee. He was also involved in Harvard's "Zero" Project, an educational program designed to help minority ethnic groups in southwest China.

Since the establishment of the center, Chou traveled between the United States and China frequently. Not until December 3, 1987, when his father died in Shanghai, was he finally able to reduce his administrative responsibilities. Chou resumed his work, by the end of 1988, completing *Beijing in the Mist* in 1987, *Echoes from the Gorge* in 1989, *Windswept Peaks* in 1990, the cello concerto in 1992, and the string quartet *Clouds* in 1996.

Chou's 1977 visit to the Central Conservatory of Music in Beijing was a landmark in the history of contemporary Chinese music. From his 1973 visit to his home city in Chang Zhou and other parts of China, Chou witnessed the negative impact of governmental censorship and control in art and music and China's isolation from the West for over half a century. He purposely brought scores and recordings of Western contemporary composers such as Bartok, Hindemith, Varèse, Babbitt, Davidovsky, Hovhaness, Shapey, Luening, Ussachevsky, Crumb, Tokemitsu, and his own works to China. He gave lectures at the conservatory, introducing contemporary music in the West and encouraging Chinese composers to use their cultural resources. As a result of Chou's visit and influence, in only two short years from 1981 to 1983, a young generation of Chinese composers produced a large number of contemporary, Western-inspired works. Coupled with the drives of economic and social reforms, the Chinese avant-garde styles emerged in the visual arts, theater, and music, creating the so-called new wave music movement. In his article, "U.S.-China Arts Exchange: A Practice in Search of a Philosophy," Chou aptly points out that "a new wave of composers, playwrights, and visual artists, most of whom have had contact with the Center, has emerged with lightening speed over the past three years. These artists have fundamentally changed the profile of their disciplines in China."[66] Besides the introduction of contemporary Western music, Chou was also responsible for bringing American musicians such as conductor David Gilbert and the violinist Isaac Stern to promote performance of Western music, and American playwright Arthur Miller to direct the theatrical production of his *Death of a Salesman* in the spring of 1983 in Beijing. The consequence of this production was the emergence of fifty new plays, which have broken away from trite formulas. From 1978 to 1989, the center-sponsored programs grew dramatically to include virtually all artistic disciplines, including architecture and writing.

Chou eventually brought several young Chinese composers to the United States to study at Columbia University. Several of them have had their works performed, premiered, and recorded in the United States. Western audiences also had an opportunity to hear works by contemporary Chinese composers. On October 27, 1991, Chen Yi and Zhou Long, students of Chou, and others such as Qu Xiao-Song, Li Bin-Yang, and Lam Bun-Ching presented a well-received New York concert, "Music from China," featuring contemporary Chinese compositions. Several of his Chinese students are now living in the United States. Some have found college teaching positions, and some are working on commissions as freelance artists.

Chou's influence on Asian composers has been evident in his students' works. The manifestation of this influence was strongly felt in China in the early 1980s as the first generation of Chinese avant-grade composers, whose artistic goals and creative energies were centered around the modernization of Chinese music, became a forceful cultural current. Once the current proponents of ideological control of musical composition were replaced by a more liberal and tolerant social and artistic visionaries, experimental music such as "new wave" could resurface and find its niche in Chinese society.

After his retirement from Columbia University in 1991, and in the last ten years, Chou became deeply involved in a cultural preservation program in Yunnan Province in southwest China through the joint sponsorship of the center and the Ford Foundation. Chou worked with teams of American and

Asian scholars, artists, educators, and their native counterparts to develop strategies to conserve the region's cultural and ecological diversity in coordination with its social and economic development, and accomplished a great deal. As a by-product, Chou learned a great deal about the meaning of heritage. He grew more conscious about his own heritage. He reflects:

> Ten years of this work has brought me into contact with those who still live and think from within their own heritage, namely, the rural masters and mentors, as well as many of Yunnan's indigenous scholars. It is they who convey to me the spirit of their legacies. It is working together with them on the issues they face that gives me a sense of interaction with their heritage, within the context of their culture, environment, and aspirations.[67]

Chou is eager to share his renewed sense of self and his concern over the revival of other Asian heritages with his colleagues by calling for a reexamination and deeper understanding of one's heritage. Chou believes that after the West borrowed musical material from the East earlier in the last century and the East borrowed from the West later in the century, the merger of the two is inevitable. In short, he advocates conceptual union, a Hegelian dialectic concept. And the substance for cross-fertilization is heritage, or aesthetics, the view Chou had already expressed in the 1966. The difference is that through his Yunnan experience, Chou felt the urgency to communicate this idea to younger Asian composers who, otherwise, might succumb to the lure of commercialism and public limelight.

In 1995, Chou attended a vocal performance of the indigenous villagers of the Ha Ni tribe in Yunnan and was impressed that the native polyphonic tradition, which contains imitation in inversion, is akin to the variable modes he developed in the 1960s. And the constant transformation of the original material is much like the constant ebb and flow of ink in Chinese calligraphy, which stresses discipline and creative spontaneity. To him, it was a true revelation. This experience must have affected his thinking while he was working on his first string quartet during this time, and it can also be seen in his second quartet, which, as homage to Bach, features imitation and eight sets of variations on a theme and has just been completed. The aesthetic ideal of the Chinese calligraphy is being worked out in both of these quartets. Chou is planning to compose his third quartet; the textual setting and characteristics of the strings in a quartet seem to be the closest media for realizing his calligraphic concepts.

Chou became acquainted with Mark Steinberg, first violin of the Brentano String Quartet, through a connection made by one of Chou's students (who was helping him to look for a group to perform his first quartet before the piece was completed).[68] Chou subsequently attended Brentano Quartet's concerts and was much impressed. Likewise, members of the quartet heard live recordings of Chou's music and regarded it very highly. With mutual respect, a cordial and fruitful working relationship developed. Steinberg and his colleagues were quite involved in the composition process; they had a unique opportunity to witness the growth of the quartet and to learn how Chou thinks and works as a composer, as Chou would send bits of the quartet to them. Through working with Chou, the musicians were able to get into his ear and find ways to achieve desired results. One example is their innovative suggestion of using guitar picks for the hard sound, which would have been impossible to produce with conventional pizzicato techniques, in the scherzo movement of the first quartet. Chou was quite pleased with this idea. Conversely, when the players could not decide how to execute the rather muted dynamics, with only mezzo forte and piano, they learned from Chou about applying the Eastern value of restraint even for explosive emotions.

Steinberg is a very insightful musician. He describes the differences between Chou's two quartets:

> The work [the second quartet] also I think is more compact than the first quartet. It is quite a bit shorter, and it feels more concise . . . whereas the first quartet feels like a huge landscape in front of you, this one feels more concentrated.[69]

Chou's second quartet has recently been performed in New York on April 23, 2004. For the second quartet, Steinberg observes:

> The quartet overall is everything we could have hoped for (when we had the initial idea for our project to ask composers to respond to Bach), because this really does seem like not only a homage to Bach but a complete absorption of what Bach is in another idiom or what Bach can mean to a very cultured musician. The way it comes out the other side, through his [Chou] eyes, through his ears, is really quite extraordinary.[70]

Chou, in his early eighties, has lately been experiencing health problems. Yet he has not slowed down in his efforts to compose and promote Asian compositional development. Despite health concerns, in September 2003, he traveled to Tokyo, Japan, to deliver his keynote speech "Beyond Identity" at the Asian Music Festival, celebrating the thirtieth anniversary of the Asian Composers League and the twentieth anniversary of the Japan Federation of Composers. In November 2003, he traveled to Taiwan to give his speech

"Commercialization and Globalization in Music" for a music festival in his name there. His trip to Beijing and Shanghai to deliver a lecture of a similar topic, planned for spring 2003, was postponed to September 2004 because of SARS (Severe Acute Respiratory Syndrome). Chou has been deeply concerned about issues, as suggested by the titles of his speeches, which may have negative impact on the stylistic development of the younger composers. Richard Pittman, Chou's long-time friend and a respected conductor, observes:

> He [Chou] felt he had to take this opportunity to speak to young Asian composers about what he saw as the wrong paths that they were taking as composers, and the kind of abandonment of the values of their own cultures in the pursuit of a new path which is really very superficial and, from his point of view, and mine, too, very wrong-headed, in really the wrong direction.[71]

Although Pittman is also critical of some of the young composers' use of their cultural resources as a way of packaging their compositions for recognition and their superficial approach to composition, he has not done anything other than complaining about it. He admires Chou's effort in "trying to take concrete steps to make changes, to speak up publicly, to take concrete steps to try to influence these negative developments in a positive way, to try to make a change."[72] In recent years, it is satisfying to see that many young composers in Taiwan, Japan, China, and elsewhere are beginning to respond to Chou's challenge to seriously explore their rich cultural resources with a firm cultural commitment and self-discipline for developing their individualistic styles, despite pressure from the lure of quick, commercial success. In Richard Pittman's words, Chou was swimming against the tide, but now the tide has begun to turn in his favor.

Notes

1. July 28, 1923, is the date on Chou's U.S. passport. According to Chou, he was born on the sixteenth day of the fifth month of the Chinese lunar calendar that may correspond to June 29, 1923. Wen-Chung Chou, correspondence with Peter Chang, April 18, 2004, 2–3.

2. From this document, Chou has found that Chou Dun-Yi or Zhou Dunyi (1017–1073), also called Zhou Lianxi was known officially in his day as a descendant of the royal family of Chou, the surname of the Chou Dynasty (1027–256/255 BC). Chou Dun-Yi received, after death, the original feudal title of the Ear of Junan (Runan), the southern part of today's Henan Province. The title was stripped from the Chou family by Qin Shi Huang, the first emperor of the Qin Dynasty (221–206 BC), after the fall of the Chou Dynasty. According to Chou, the *Tang* (family tem-

ple), with brick pillars decorated with the family insignia and a bundle of books tied with silk cords, was still standing at the time of his visit in 1996, and there were two original copies of his own family branch (Ai Lian or loving the lotus) genealogical record kept in his ancestral home, but both were lost. One was taken by the Japanese army during World War II, and the other was burned by the Red Guards during the Cultural Revolution. Chou, correspondence, April 18, 2004, 3.

3. The civil service examination was the traditional way to select government officials. It was established in the Sui period (ca. 606 AD), perfected in the Song period (ca. 975 AD), and finally abolished in 1905.

4. Known as the *Ba Gu Wen* or "eight-legged essay" with eight main headings and no more than 700 characters.

5. This is *Zi*, which is one's second name that is derived from the interpretation of his given name (*Zhengming*). For example, Chou's father's given name is Chou Miao, and his *Zi* is Zhong Jie, or *Miao*, meaning vast body of water, as *Jie* means pure or clean. *Zhong* means the second child in the family. Before 1949, most educated Chinese men had a *Zhengming*, a *Zi*, or a *Hao*, which was sometimes used indiscriminately with *Zi*. *Hao* means nickname. However, another name for Chou Xue-Qiao is Chou Wei-Han.

6. A letter to Chou from the Xun Yaping of the Municipal Library of Changzhou, referencing to *Cultural and Historical documents of Changzhou*, book 9, edited by the Cultural and Historical Research Committee of the Commission for Changzhou, Jiangsu Province: People's Political Consultation Council of China, December 1989. Letter and documents translated by Wen-Chung Chou.

7. Between the 1860s and 1890s, the Manchu government initiated a movement known as the *Yang wu*, or foreign affairs movement, to empower itself by adopting Western technology and encouraging Western financial investment for building factories, railroads, a navy, a defense industry, and to set up departments for handling foreign affairs movement. However, this effort failed to protect China from defeat by Western powers, including the Japanese. Almost concurrently, there was an intellectual movement lead by Kang You-Wei (1858–1927), who reinterpreted Confucianism with the Western view of a just and functioning society, and laid a philosophical foundation for modern Chinese intellectuals. Kang advocated parliamentary monarchy rather than republican revolution.

8. Since 1627, Aristotle's works had been translated into Chinese by Portuguese missionaries and Chinese translators. Some of the translations were published (e.g., 1631 Hang Zhou edition of Aristotle's *Ming Li Tan*). See Shen Fu-Wei's *Zhongxi Wenhua Jiaoliu Shi* [History of Cultural Exchanges between East and West], 3rd ed. (Shanghai: Shanghai People's Publisher, 1988), 427–28. Whether Chou's grandfather became acquainted with Western philosophy from Japanese sources or from the published translation in China is not determined.

9. This information came from a letter to Chou from Xun Yaping of the Municipal Library of Changzhou, containing information provided by the Museum of Jiangsu Province (Wen-Chung Chou's translations).

10. Letter to Wen-Chung Chou from Xun Yaping of the Municipal Library of Changzhou (translation by Wen-Chung Chou).

11. Letter to Wen-Chung Chou from Xun Yaping of the Municipal Library of Changzhou (translation by Wen-Chung Chou).

12. Letter to Wen-Chung Chou from Xun Yaping of the Municipal Library of Changzhou (translation by Wen-Chung Chou).

13. See Ssu-yu Teng and John Fairbank, *China's Response to the West: A Documentary Survey 1839–1923* (New York: Athenan, 1966). Six forces were operational after the 1840 Opium War through the 1920s: nationalism (the boxer and Heavenly Peace rebellions), party dictatorship, the cult of the masses, worship of Western science and technology, the leadership of the youth, and liberation of women.

14. In the seventy-fifth anniversary of the 1911 revolution, Chou's father was recognized as one of the surviving members of the participants. He participated in the 1911 revolution in Shanghai.

15. The 1903 adoption of a Western education system was the earliest and was based on the German-Japanese models. The 1911 revision consisted of an eight-year elementary school, a four-year secondary school, and a four-year college, somewhat similar to the American system. The final revision came in 1922 in which the elementary school was reduced to six years and secondary school was divided into two three-year levels, reflecting American influence.

16. In terms of his interest in studying *I-Ching*, Chou was influenced by his father, and in a traditional Chinese family, passing on the family tradition from one generation to another is extremely important.

17. Chou's father never joined Guomindang [the Nationalist Party].

18. This was known as the famous "8.13 Songhu Campaign." The fighting was fierce—700,000 Chinese troops fought bravely but were forced to retreat in early November. Songlin Li et al., eds., *The Chronology of Major Events of the Chinese Nationalist Party (1894.11–1986.12)* (Beijing: PLA Press, 1988), 272.

19. Chou, correspondence, April 18, 2004, 2.

20. Kuo-Huang Han, "Shanghai Gongbuju Yudui Yanju" [A Study of the Shanghai Municipal Orchestra], *Study of the Arts* 14 (1995): 163–64.

21. Han, "Shanghai Gongbuju Yudui Yanju," 164–65.

22. Zhongguo Yinyue Cidian Editorial Committee, *Zhongguo Yinyue Cidian* [Dictionary of Chinese Music] (Beijing: People's Music Publisher, 1984), 343.

23. Han, "Shanghai Gongbuju Yudui Yanju," 163.

24. Editorial Committee, *Zhongguo Yinyue Cidian*, 343.

25. Han, "Shanghai Gongbuju Yudui Yanju," 163.

26. Alexander Tcherepnine, "Music in Modern China," *The Musical Quarterly* 21, no. 4 (October 1935): 391–400.

27. With Ding Shan-De, Chen founded the Shanghai Music Institute for the training of musically inclined teenagers.

28. Xu studied in Belgium.

29. Chou, correspondence, April 18, 2004, 2.

30. Songlin, *Chronology of Major Events*, 329.

31. Chou fled Guilin via a freight train. He later recalled that it was hard to recognize outbound freight cars, and it was a coincidence that he had just completed a course on railroad construction, which allowed him to recognize the freight that would take him and his friends to safety. He said jokingly, "this is why I studied civil engineering, to save my life." Chou, correspondence, April 21, 2004. 3–4.

32. The Chiang Kai-Sheck regime, as opposed to the Communist party and government, had headquarters in Yanan, Shanxi province.

33. During the Japanese occupation in Shanghai, the puppet Chinese government took over the Shanghai Conservatory. Some faculty members and students moved to Chungqing, and some separated from the existing one to form a private one. See "Guoli Yinyue Yuan" [The National Conservatory of Music], *Zhongguo Yinyue Cidian*, 138.

34. Wang asked Chou about the possibility of joining the orchestra. Chou was interested. But because of his impending trip to Shanghai, he could not accept the offer. He later reflected that the orchestra's repertoire was too limited for an adequate orchestral experience. Chou, correspondence, April 18, 2004, 2.

35. Chou, correspondence, April 18, 2004, 1.

36. Robert Kyr, "Between the Mind and the Ear: Finding the Perfect Balance," *League-ISCM*, Boston, April 1990, 14.

37. Nicolas Slonimsky, "Chou Wen-Chung," in *American Composers Alliance Bulletin* 9, no. 4 (1961): 3.

38. Chou, correspondence, April 21, 2004, 4.

39. Chou, correspondence, April 21, 2004, 4.

40. Kyr, "Between the Mind and the Ear," 14–15.

41. Slonimsky, "Chou Wen-Chung," 3.

42. Carol Oja, *Colin McPhee: A Composer in Two Worlds* (Washington, D.C.: Smithsonian Institution Press, 1990), 202.

43. This implies traditions of Busoni's objectivity and Debussy's architectural formal design.

44. Kyr, "Between the Mind and the Ear," 15.

45. Kyr, "Between the Mind and the Ear," 15–16.

46. Kyr, "Between the Mind and the Ear," 16.

47. Kyr, "Between the Mind and the Ear," 17.

48. His most revered early Baroque composers were Monteverdi and Schütz, and through his association with *Schola Contorum* in Paris, he developed a strong interest in early music.

49. Slonimsky, "Chou Wen-Chung," 3.

50. Kyr, "Between the Mind and the Ear," 20.

51. Kyr, "Between the Mind and the Ear," 24.

52. See Wen-Chung Chou, "Chinese Historiography and Music: Some Observations," *The Musical Quarterly* (April 1976): 218–40; and "Review of *The Lore of the Chinese Lute*: An Essay in the Ideology of the Ch'in," *The Musical Quarterly* (April 1974): 301–5.

53. This is largely due to the activities and the publications of several scholars such as McAllester, Kurath, Merriam, and Rhodes. For more on this, see Bruno Nettl, *The Study of Ethnomusicology* (Chicago: University of Illinois Press, 1983), 360.

54. Wen-Chung Chou, "Sights and Sounds: Remembrances," www.chouwenchung.org, 5.

55. Wen-Chung Chou, "Beyond Identity" (keynote lecture, Asian Music Festival, Tokyo, Japan, September 18, 2003), 3.

56. Wen-Chung Chou, interview transcriptions by Peter Chang at Chou's New York home, November 8, 1991.

57. Slonimsky, "Chou Wen-Chung," 2.

58. Announcement, *American Composers Alliance Bulletin* 11, no. 24 (December 1963): 20.

59. Reprinted from a *New York Herald Tribune* announcement, *American Composers Alliance Bulletin* 10, no. 3 (September 1962): 15.

60. Chou, "Sights and Sounds," 4.

61. Paul Griffith, *Modern Music* (London: J. M. Dent and Sons, Ltd., 1981), 196–200. Eric Salzman attributes this trend as an Asian response to Cage's influence and appropriation of oriental ideas. See Eric Salzman, *Twentieth-Century Music: An Introduction* (Englewood Cliffs, N.J.: Prentice-Hall, 1974), 156, note 2.

62. Chou, interview, 1991.

63. According to Chou, for *Metaphors*, in addition to the Chinese modal system as a source, there is also the influence of the Indian raga from an Indian concert. Wen-Chung Chou, correspondence with Peter Chang, May 4, 2004, 2.

64. Richard Pittman, Interview with Richard Pittman on the subject of Wen-Chung Chou, February 5, 2004, 4.

65. Will Crutchfield, "Columbia to House a Reiner Archive," *New York Times*, November 25, 1984.

66. Wen-Chung Chou, "U.S.-China Arts Exchange: A Practice in Search of a Philosophy," in *Intercultural Music Studies Volume 2: Music in the Dialogue of Cultures: Traditional Music and Cultural Policy*, ed. Max Peter Baumann (Berlin: Lorian Boetzel Edition, 1990), 156–57.

67. Wen-Chung Chou, "Music—What Is Its Future?" (keynote speech delivered at the "Search Event III," University of California, San Diego, April 21, 2001), 3.

68. Mark Steinberg, interview with Mark Steinberg on the subject of Chou Wen-Chung, February 27, 2004, 1.

69. Steinberg, interview, 4.

70. Steinberg, interview, 4.

71. Pittman, interview, 5.

72. Pittman, interview, 5.

CHAPTER THREE

~

Chou's Works of the 1940s and 1950s

A common characteristic among Chou's works of the 1940s and 1950s is the use of poetry as inspiration and the direct employment of Chinese melodies with decorative harmony. Chou tried to "recapture the color, mood, and emotion implied in the seemingly simple material."[1] During this period, Chou worked with one idea for several pieces and, then, abandoned it to start a new one. To appreciate the qualities of these Chinese melodies, Chou wanted to learn to generate musical structure, voice leading, supporting sonorities, as well as timbre and emotion for each composition.[2]

There is a sharp distinction between the use of Chinese melody in *Landscapes* and Chou's early attempts to write "Chinese-flavored" fugues while he was still a student at the New England Conservatory. In *Landscapes*, Chou was able to project his realization of Chinese aesthetic values expressed in classic Chinese poetry, water-ink paintings, and calligraphy impressionistically and to avoid subjugating Chinese melody under the Western harmonic framework. In other words, quartal harmony and Western instrumentation were used only to help create the mood and overall sound quality of the piece. Chou revealed that this was the result of his teacher Slonimsky's suggestion that he should study Chinese music seriously. In his letter of July 16, 1960, to Slonimsky, Chou writes:

I was stimulated by your suggestions when I began in 1949 to make a serious study of classical Chinese music and subsequently other Eastern music as well. In the meantime, I tried to integrate the result of these studies with the most advanced contemporary musical techniques. I believe the foundation of my musical thinking was formed beginning with *Landscapes* written in 1949 and culminating with the composition of *And the Fallen Petals*.[3]

Slonimsky wrote in retrospect, "I encouraged him to cultivate his knowledge of traditional Chinese music because I felt that he had the unique chance of creating an oriental style in a twentieth-century idiom."[4]

Landscapes (1949)

Landscapes, Chou's first major work or his opus one, relates to several of his lesser-known works in a particular way. In this work, Chou experimented with working out Chinese thematic materials for different media, that is, for a large orchestra, small chamber group, and a solo instrument. The theme used in the second section of the first poem also appears in the first movement of *Suite for Harp and Wind Quintet* (1951; see examples 3.1 and 3.2), and the thematic material used in the second poem "The Sorrow of Parting," arranged for solo harp, is recycled in the second song of "Three Folk Songs"

Example 3.1. *Landscapes* mm. 13–17

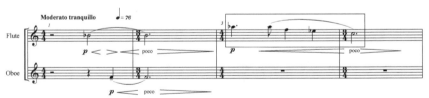

Example 3.2. *Suite for Harp and Wind Quintet* mm. 1–4

Example 3.3. *Landscapes* mm. 44–48

Example 3.4. *Suite for Harp and Wind Quintet* mm. 53–57

(1950), for harp and flute or for solo harp, and in section 4, mm. 79–101 of *Suite for Harp and Wind Quintet* (example 3.3).

The melody used in the third piece of *Landscapes* mm. 84–86 again appears in mm. 55–56 of the first piece of *Suite for Harp and Wind Quintet* (examples 3.4 and 3.5).

Among Chinese tunes explored by Chou, the "Flower and Drum Song of Fengyang" characterized by drum rhythm is used repeatedly. Besides Chou, this melody was also used by Qu Wei in his 1946 piano piece "Flower Drum" in which Qu Wei combines it with "Moli Hua," or Jasmine Flower, characterized by syncopation (examples 3.6–3.8).[5] Together, "Fengyang Huagu" and "Moli Hua" also appeared in a 1934 Hollywood movie *The Good Earth* based on a novel by Pearl Buck (1892–1973). The difference between Chou's settings and the rest is that Chou allowed more rhythmic freedom and consciously avoided triadic harmony. Example 3.9 (m. 113, piano and bassoon) shows the abrupt transposition, fifth higher, from *zhi* mode, that is, sol–la–do–re–mi or sol=F, on pitch F to *zhi* mode on pitch C or sol=C without harmonic preparation. This technique in Chinese is called *lidiao*, or

Example 3.5. *Landscapes* mm. 82–86

Example 3.6. Chinese Folk Song "Fengyang Huagu" [Flower and Drum Song of Fengyang] mm. 7–12

Example 3.7. Qu Wei's Piano Piece "Huagu" [Flower Drum] mm. 13–30

Example 3.8. *Three Folk Songs* mm. 40–42

Example 3.9. *Suite for Harp and Wind Quintet* **mm. 109–115**

temporary deviation from the tune or the mode. In Chou's terms, this is the change of tonal plane.[6] Because in traditional Chinese music there is no functional harmony, the modulation between pentatonic modes does not require harmonic support. Chou experimented with this technique in *Landscapes* (mm. 76–77) and again in *Willows Are New* (1957) (mm. 23–34; example 3.10). This is seen in a shift of tonal centers from *yu* mode on F♯ to *yu* mode on G, a semitone higher. Coupled with a brisk tempo, the effect in this passage is a dramatic shift of mood, illustrating a person's internal conflict between leaving and wanting to stay.

LORETTE WILMOT LIBRARY
NAZARETH COLLEGE

Example 3.10. *Willows Are New* mm. 23–34

In comparison with *Three Folk Songs* (1950), the *Suite for Harp and Wind Quintet* (1951) and *Landscapes* mark Chou's early success in writing for a large orchestra or small chamber group. *Three Folk Songs* represents an intermediate stage between these two. There is another piece, *Two Chinese Folk Songs*, which is the 1950 arrangement of *Three Folk Songs* for solo harp by Lucile Lawrence, published, with Chou's permission, by C. F. Peters in 1964. A shared characteristic in these early works is the principle of theme and variation in which Chinese themes have structural significance. In these works themes become the center that determine the length, form, rhythmic character, and texture of the piece. These structural constituents are generated from thematic material, not the other way around. Other compositional components such as harmony and counterpoint are generally given to expand the expression of melodic material. In these works, a single theme would appear many times in cyclic fashion. Chou's intention in working out the innate quality of the Chinese melody is revealed through the projection of the oriental mood, often evoked through Chinese poetry, paintings, and classical music, and through the audience's association of the music with the mood and artistic expressions in classical Chinese poetry and painting. This objective is often achieved through contrasts in orchestral timbre, sparse or thin orchestration, subtle dynamic contrasts, and the alternation between quartal consonance and dissonant dyads such as major second and minor second.

Landscapes is a trilogy, which is based on three Chinese poems of the Ming (1368–1644) and Qing (1644–1911) periods. For each movement of the work, Chou supplied the new program titles to express his own sentiments toward the poems. The form of the piece is outlined below:

Movement I, mm. 1–43, based on a poem by Cheng Hsieh (1693–1765), "Old Fisherman." Chou added a program title, "Under the Cliff in the Bay," to the movement.

Movement II, mm. 44–66, based on a poem by Ting P'eng (ca. 1661), "My Carriage Has Barely Paused." Chou's program title is "The Sorrow of Parting." The movement features a dialogue between an oboe and an English horn.

Movement III, mm. 67–101, based on a poem by Liu Chi (1311–1375), "Green, Green the Grass West of the Pavilion." Chou's title is "One Streak of Dying Light."

All in the Spring Wind (1952–1953)

Somewhat analogous to Chou's second major work, *And the Fallen Petals* (1954; or *Petals* hereafter), *All in the Spring Wind* is also based on a Tang poem, "Yi Jiangnan" or "Reminiscence of Southern Territories" by Li Yu, the last emperor of the Nan Tang courts (937–978 AD). The poem reads:

> [Hateful and regretful],
> Last night, amid broken dreams,
> I was again in the Imperial City as in the days of old.
> [The flow of carriages and horses]
> The flowers, the moon,
> All in the Spring Wind.[7]

The work was completed in 1953, and it was then submitted to Columbia University by Chou in lieu of a thesis for his MA degree, which was conferred in 1954. Oddly, it took almost eight years to have the work publicly performed. The premiere took place on December 7, 1960, by the Louisville Orchestra under the direction of Robert Whitney.[8]

Unlike *Petals*, *All in the Spring Wind* (*All in* hereafter) has not been extensively performed and reviewed in the United States and abroad. In contrast to the optimistic and naive expression of Meng Hao-Ran's poem, which inspired *Petals*, Li Yu's poem is gloomy and nostalgic. Generally, the texture in *All in* is thicker than in *Petals*, but the shift of moods is more frequent, and thematic contrast is greater in *Petals* than in *All in*. In his review of *All in*, in comparison to Chou's *Landscapes* and *Petals*, Karl Kroeger points out that *All in* did not make the same strong impression because it lacked subtlety and the expression was too direct.[9]

The concert in which the work premiered was an interesting combination: Gabrieli's "Sonata Pian e Forte," Chou's *All in the Spring Wind*, Beethoven's First Symphony, and Mendelssohn's Violin Concerto. Clearly, it was a little strange that Chou's work, the only contemporary one, was senselessly thrown in with classical masterpieces in one program. The concert was repeated on December 8, 1960, in Louisville. William Mootz, music reviewer for the Kentucky *Courier-Journal*, found himself caught in an imbroglio. Mootz thought that Chou was quite an innovator and was "just as daring as was Gabrieli back in the days of Venice's musical glory."[10] Mootz further thought that this work "is to be absorbed like an exotic aroma," and "old listening habits must be discarded."[11]

In his article on Chou's promotion of a U.S.-China arts exchange, Chinese composer Chen Gang has paired *Petals* and *All in* as "two flowers" due to the mention of flowers in both Tang poems.[12] In contrast to *Petals*, which is constructed as a triolet, *All in* is a rondelet or rondo:

A B C B A B C B A

It contains:

A1 B1 C1 B2 A2 B3 C2 B4 A3 coda

The structure of the piece consists of four couplets, AB, CB, AB, CB, an A section, and a coda. This can be seen as two alternating couplets, AB and CB. The refrain B, only six measures long, is sparsely orchestrated and so creates a dreamy atmosphere. The lucid structural plan is carefully thought out and calculated. Chou's subsequent use of orchestra as percussion in *Petals* is clearly seen in the coda of this piece, for a machine-like motor rhythm is prominent, and pitch changes are minimized.

The intervallic pattern for the thematic material used in section A consists of a descending minor ninth and two ascending octaves (example 3.11). This is assigned to the upper strings. The B material consists of a tritone (C♯–G), an ascending fourth (C♯–F♯), and a descending minor ninth (E♭–C♯), also verticalized major ninth (F♯–G, A–B♭, and C♯–D). The C section begins with thematic fragments of section A that is played on xylophone with double dotted rhythm and an intervallic pattern of an ascending and a descending major ninth, plus a descending minor ninth (example 3.12).

Thematic unity is also achieved through recycling basic thematic fragments in different sections of the piece, a practice found also in *Petals*. It seems that in terms of intervallic patterns, *All in* signifies a break from Chou's penchant for fourth, major second, and minor second in his earlier and later works because it makes extensive use of major ninth, minor ninth,

Example 3.11. *All in the Spring Wind* mm. 1–6

Example 3.12. *All in the Spring Wind* mm. 27–31

and octaves. For the thematic material used in these two orchestral works, Chou commented:

> In both of these works, Chinese material is used as a kind of cantus firmus as a result of my having been in a seminar on medieval music. In these pieces, the pitches of the Chinese melodies are spread throughout the register and texture, with each pitch serving as the principal tone for a particular segment of the music.[13]

This most recent comment, the first time in five decades, is indeed revealing for it brings audiences' vague feelings into sharp focus.

And the Fallen Petals (1954)

This work, commissioned by the Louisville Orchestra, was composed in 1954. Its premiere on February 9, 1955, in Louisville was an instant success. The work signifies Chou's technical maturity and marks a new stage in his career. In fact, this work has been performed in the United States and foreign countries more than any other of his works, establishing Chou as a successful model for musical synthesis for contemporary music worldwide.

Apparently, the work extends the three-part formal construction already seen in *Landscapes*:

Prologue mm. 1–17
Part I. mm. 18–46
Part II. mm. 47–186
Part III. mm. 187–227
Epilogue mm. 228–251

The difference between these two works is that, instead of using different thematic materials for each part, there is a clear sign of thematic unity in *Petals*. The theme, or in Chou's words "cantus firmus"—derived from several Chinese folk tunes that were quite popular in Chou's college days during the war—is constructed on a sequence of descending fourths that is derived from traditional Chinese grace-note figures, either descending minor second or perfect fourth (example 3.13). In the middle part of the piece, *Gioioso* mm. 47–186, the theme is used in a fragmented and extremely sparse manner and is tossed around here and there among different voices. Example 3.14 shows just one appearance of the thematic fragment

Example 3.13. *And the Fallen Petals* **mm. 1–7**

in part II. Much of the rhythmic vitality of the piece is generated through rapid alternation of duple, triple, and asymmetrical meters. The alternation can be seen from measures 27 to 37 where meter changes in every measure. This is also seen in the second poem of *Landscapes* (example 3.15). Several rhythmic figures such as triplets have structural meanings and are usually assigned to percussion, lower strings, or French horns. Combined with rests or longer sustained notes, they propel the middle section of the piece that requires agitated motion.

A major concern of the piece is sonority, often in the form of single chords, which are distributed to different instruments, either juxtaposed on one another to create dense sound or spaced sparsely according to the mood of the section. Throughout the piece, the articulation of each sonority begins and sustains an attack either on percussion or melodic instruments, and frequent shifts in dynamics play important roles in providing timbral variety.

Structurally, an important consideration of the piece is the interplay between layers of sounds in which the Varèsean idea of sound as a moving mass and the idea of controlled flow of ink in Chinese calligraphy are merged. There are five kinds of sound layers:

1. The prologue starting with the flute playing a single line of melody, which is then imitated a fourth lower on the oboe, with the same idea repeated in the epilogue with different ending pitch E♭ as opposed to B♭ in the prologue
2. Sustained notes on the upper strings with harmonics in horns and harp often with quartal harmony
3. Sparse short punctuating notes alternating with the woodwinds, strings, and brass sections

Example 3.14. *And the Fallen Petals* mm. 65–69

Example 3.15.   *And the Fallen Petals* mm. 29–34

4. Decorative figures in upper strings, harp, and woodwinds around the melodic fragments in oboe (m. 106), English horn (mm. 28, 128), and trumpet (m. 159)
5. Long notes plus scale figures

Except for the prologue and epilogue, these layers are manipulated through juxtaposition, linear elaboration, and verticalization. Linear elaboration results in the expansion of sonority without increasing rhythmic activity, while verticalization refers to the stacking of chords chosen from different layers by maintaining their identity. These layers are the basic building material for the piece, and the thematic unity and textural diversity are created and maintained by alternating different layers of sonorities, that is, stasis versus activity, and thinness versus density.

Often, a layer is expanded linearly and is stacked on top of another layer (specific combinations of instruments) or layers without sacrificing the identity of any layer. Furthermore, a particular type of texture has direct relationship to the increment of rhythmic activity, which is characterized by rapid alternation of duple and triple meters.

Another distinctive feature of the piece is the reduction of linear pitch variation. For example, for the horns, tuba, and lower strings, the change of pitch occurs only once in ten measures (mm. 27–37). This is true elsewhere throughout the piece. This melodic inertia or slow pace in changing pitch suggests that the composer is treating the orchestra as a large percussion ensemble in which the pitch variety is limited. The composer's major concerns are on the contrast among vertical sonorities and between rhythmic stasis and activity.

This concept of using the orchestra as a percussion ensemble reflects the influence of Varèse,[14] and the acknowledgment of the independence of certain sonorities shows the influence of Webern, in addition to the concept of textural stratification from Korean and Indian music. Yet, above all, these ideas are dictated by the expressive requirements of the poems, which were the source of inspiration that molded Chou's musical thinking.

At another level, through his study of classical Chinese music, Chou realized that these Western concepts have precedents in Chinese musical tradition. In the absence of harmony, the timbre of each individual tone has become highly elaborated and constituted an important aspect of Chinese classical music, especially in the music of the qin, whose timbral palette extends to at least twenty-six varieties through different playing techniques. Such a great variety on a single instrument is rarely seen on Western instruments with the exclusion of electronic devices.

Timbre, an underdeveloped area in earlier times, has been explored much more rigorously during this century in the West. The definition of timbre involves register, articulation, and vibratory characteristics of an instrument or group of instruments. In terms of defining vibratory and articulatory aspects of timbre, the Chinese are more specific and clear than their Western colleagues. Although there have been attempts to define timbre by acoustic science in more precise ways in the West,[15] the generic term for the definition of "timbre" (no specific names of hues are applicable for tones) or "tone color" (and a list of the associated adjectives such as bright, dark, and mellow) has not yet established by the results of these experiments.

Varèse's contribution in elevating rhythm and sonority to the status of melody and harmony has much to do with his association with painters and poets. Varèse maintained a cordial relationship with both Cocteau and Picasso during the 1910s.[16] He knew the cubist painter Fernand Léger's work well. He had even quarreled with him over private affairs.[17] Other influential painters in Varèse's circle included André Derain, who illustrated Apollinaire's poems L'Enchanteur (1909), Raoul Dufy, André Lhote, and Robert Delaunay.[18] According to Ouellette, Varèse's most admired painters were Goya, Picasso, Chagall, Dubuffet, the Tachists, Kandinsky, and Klee in their early works. Varèse and Italian sculptor Giacometti were also friends.[19] Varèse's close association with modern visual artists and poets rather than with composers was based on his belief that the visual arts and literature were far more innovative than music and that leadership in visual and literary arts was at the forefront of a stylistic revolution. A visible element in modern visual arts is the intensification of contrast through color and shade, an important achievement in moving away from traditional use of light as a way of creating dimension and depth in a flat surface. The play between light and color is evident in the works of impressionist painters most visibly, in Monet and Renoir, and more so in the works of Kandinsky, who formulated a theory that articulates the role of color as dependent on form.[20] Varèse heard about the theoretical writings of Blaue Reiter through his friends at L'Abbaye de Créteil. The Blaue Reiter artists, cubists, and futurists shared a principle that color and texture are the agents of contrast; they also shared a view that despite the new art's elevation of color, color is still subjugated under form, which could stand alone.[21]

Varèse realized that, in terms of the exploration of color, there is a disparity between visual art and music because the concept of color has not been explored by modern composers as extensively as it has in modern paintings. For example, Fernand Léger expounded on the specific role of color in painting for providing contrast.[22] With his familiarity with Léger's and Picasso's cubist theories about color and simultaneous representation of the same object by juxtaposition, Varèse was able to translate these theories from modern painting to music. Varèse's view on the function of color in music is expressed in his lecture "The Liberation of Sound":

> The role of color or timbre would be completely changed from being incidental, anecdotal, sensual or picturesque; it would become an agent of delineation, like the different colors on a map separating the different areas, and an integral part of form. These zones would be felt as isolated.[23]

Varèse maintained his association with new ideas in the visual arts; everything he found interesting in visual arts would be referred to music later. He used to echo his painter-friend André Derain's often-quoted saying, "painting is made of light [as] music is made of sound."[24] He was also susceptible to art critics' use of the term geometric, which he later used to describe the sound of his music. His embracing of cubist concepts of form, color, and multiple viewpoints and simultaneity is reflected in his view on the structural components of music.

Chou's affinity to classical Chinese visual arts, particularly painting, calligraphy, and poetry, parallels Varèse's. In other words, he learned from Varèse not only specific composition techniques but also, more importantly, how to discover the links between visual and musical arts and use them as a point of departure for each work and as a theoretical base for his music. For a Chinese classical painting, there is always a poem in the calligraphy inscribed upon it. Thus, painting, poetry, and calligraphy are presented on the scroll simultaneously. And the subject of the painting, usually a landscape, and the poem are integrated to suggest the interaction between man and nature. The painting usually determines the content of the poem. By allying himself with visual and fine arts, Chou's compositional resources were greatly expanded.

The connection between every domain in a culture was earlier suggested by structural-functionalist anthropologists Malinowsky and Radcliffe-Brown.[25] This connection or mutual influence is seen clearly in Chinese culture, and, as seen in Varèse's case, it is extraordinary in Western culture as well.

In comparing the sophistication in the variety of sonority and formal design, *Petals* is more complex than *Landscapes*, and Chou himself observed that his first venture in fusing Western and Chinese elements began with *Landscapes* and ended with *Petals*; the latter signifies Chou's maturity and sophistication in looking for compatible theories not only between visual and musical arts in Western culture but also in their Chinese counterparts. In *Petals*, although the use of Chinese melody as used in *Landscapes* is retained, such melody functioned only ironically, establishing the context and setting the mood rather than as basic thematic material to be worked out harmonically and orchestrated. The use of motivic cells in the first and third movements of *Landscapes* appeared again throughout *Petals*, but instead of making them thematic and lyrical orchestral accompaniments, these cells are interwoven with only thematic fragments and percussive orchestral sonorities. Even though these two works represent different styles, it is clear that there is no break between this group of Chou's early works. Instead, a continuous line of evolution can be observed.

Like the sonorous aspect of the piece (comparable to the calligraphic-controlled flow of ink), *Petals*'s tripartite structure is inspired by Meng Hao-Ran's (689–740 AD) short poem "Chun Xiao" or "Dawn in Spring" and Chen Tzu-Ang's (661–702 AD) "Deng Yuzhou Tai Ge," which was Chou's source of inspiration for the prologue and epilogue of the piece. The last line of "Chun Xiao" became the title of the piece. Meng's poem reads:

> Spring sleeps,
> Not knowing the dawn.
> Bird songs are heard everywhere
> All through the night,
> Such noise of wind and rain,
> And the fallen petals,
> Who knows how many![26]

Chen's poem reads:

> I can see no one gone before me,
> I can see no one coming after me;
> All alone, I am overwhelmed by the thought of the eternity of
> Heaven and earth
> And my tears fall.[27]

The moods of the poems, which are self-evident, express the sentiment of the T'ang poets of the seventh and eighth centuries, the time Chinese poetry attained its highest artistic perfection and when Chinese culture was at its golden age. However, it must be pointed out that Chou uses the T'ang poems only to express a general sentiment, sadness and nostalgia. Yet, the specific images of solitary man in nature suggested in this work are derived from *wenren* style painting, which flourished during the Song (960–1279) and later periods in Chinese history. It was only during the Song period that the *wenren* style, as opposed to the *gongbi* or court-artisan style of the T'ang and earlier periods, became prominent. Instead of court style's refined lines, conventionalized images, and extremely detailed descriptions, such as individual hairs in a mustache, the *wenren* style puts much emphasis on *xieyi* or expression of the emotional state of the painter, his response to nature, and his personality.[28]

In *Petals*, the descriptive content is subtler and the projected image more sophisticated and animated than those in *Landscapes*, which projects static images of solitary man and his natural surroundings based on the poems of the Ming and Qing periods.

In the Mode of Shang (1956)

In the Mode of Shang, an orchestral piece completed in December 1956, is related to *Two Miniatures from T'ang Dynasty* (1957). In terms of melody, both works feature grace notes and an intervallic pattern of major second (D–E) with a upper neighbor F, that is, D–^{F}E (example 3.16). The sixteenth note scale figure was later used in *Two Miniatures from T'ang Dynasty*. Harmonically, perfect fourth or tritone, minor third, and octave doubling can be frequently observed. As indicated by the title, the piece is in the *shang* mode, that is, re–mi–so–la–do with starting pitch of re on D in English horn and C in flute, harp, and first violin (example 3.17). Another prominent feature of the piece is the dotted rhythm that has become a trademark of a group of Chou's works from the mid- and late 1950s, namely, *In the Mode of Shang*

Example 3.16. *Two Miniatures from T'ang Dynasty* mm. 18–21

Example 3.17. *In the Mode of Shang* mm. 20–25

Example 3.18. *Two Miniatures from T'ang Dynasty* mm. 14–17

Example 3.19. *Soliloquy of a Bhiksuni* **mm. 19–25**

(1956), *Two Miniatures from T'ang Dynasty* (1957), and *Soliloquy of a Bhiksuni* (1958; examples 3.17–3.19).

Two Miniatures from T'ang Dynasty (1957)

In 1957, Chou received a commission from Sarah Lawrence College to compose a piece for chamber ensemble. The composer and conductor Meyer Kupferman specified the instrumentation for what was available at that time at the college—violin, viola, cello, clarinet, French horn, harp, two flutes, percussion, and piano—and student players' ability was also a consideration.[29] The result was *Two Miniatures from T'ang Dynasty* (1957). Structurally, the first miniature (mm. 1–37) is in a tripartite form, that is, A–B–A. The second one (mm. 38–76) consists of two melodic sections preceded by a refrain and a coda (mm. 77–83). The thematic material in the first miniature, later used in *Soliloquy of a Bhiksuni* (1958), concludes the piece, and the harmony is basically quartal. The metric alternation between 4/8 and 5/8 continues to be present here, and a rhythmic figure that was used in *Petals* (mm. 131–134) and *In the Mode of Shang* (mm. 2–7) is also used in this work. The work premiered in New York on April 30, 1957, by Sarah Lawrence College Chamber Orchestra, conducted by Meyer Kupferman. Of the eight pieces premiered, the composers of three works, Miriam Gideon for *Danza*, Chou for *Two Miniatures from T'ang Dynasty*, and Erza Laderman for *Theme and Variations* were present at the concert. Recordings of the concert were later used in classrooms for discussion. For an inexperienced student orchestra to perform a contemporary piece, it was an exciting experience. The student audience was just as enthusiastic as the orchestra members.[30]

Soliloquy of a Bhiksuni (1958)

Chou experimented with his melodic and rhythmic ideas in the works mentioned above, ideas that were finally solidified in *Soliloquy of a Bhiksuni*. While a composer-in-residence at the University of Illinois, and with *Two Miniatures from T'ang Dynasty* (1956) and *In the Mode of Shang* (1957) as prelude, Chou composed *Soliloquy of a Bhiksuni* in 1958. The piece is for solo trumpet and wind ensemble and is based on a scene from a sixteenth-century Chinese drama, the famous *Kunqu* tune, Si Fan. Initially, Chou planned to use this material for a one-act opera and wrote most of the libretto but later decided to compose an instrumental piece instead. According to Chou, the piece relates to an imagined experience of a Buddhist nun at worship in a dark temple. The text describing her thoughts at worship follows:

> I am only sixteen,
> In the early spring of life.
> Yet I am thrust through the Gate of Emptiness.
> Hearing only the sound of temple bells and ritual pipes,
> Striking stone chimes,
> Endlessly, endlessly,
> Ringing bells.
> Blowing the shell trumpet,
> Beating the drums,
> Trying vainly to communicate with
> The land of the Dead.[31]

The work was premiered on December 18, 1958, in the University of Illinois's Smith Hall with the University Wind Ensemble conducted by Robert Gray and with Richard Tolley as the soloist. Three months later, the piece was again performed on March 3, 1959, as part of the University of Illinois's Festival of Arts concerts.[32] Its July 10, 1960, Pittsburgh performance with the American Wind Symphony conducted by Robert Boudreau elicited an enthusiastic response. Ruth Heimbuecher wrote, "Sometimes harsh, the composition was constantly interesting."[33]

The work is a continuation of Chou's interest in maintaining thematic unity through its interpenetration of a varied textural environment and the variation of sonority in a directionally controlled movement of sound mass. The interplay between the flow of the melody and the textural density can be seen in the A section in which the two-phrased melody in the solo trumpet flow is interrupted by stagnant dense accompaniment (example 3.20). Such interplay creates an aural impression of a controlled ebb and flow of sound, thereby approximating the control of ink flow in Chinese calligraphy and realizing this effect in music.

Although the form of the piece can be tabulated as a tripartite A–B–A–coda type, the textural treatment of the piece exemplifies the

Example 3.20. *Soliloquy of a Bhiksuni* mm. 12–25

baroque concerto principle, that is, alternation between solo(s) and the orchestra:

A Section:
tutti	solo	tutti	solo	tutti	solo	tutti	solo
mm. 1–8	9–11	13–20	20–25	25–32	33–37	38–40	41–44

B Section:
tutti/solo	solo	tutti/solo
mm. 45–48	49–50	51–79

A Section:
tutti	solo	tutti	solo	tutti
mm. 80–86	87–91	92–99	99–104	105–107

Coda:
tutti/solo	tutti	solo	tutti
mm. 108–114	115–121	122	123

Both the melodic and harmonic materials are based on the Chinese pentatonic mode, specifically, the *yu* mode, that is, la–do–re–mi–so, and minor second, perfect fourth, and minor ninth are again featured prominently.[34]

Willows Are New (1957) and To a Wayfarer (1958)

Two weeks before the premiere of *Soliloquy* on December 3, 1958, Chou's other work *To A Wayfarer*—composed in 1958 for clarinet, strings, harp, and percussion—was premiered at Metropolitan Museum of Art in New York City at a concert of the Contemporary Music Society[35] conducted by Leopold Stokowski. Of all the works on the program, including those by Henry Cowell, Colin McPhee, Halim El-Dabh, Shukichi Mitsukuri, and Oden Partos, Chou's made the "deepest impression" on Ross Parmenter, music critic for the *New York Times*, due to its poetic expression. Though the poems inscribed on the scores of the two works are different, namely, the anonymous one for *To a Wayfarer* and Wang Wei's *Yangguan Sandie* for *Willows Are New* (1957), *To a Wayfarer* was the orchestral version of *Willows Are New*, which was composed for piano solo in 1957. The work premiered on February 2, 1958, in New York by Don Shapiro and was later recorded by Yi-An Chang. Other pianists who have performed the piece include, among others, Dorothy Escosa at Fort Wayne Art Museum, Indiana on January 24,

1960; Albert Faurot at the American Music Festival's Mu Phi Epsilon concert in New York City in February 1960; Selma Epstein at the National Gallery of Art, Washington, D.C., on October 21, 1962, at Palo Alto on April 11, 1964, and at Portland on April 16, 1964; and Yi-An Chang at Abbott Academy at Andover Massachusetts on April 8, 1962, and on February 17, 1964, at the 25th Annual WNYC American Music Festival, Hunter College concert. The work was also performed at Brooklyn Museum on June 23, 1963, at the College of William and Mary on May 19, 1963, and at Southern Connecticut State College on May 9, 1963.

Willows Are New was inspired by a traditional Chinese *qin* piece, "Yangguan Sandie" or "Parting at the Yangguan Pass," which was based on the poem "Seeing Yuaner Off to Anxi" by Wang Wei (699–759 AD).[36] Variant names of this poem are "Zengbie" or "Parting," "Weicheng Qu" or "Song of the Wei City," and "Yangguan Qu" or "Song of the Yangguan Pass." Concerning the genesis of the music, Chou has pointed out that the music "is believed to be an adaptation of a movement from 'I-Chou Ta Ch'u,' type of orchestral work of the T'ang dynasty, with Wang Wei's poem as its text."[37] In other words, it is possible that Wang Wei himself actually adapted the poem to *qin* music, which was to be sung while playing. As a separate genre, *qin* music with text has been classified in the *Dictionary of Chinese Music* (1984) as *qinge*, meaning *qin* piece with lyrics. Wang Wei's poem has only four lines:

> In this town, morning rain has cleared the light dust.
> Green, green around the tavern, the willows are new.
> Let us empty another cup of wine.
> For, once West of Yangguan Pass, there will be no more friends.[38]

The following is a translation of later-added text to the original four-line poem, which then appears, as refrains, three times in the piece:

> Refrain 1. Wang Wei's four-line poem
> Verse 1.
>> Through cold mornings and nights,
>> Galloping
>> A long journey over the passes and rivers,
>> With loneliness.
>> Toiling along,
>> please preserve yourself.
> Refrain 2. Wang Wei's four-line poem
> Verse 2.
>> We can no longer comfort each other.
>> How sad.

You will be on my mind day and night.
We will be so far apart,
Whom shall I seek?
No one, but you.
Refrain 3. Wang Wei's four-line poem
Verse 3.

Green grass creeps everywhere.
Delightful wine
that imbues the heart before a swig.
Galloping
When will your carriage return?
How many more times can I fill up your wine cup?
There is an end to thousand drinks,
but none for my sadness.
Endless sorrow,
We are so far apart
as if state of Chu from sky and Xiang River from sea.
Write soon;
tell that we have never parted.
Coda.

Alas! once parted
our thoughts will meet only in dreams.
Wild geese will become our messengers.[39]

Interestingly, although *qin* pieces are not generally intended for singing, this *qin* piece with its text is meant to be sung by the *qin* player. This practice goes back as far as the T'ang period (618–907); two well-known T'ang poets, Bai Ju-Yi and Liu Yu-Xi, described the playing and singing of this very piece.[40] The structural features are very much in line with strophic song form in Western view. Figure 3.1 shows the *qin* tablature with text.

Comments on the Music and the Text

The association of either *qin* music with poetry, called "xuange," or songs with string accompaniment has long been documented in *Shangshu* (ca. eleventh century BC), one of the oldest treatise of arts.[41] In a chapter entitled "Yiji," *Shangshu* reports the performance of *qin* and *se* (type of zither up to twenty-five strings) music with human voice as "bofu qinse yiyong," meaning singing with *qin* and *se* accompaniment.[42]

Besides other inspirational sources for new *qin* compositions such as anecdotes of historical personages, myths and legends, and historical events, preexisting *qin* pieces were often reworked by later poet-musician-calligraphers and painters. Cai Yong (132–192 AD) was a well-known mu-

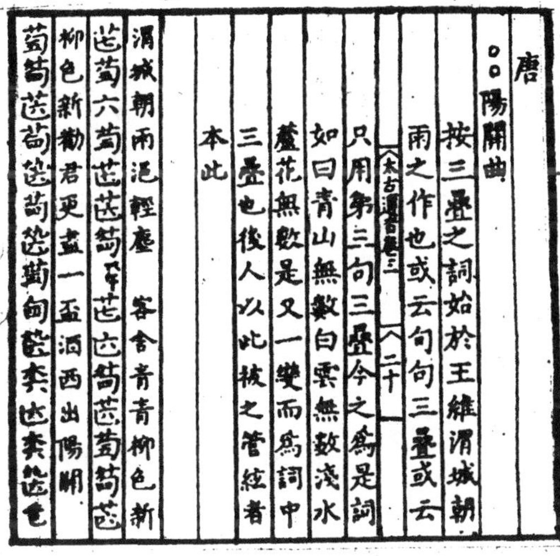
唐
〇〇陽關曲
按三疊之詞始於王維渭城朝
雨之作也或云句句三疊或云
只用第三句三疊今之爲是詞
如曰青山無數白雲無數淺水
蘆花無數是又一變而爲詞中
三疊也後人以此被之管絃者
本此
渭城朝雨浥輕塵　客舍青青柳色新
柳色新勸君更盡一盃酒西出陽關

Figure 3.1. A *Qin* tablature "Yangguan Sandie" with text; *Zhongguo Yinyue Cidian* (1984), 454.

sician of the late Han dynasty. Cai's five-*qin* compositions, "Youchuen" or "Spring Sightseeing," "Lushui" or "Green Water," "Yousi" or "Solitary Thoughts," "Zuochou" or "Gloom," and "Qiusi" or "Autumn Thoughts," were classified as popular pieces by the Wei philosopher, poet, and musician Ji Kang (223–263 AD) in his *Qinfu*, an anthology of *qin* pieces. These works were also listed in the *Qinli*, an *qin* handbook of the Sui period (589–618 AD), and *Yulan*, a set of *qin* tablatures of the Tang period (618–960 AD), were collected in an anthology, *Caishi Wunung*, which was later printed during the Ming period (1368–1644).[43] Cai's works had become an important source for Tang poets like Li Bai, Li He, and Wang Wei to draw upon and for later *qin* players to emulate.[44] Cai's treatise *Qincao* contains over fifty *qin* pieces, the subjects of these pieces were pre-Qin period (ca. 221 BC), and most pieces have texts.[45] Another example of *qin* music with text is the well-known *qin* piece "Jieshidiao Yulan" (text by Bao Zhao, 414–466 AD), the oldest surviving *qin* tablature, which has been preserved in Japan. Also, in the chapter on song lyrics for *qin* music in a historical anthology of poems and music entitled *Yuefu Shiji* [*Poems and Songs from the Music Bureau*] by Guo Mao-Qing of the Song period (960–1279) has a long listing of *qin* pieces with song lyrics.

The setting of poems to *qin* music became common during the Southern Song period (960–1027) and in later periods; several of such pieces have survived. Su Shi (1037–1101), a well-known poet, for example, wrote three different poems as texts for the *qin* piece "Yangguan." Su also composed the text for Shen Zun's *qin* piece "Zuiwong Yin" or "Lament of the Drunken Sage," which was initially inspired by Ouyang Xiu's prose, remained a pure instrumental piece until after Shen's death.[46] Although, today, the text is generally not to be sung while the music is played, the music continues to evoke the emotional states and mood of the performer.

Structure

A comparison between the version of "Yang Guan" from the *qin* handbook, *Qin Xue Rumen* by Zhang He (1864) and Chou's (1957) *Willows Are New* reveals that except for alternations in rhythmic figures, the truncation of the third variation and tonal plan, the content of Zhang's version is basically preserved:

Zhang's Version:

Intro	I			II				III				
	A	B1	B2	A'	(new)	B1	B2	A'	B1	(new)	B2	Coda
mm. 1	2–12	13–18	19–30	31–42	43–46	47–52	53–64	65–76	77–82	83–94	95–107	108–114

Chou's Version:

Intro	I			II					
	A	B1	B2	A'	(new)	B1	(new)	B2	Coda
mm. 1	2–22	23–30	31–47	48–68	69–74	75–82	83–106	107–124	125–145

Tonal Material

The basic mode of the piece is *shang* (re) in B, that is, B=re, C$\sharp$=mi, E=sol, F$\sharp$=la, and A=do. Two major seconds (A–B) and (B–C$\sharp$), above and below the tonic (B or re), make the *shang* mode readily discernible. The opening melody begins on sol (E or subdominant) and cadences on re (B or tonic). Both sections B1 and B2 are in the *yu* (la) mode with B1 in F$\sharp$ and B2 in G respectively. However, in mm. 27–28, a transposition of the *yu* mode, a half step higher, occurs (example 3.21). Here, the basic intervallic patterns of the mode are retained, while pitches are changed. Because the Chinese modal structure is not based on triads, there is no need for harmonic support for either modulation or transposition; this phenomenon is essentially linear. The A and B sections are related somewhat like tonic (*shang* mode [re] on pitch B) and dominant (*yu* mode [la] on pitch F$\sharp$). This kind of modulation is

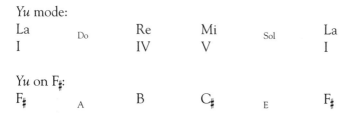

Example 3.21. *Willows Are New* mm. 23–34

achieved only through linear emphasis of the intervallic patterns between certain characteristic tones and the tonic:

Shang mode:

Re		Sol	La		Re
I	Mi	IV	V	Do	I

Shang on B:

B		E	F♯		B
	C♯			A	

(In *Shang* mode, mi and do are characteristic tones, and the emphasis on the major second above and below the tonic creates the aural impression of the mode.)

Yu mode:

La		Re	Mi		La
I	Do	IV	V	Sol	I

Yu on F♯:

F♯		B	C♯		F♯
	A			E	

(In *Yu* mode, do and sol are characteristic tones, and the emphasis on the minor third above the tonic and major second below it creates the aural impression of the mode.)

Rhythm and Meters
In comparison with Zhang's version of the piece, Chou's rhythmic treatment in his adaptation is worth noting. In order to simplify the subtle tone

inflections produced by a specific way of plucking and stopping the strings on the *qin*, Chou contracts and augments the rhythmic figures and alternates different meters, thereby making the grace notes clearly heard and, at the same time, avoiding regular rhythmic pulsation (compare the *qin* piece with Chou's version in example 3.22 and 3.23). The aural effect of the rhythmic, metric, and temporal designs here is the middle ground between strict, regular rhythmic pulsation and an improvisatory type of rubato. In

Example 3.22. *Willows Are New* mm. 1–22

Example 3.23. *Yangguan Sandie* mm. 1–12; *Qin* tablature realization by Guan Ping–Hu, transcription by Wang Di.

fact, the performance of the *qin* does require adherence to the tablature on the one hand and personal interpretation of the tablature by slight rhythmic and melodic alteration on the other.

Texture

The textural design of the piece features right-hand melody plus a left-hand drone with dissonant minor second doubling of the right hand (example 3.24). Here, the dissonant minor second in the left hand is emulated from the upper grace note from the melody. This sonority persists throughout the piece, and it actually enhances the aural impact of the descending upper grace notes and especially the sliding sound effect on the listener. Anyone who has heard *qin* music, especially this particular piece, would agree that Chou's *Willows Are New* is successful in approximating the traditional Chinese *qin* music on the piano and fascinates the listener with the capabilities of Western instruments and performance settings for recreating a piece of ancient Chinese music.[47] There were previous instances of approximating Chinese instrumental music on Western instruments such as the violin concerto "Liang Shan-Bo Yu Zhu Ying-Tai," known as the "Butterfly Lovers Concerto," which was jointly composed by Chen Gang and He Zhan Hao in 1959 at Shanghai Conservatory for Chinese audiences; however, the recreation of this well-known *qin* piece on the piano provides a new listening experience in which the subtlety of the sound of *qin* music can be explored by a single Western instrument to an unprecedented degree.

Timbre

The subtlety and variety of the timbral aspect of *qin* music have always been important sources of literary and spiritual inspiration and an important

Example 3.24. *Willows Are New* mm. 1–11

measurement for the overall scholarly accomplishments for the Chinese literati. Over the centuries, the sound of the *qin* has been described in various historical documents such as musical treatises and memories, and codified in the famous *qin* treatise *Qinsheng Shiliu Fa* or "Ways to Produce Sixteen Kinds of Sound on the *Qin*" by Leng Qian (1368–1398) of the Ming period.[48] Leng's codification of the timbral variety of the instrument indicates the *qin* players' sophisticated taste, which resulted from centuries of refinement in playing techniques up to the Ming period. According to Xu Jian, a contemporary Chinese music scholar with specialty in the music of the *qin*, Zhang He's 1864 version and the version in Yang Lun's (1609) *Taigu Yiyin* are identical and are widely known today as *Yangguan Sandie*.[49] We now have a modern transcription of the piece based on *Yangguan Sandie* that shows how and where a particular sound is produced, allowing us to compare it with Chou's recreation of the *qin* sound on the piano.

Four kinds of sounds constitute the basic timbral elements in a *qin* piece: (1) *sanyin* (open-string sound), (2) *shiyin* (solid, finger-stopped sound), (3) *fanyin* (floating sound or harmonics), and (4) *huayin* (sliding sound or glissando). *Sanyins* are the most sonorous and are often used emphatically for notes to be stressed in a melody. *Shiyins* are used for embellishing notes such as upper neighbors and because tones produced by finger-stopped notes are easier to control than open-string tones. *Shi yins* are most suitable for double stops, such as fifths and octaves, and vibrato. *Fanyins* are customarily used in the *weisheng* or coda section of a piece. *Sanyin* in Chou's piece is produced by octave doubling of the melody and *fanyin* or harmonic by three-octave doubling of the melody. Because *qin* uses silk strings, which has a unique dark and dissonant sound as the player's left finger slides on it, Chou has used abundant minor ninths in *Willows Are New* to approximate this particular timbre.

Melody

The melody of Chou's version is distributed among different registral ranges for timbral contrasts. This is a salient feature of the piece (example 3.25). The variety of sonorities are produced by octave doubling over a wide range of a single tone in the melodic flow, and by verticalizing the dissonant semitone grace notes throughout the piece, together with the avoidance of metric accents and frequent shift of melodic registral ranges; by these means, Chou has achieved what he calls "the modulation of line and texture," a typical Varèsean concept. *Willows Are New* is Chou's first work in parodying a Chinese instrument on a single Western instrument. His *Yu ko* (1965) was also designed to recreate the sound of *qin* on a group of nine Western instruments including violin, alto flute, English horn, bass clarinet, two trom-

Example 3.25. *Willows Are New* mm. 125–145

bones, piano, and percussions. The interpretation of Chinese poems in musical terms in Chou's works of the 1950s paved the way for further exploration into combining traditional Chinese thoughts and aesthetic principles with Varèsean ideas in his compositions of the 1960s.

Chou's Vocal Works

In his entire career, Chou composed only two vocal works: *Seven Poems of T'ang Dynasty* (1951–1952)[50] for solo high voice (tenor) and instrumental ensemble and *Poems of White Stone* (1959) for mixed chorus. The former premiered in New York City at the International Society for Contemporary Music's concert on March 16, 1952, under the baton of John Clark; the latter was composed in conjunction with Merce Cunningham for the Festival of Contemporary Arts at the University of Illinois. It was performed on March 14, 1959, with Cunningham and his dance company conducted by John Garvey at the University of Illinois. After its premiere in 1952, the *Seven Poems of T'ang Dynasty* was performed in Darmstadt with Kranichsteiner Kammerensemble at Internationale Ferienkurse für Neue Musik Kammerkonzert on September 2, 1961.

Seven Poems of T'ang Dynasty (1951–1952)
Seven Poems of T'ang Dynasty is based on Chou's and Louise Varèse's collaborative translations of seven four-line Tang poems. Two poems are by Wang Wei (699–759); the other five poets include Liu Yu-Xi (772–842), Jia Dao

(788–843), Li Bai (705–762), Liu Zong-Yuan (773–819), and Liu Chang-Qing (ca. 710–780). The work shows strong Varèsean influence in terms of long sustained single pitches, verticalized linear sonorities, and the contrast between movement of voice in semitones and in wide leaps, that is, minor sevenths or tritones. Rhythmically, regular pulsation is again avoided by asymmetrical rhythmic figures.

Poems of White Stone (1959)

In contrast to *Seven Poems*, the poems used for Chou's *Poems of White Stone* came from Jiang Gui (1155–1221) of the Song dynasty, a musician and *ciren* or writer of a kind of poetry containing fixed titles, numbers of lines of unequal length in a stanza, and a fixed number of words per line. White Stone and White Stone Monk are Jiang Gui's pseudonyms. The poems in this work are meant to be sung in original Chinese even for Western choirs. Another difference between *Seven Poems* and *Poems of White Stone* is that, in the latter, the original music in *gongche* notation written alongside the seventeen poems has survived and has been transcribed to Western staff notation by Chinese scholars.[51] According to Yang Yin-Liu, the music was mainly collected and adapted to the poems by Jiang himself.[52] However, the second poem, "Yumei Ling" or "Spring Snow and Plum Tree," was allegedly composed by Fan Cheng-Da (1126–1193). Chou's adaptation of Jiang Gui's poems basically follows the metric foot of the poems, yet in order to avoid regular pulsation and make the music less marked by metric accents, syncopation has been employed extensively. Like other Chou's early works, the grace note, upper-neighbor figure is readily recognizable here. The overall structure is symmetrical:

Poem 1	Poem 2	Poem 3	Poem 4	Poem 5	Poem 1
"Guyuan"	"Yumei Ling"	"Geximei Ling"	"Shuying"	"Anxiang"	"Guyuan"
mm. 1–107	124–171	179–222	223–280	281–345 (cut)	603–725

Alternating four basic types of texture provides textural variety:

    I. single line
   II. 2-part counterpoint
  III. 2-part counterpoint with drone (or double counterpoint)
  IV. 4-part chordal

Chou's melodic treatment for the work is based on the idea that in order to create new melodic phrasing, the text needs to be regrouped by breaking up

Example 3.26. Rulan Pian's transcription of White Stone's Song "Geximei Ling" Pian (1967: 101)

the main tune and then using the fragments to punctuate or reinforce each phrase. A comparison between Jiang Gui's original melody transcribed by Yang Yin-Liu and Yin Fa-Lu and by Rulan Pian and the melody in Chou's work shows that the basic melodic ideas of Jiang Gui's songs have been adopted in Chou's work. Examples 3.26–3.28 compare the melodic motif E♭–G–F in Jiang Gui's transcribed version with Chou's modification of this figure with his usual grace-note, upper-neighboring tone

^{G}F♯–A♯–G♯

The harmony of the piece relies heavily on octave doubling. Verticalized intervals of minor second, major second, minor third, major third, fourth,

Example 3.27. Yang Yin–Liu/Yin Fa–Lu's transcription of the same piece Pian (1967: 101)

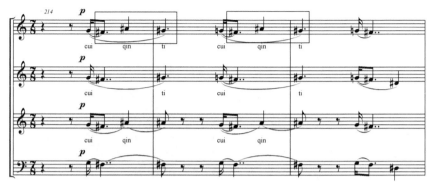

Example 3.28. *Poems of White Stone* mm. 214–216

Example 3.29. *Poems of White Stone* mm. 318–330

and fifth, minor sixth, and minor seventh at the cadential points result from prolongations of particular voices, often in pairs, which overlap with other voices (mm. 58–59, 101–107, and 708–709). The piece reveals a great deal of the composer's interest in contrapuntal treatment of melodic material. Thematic unity between sections is achieved through repeated use of a basic syncopated rhythmic figure (example 3.29).

Commenting on this work, Edward Wolf, reporter of the *Daily Illini*, wrote, "The music exploited many unusual tone colors of an impressionistic nature. Its greatest drawback was a feeling of contrived symmetry. Rhythmic, melodic, and color motives had frequent repetition within clearly defined sections and the sections themselves fell into a rather stiff pattern."[53] The constraints of preexisting melodies, the avoidance of treating the Chinese text in the style of a stereotypical Chinese text and melody-plus-Western harmony, and the accommodation of the music to dance choreography have indeed created a sense of monotony. However, after this last work of the 1950s, Chou was able to reach a new plateau by leaving his old habit of working with Chinese poetry behind and by finding new sources of inspiration in philosophical aspects of Chinese culture and by synthesizing it with its compatible counterpart in the Varèsean concept of sound and certain techniques.

Notes

1. Wen-Chung Chou's preface to the 1953 edition of *Landscapes* (1949) by C. F. Peters.

2. Chou reflected on his repeated use of certain Chinese melodies in several works as a remembrance of his childhood and roots or a source of inspiration. He quoted these Chinese melodies purely out of memory (he did not bring any Chinese music with him to America). Wen-Chung Chou, correspondence with Peter Chang, May 7, 2004, 1.

3. Nicolas Slonimsky, "Chou Wen-Chung," *American Composers Alliance Bulletin* 9, no. 4 (1961): 3.

4. Slonimsky, "Chou Wen-Chung," 3.

5. For Qu Wei's piano piece "Huagu" [Flower Drum], see *Gangqin Qu Xuan* [*Anthology of Piano Pieces*] (Beijing: Yinyue Chubanshe [Musical Press], 1960); for the printed traditional melody "Moli Hua" [Jasmine Flower], see Jin-Sheng Li's edited version in *Zhongguo Minge* [*Chinese Folk Songs*], vol. 1 (Shanghai: Shanghai Wenyi Chubanshe, 1964) or Wu-Jun Shen's edition in *Zhongguo Minge Ershi Shou* [*Twenty Chinese Folk Songs*] (Beijing: People's Music Publications, 1981); and for Wen-Chung Chou's "Fengyang Huagu" [Flower Drum Melody from Fengyang], see the version edited by the Research Institute of Literature and the Arts (Ministry of Culture) in *Zhongguo Minge* [*Chinese Folk Songs*], vol. 3 (Shanghai: Shanghai Wenyi Chubanshe, 1982).

6. *Zhongguo Minge* [*Chinese Folk Songs*], vol. 3 (Shanghai: Shanghai Wenyi Chuban-she, 1982), 4.

7. Lines omitted by Chou are supplied here in brackets.

8. Slonimsky and *ACAB* (1969) were incorrect on the premiere date of the work. See William Mootz's review of the premiere "Concertmaster Kling Star As Soloist in Mendelssohn's Violin Concerto," *The Courier-Journal* (December 8, 1960): 18.

9. Karl Kroeger, "Review of Scores," *Music Library Association Notes* 20, no. 2 (Winter–Fall 1962–1963): 407.

10. Mootz, "Concertmaster Kling Star," 18.

11. Mootz, "Concertmaster Kling Star," 18.

12. Gang Chen, "Zaochuen Eryue Liuse Xin" [New Willows in Early February], *Peoples Music* 11, no. 12 (1979): 68–69.

13. Chou, correspondence, May 7, 2004, 2.

14. According to Chou, Varèse was also influenced by Asian music. There are references in his *Intègrales*, for example, to the Japanese *gagaku* music in the opening and to the Korean court music or the *gamelan* music in subsequent sections. Chou, correspondence, May 7, 2004, 2.

15. This refers to Alexander Scryabin's *Prometheus* (1910), which is scored among other instruments also for "clavier à lumières," an imaginary instrument for bringing intense colored light beams into the concert hall. This is also seen in the concept of synesthesia, which associates pitches with colors, a concept derived from psychology. For more on synesthesia, see Alan Merriam, *The Anthropology of Music* (Evanston, Ill.: Northwestern University Press, 1964), 85–101. For a recent acoustic study of timbre by a Chinese composer, see Jin-Min Zhou, "Timbre, Playing Technique and Structure: A Microscopic Analysis of Samples from Two Works for the Qin," *Progress Reports in Ethnomusicology* 3, no. 3 (1991): 437–88.

16. Louise Varèse, *Looking Glass Diary* (New York: Norton, 1972), 117.

17. Louise Varèse, *Looking Glass Diary*, 108.

18. Louise Varèse, *Looking Glass Diary*, 104–5, 108–9.

19. Fernand Ouellette, *Edgard Varèse* (New York: Orion, 1968), 175.

20. Wassily Kandinsky, "Content and Form," in *Complete Writings on Art*, vol. 1, ed. Kenneth C. Lindsay and Peter Vergo (Boston: G. K. Hall and Co., 1982), 89; also see his "Color Course and Seminar," vol. 2, pp. 501–4 of the same book.

21. Jonathan Bernard, *The Music of Edgard Varèse* (New Haven: Yale University Press, 1987), 35.

22. Fernand Léger, "Contemporary Achievement in Painting," in *Cubism*, ed. Edward Fry with excerpts from documentary texts (New York: Oxford University Press, 1966), 138.

23. Edgard Varèse, "The Liberation of Sound," in *Contemporary Composers on Contemporary Music*, ed. Elliot Schwartz and Barney Child (New York: Da Capo, 1978), 195–208.

24. Louise Varèse, *Looking Glass Diary*, 108.

25. Bruno Nettl, *The Study of Ethnomusicology: Twenty-nine Issues and Concepts* (Chicago: University of Illinois Press, 1983), 137.

26. The first three lines of the poem translated by me and the rest by Chou Wen-Chung. See *Tangshi Xuanzhu* [*Selected and Annotated Tang Poems*], vol. I (Beijing: Beijing Publications, 1978), 39.

27. Wen-Chung Chou's translation.

28. Li-Pu Wu, *Zhongguo Guohua Lun Yanjiu* [*A Study of the Chinese Classical Painting Theories*] (Beijing: Beijing University Press, 1985), 109.

29. Announcement, *American Composers Alliance Bulletin* 6, no. 4 (1957): 22.

30. Announcement, *American Composers Alliance Bulletin* 6, 22.

31. Wen-Chung Chou, "Introduction," *Soliloquy of a Bhiksuni* (New York: C. F. Peters Edition, 1961), 2.

32. Announcement, *American Composers Alliance Bulletin* 9, no. 1 (1959), 19.

33. Ruth Heimbuecher, "Soliloquy of a Bhiksuni," *Pittsburgh Press*, July 12, 1960.

34. Chou sees the half-step grace note as part of the mode. Thus, instead of five tones, he would call it "hexatonic" or six-tone mode, and he traces the origin of this back to the central Asian–influenced music of the T'ang period (618–907 AD).

35. The society was founded on October 21, 1952, with sponsorship by several musical organizations including ACA and BMI. The concerts of the society are often held at the Museum of Modern Art in New York. See Oliver Daniel, *Stokowski* (New York: Dodd, Mead, and Co., 1982), 575–89, 696.

36. Anxi was the name of the place now located at Kuche county, Xinjiang Automous Region in northwestern China.

37. Wen-Chung Chou's program notes for *The Willows Are New* (New York: C. F. Peters Edition, 1960), 2.

38. This is Chou's own translation, which, while being precise and concise, also preserves the subtle shadings of the poem. No better translation is found to date.

39. Based on a version of a nineteenth-century *qin* book, by He Zhang *Qinxue Rumen* [*Elementary Learner's Book of Playing the Qin*] (1864) of the Qing period. My translation.

40. Jian Xu, *Qinshi Chubian* [*History of the Qin: A Preliminary Study*], 2nd ed. (Beijing: People's Music Publications, 1987), 73

41. Xu, *Qinshi Chubian*, 7.

42. Xu, *Qinshi Chubian*, 7.

43. Xu, *Qinshi Chubian*, 16.

44. Xu, *Qinshi Chubian*, 16.

45. Xu, *Qinshi Chubian*, 18. The authorship of this treatise has been a subject for debate between authors of *Yiwen Zhi* in *Tangshu* (by the Jin period Kong Yan, who held a negative view) and *Wenxuan* (by Li Shan, who held a positive view). Rei-Chen Ma of Qing period (1644–1911) believed that the work was part of Cai's *Xuyue* and Kong Yan was only a copier of the work.

46. Shen was a musical official in the music administration of the Southern Song period. See Xu, *Qinshi Chubian*, 18.

47. The word "parody" is defined as a composition that seriously reworks the musical material of another composition seen in the cases of Stravinsky, Peter Maxwell Davis, and George Rochberg, who reworked earlier musical material in contemporary contexts.

48. Zhongguo Yinyue Cidian Editorial Committee, *Zhongguo Yinyue Cidian* [*Dictionary of Chinese Music*] (Beijing: People's Music Publications, 1984), 222, 309.

49. Xu, *Qinshi Chubian*, 74.

50. Published by *New Music Edition* 25, no. 4 (July 1952). *New Music Edition* was a nonprofit corporation aimed at serious new compositions that might not have a chance of distribution through ordinary channels. Vladimir Ussachevsky was the chairman of the editorial board; its members consisted of John Cage, Lou Harrison, Elliott Carter, Peggy Lanville Hicks, and Richard Franko Goldman. Otto Luening, Henry Cowell, and Virgil Thomson were among the Board members.

51. Yin-Liu Yang and Fa-Lu Yin, *Song Jiang Bai-Shi Chuangzuo Gequ Yenjiu* [*Study of Composed Songs by Jiang Bai Shi of Song Dynasty*] (Beijing: People's Music Publications, 1957). Also see Cheng-Tao Xia, "Baishi Daoren Gequ Kaozheng" [Investigation of Baishi Monk's Songs], *Yanjing Xuebao* 16 (December 1934); Qong-Sun Qiu, *Baishi Daoren Gequ Tongkao* [*A Comprehensive Investigation of Baishi Monk's Songs*] (Beijing: People's Music Publications, 1959); Rulan Chao Pian, *Song Dynasty Musical Sources and Their Interpretation* (Cambridge, Mass.: Harvard University Press, 1967), 147–54.

52. Yin-Liu Yang, *Zhongguo Gudai Yinyue Shigao* [*History of Chinese Music in Antiquity*], vol. 1 (Beijing: People's Music Publications, 1981), 293.

53. Edward Wolf, "Imagination in Music, Dance," *The Daily Illini*, March 17, 1959, 7.

CHAPTER FOUR

~

Chou's Works of the 1960s

From 1960 to 1969, Chou completed twelve works, mostly for wind, piano, and percussion. Among these, five were incidental music written for documentary films such as the "Music for Hong Kong" (1960), "Tomorrow" (1961), "White Paper of Red China" (1962), "A Day at the Fair" (1964), and "Red China: Year of the Gun?" (1966). Except for "A Day at the Fair," which was based on a series of traditional material from different cultures around the world for the World's Fair, Chou did not consider these his regular repertoire. These works were not performed again after recording for the films, and scores were not published.

In his works of the 1950s, Chou sought ways to express Chinese sentiment through direct or indirect musical references to Chinese music and through developing a mode of musical thinking in terms of Chinese visual and literary artistic principles such as the emphasis on the control of ink flow in calligraphy, brevity in landscape paintings, poetry in musical form, and pictorial depiction of the *qin* playing gestures and their relations to timbre. During this time, Chou also tried to demonstrate the validity of the basic Chinese musical concept that each individual tone has a life of its own and is capable of a variety of subtle timbral changes and expressions.

Since the turn of this century, the obsession with musical timbre has become increasingly prominent in the West. In light of Western interest in exploring the timbral aspect of music, Chou was able to discover this important Chinese concept and articulate it as an example in his *Willows Are New* and other works of the 1950s. Chou's interest in rendering Chinese sound on

Western instruments was elevated to explore the integration of structural constructs such as articulation, pitch and timbre modification, and rhythmic elasticity by absorbing specific Chinese instrumental performance techniques in his works of the 1960s. And instead of using Chinese poems as inspirational sources, Chou turned to the kind of philosophy expounded in one of the oldest surviving classic books, the *I-Ching* or Book of Changes.[1]

Chou applied the *I-Ching* principal in *Metaphors* (1960–1961) for wind ensemble, a piece that demonstrates Chou's maturity of techniques and an assured philosophical foundation for his compositional approach. There is a marked difference between Chou's and John Cage's use of *I-Ching* theory in compositions. Unlike Cage's interest in relegating composers' responsibilities for structure to that of dice, Chou was interested in devising a musical, structural model whose germinating power would lie in the interaction between two opposite poles: change and constancy. Instead of relying on die operation, Chou followed the *I-Ching* principle that everything is generated from the interaction between two forces in treating melodic, rhythmic, and harmonic materials.[2] In specific terms, the basic component of the *bagua* or eight trigrams consists of three lines, two solid and a broken horizontal line or vice versa; different arrangements of these two kinds of lines could generate sixty-four hexagrams from the initial eight trigrams:

a. __ b. -- c. --̲ d. =̲= e. *bagua* f. 64 hexagrams

Chou criticized Cage for his practical use of the eight trigrams as the determinant for the structural design of a composition without an understanding of the Chinese text and its philosophical implications. He wrote,

> Cage's application of *I-Ching* does not take the text into consideration but merely translates each hexagram into a preassigned musical value. . . . Iannis Xenakis's idea of a "stochastic music" is closer to the concept of *I-Ching* than Cage's. . . . György Ligeti speaks of "global categories" involving the interrelationship of "register and density, distribution of various types of movement and structure," and of "compositional design of the *process* of change"; he too is closer to applying the principle of events and processes of *I-Ching*.[3]

In fact, the *I-Ching* can be viewed, in Joseph Needham's term, as a "cosmic filing system" based on binary arithmetic or as a "repository of concepts" to which all events and processes in nature can be referred.[4]

With his studies in Webern's works, Chou was familiar with the development of the European serial principles and methods. The basic concepts of the serial method, such as generating a variety of combinations of pitches from a basic set by pitch aggregation, inversion, rotation, and transposition, are comparable to those of generating a variety of hexagram from two basic types of lines by line aggregation and rearrangement discovered by Chou.

Metaphors (1960–1961)

The principle of unity through constancy and change was first applied in *Metaphors*. The work, which was commissioned and premiered by the American Wind Symphony Orchestra, is in four movements, each with a symbolic title: (1) "Awakening," (2) "Sprouting," (3) "Clinging," and (4) "Receiving." The interaction of eight composite images of the *I-Ching* represents "the germinal elements of all that happens in the universe, including natural phenomena, human affairs, and ideas."[5] Movements 1 and 2 and also 3 and 4 are related in that each of the two pairs evokes a specific mood: the first pair, spring, and the second pair, summer. There are eight scale modes used in the piece, a pair in each movement:

Movement 1. Awakening Pair I
Modes   I C–D–A♭–B♭–E♭
             II B–A–E♭–D♭–G♭
Movement 2. Sprouting Pair II
Modes   III A♭–B♭–C–E♭–G♭
             IV A♭–B♭–C–D–F
Movement 3. Clinging Pair III
Modes   V B♭–E♭–F–D♭
             VI A♭–E♭–F–D♭
Movement 4. Receiving Pair IV
Modes   VII D♭–G–A–E♭
             VIII F–E♭–A–G

The modal design of the work reflects a principle in which subtle changes take place in a seemingly unchanging microcosm, the basic view of the *I-Ching* that change and constancy always complement each other. The first two modes in movement 1, for example, share a basic intervallic cell, that is, major second.[6] While everything else remains constant, a minute change, in this case, the change of interval from minor second (D–E♭) in mode I to minor third (E♭–G♭) in mode II, is almost imperceptible. In movement two, the basic intervallic cells are major second and minor third. While the rest of the intervallic patterns remain identical, the change takes place between the ordering of major second and minor third (M2 and m3 hereafter):

Mode III M2–M2–m3–m3
Mode IV M2–M2–M2–m3

This fact can be seen also in mode IV between two complementary modes: mode V, m3–M2–M3, versus mode VI, P4–M2–M3. In the last movement, modes VII and VIII appear to be identical at the beginning, with no change occurring until measure 10 when the intervallic pattern of the descending mode VIII changes from major second to minor second:

Mode VII G–A–E♭–F–B
Mode VIII G–F–B–A/A♭–E♭

Interestingly, the triadic harmonic implications of the piece signify a sharp break from Chou's earlier harmonic approaches in which quartal harmony and verticalization of thematic material dominate. Mode II and IV, in the second movement, for example, can be viewed as A=minor ninth chord and B=minor ninth chord:

Mode III A♭–B♭–C–E♭–G♭ or A♭–C–E♭–G♭–B♭ (A♭ minor ninth chord)
Mode IV A♭–F–D–C–B♭ or B♭–D–F–A♭–C (B♭ minor ninth chord)

Triadic structural implications in other modes of the piece are illustrated as follows:

Mode		Triads
I C–D–A♭–B♭–E♭	or	A♭–C–E♭ + B♭–D
II B–A–E♭–D♭–G♭	or	G♭/F♯–A–D♭/C♯ + B–E♭/D♯
V B♭–E♭–F–D♭	or	B♭–D♭–F (augmented triad)
VI A♭–E♭–F–D♭	or	F–A♭ + F–D♭
VII A–E♭–F–B	or	F–A + B–E♭/D♯

In this work, Chou's interest in working with intervallic cells or a collection of pitches shows the influence of serial compositional procedures and his unique way of interpreting this procedure in Chinese philosophical terms, that is, the I-Ching. To explain how he was inspired by the I-Ching, Chou wrote a program note in the score that the meaning of the images presented in the I-Ching is "interpreted through metaphors, hence the title of this composition."[7] Chou's interpretation of the *I-Ching* principal, composite dualistic cycles, is close to that of the Taoist philosopher Lao Zi (ca. 600 BC), who was an exponent of it.

Form and Timbre

The formal design of the piece, like all other Chou's works of the 1950s, again exhibits the principle of symmetry. The first movement is constructed in an arch form in which each thematically, timbrally, and rhythmically distinct section is echoed by a section at the right side of the center (measure 70) in retrograde order:

	mm.	segments
Left	1–13	1
	14–17	2
	18–33	3
	34–47	4
	48–51	5
	52–63	6
Center	64–76	
Right	77–88	6
	89–92	5
	93–106	4
	107–122	3
	123–125	2
	126–130	1

Structurally, the second movement features the alternative of two timbrally, rhythmically, and harmonically distinct sections. Measures 21–33 represent one section which features syncopation in oboes and English horns, sixteenth-note figures in flutes, horns, and piccolos, and two notes in alternation in bassoons, English horns, and harp. The other section consists of a combination of two groups of descending triplets, and two groups of ascending triplets in oboes, English horns, and single-triplet figures in piccolos, trumpets, vibraphones, and harp (seen in mm. 34–68). The basic idea of alternating these two sections by maintaining two basic intervallic patterns of these pitch collections represents the constant cycles of microcosmic change in nature. Here, the change in instrumentation and pitch are almost imperceptible. The two complementary forces or ideas are presented at the beginning of the third movement, that is, constant flow of eighth notes in two harps and pianos and verticalization of the harp parts

Example 4.1. *Metaphors* movement 3, mm. 13–17

by gradual thickening and thinning of the sonority in the brass and woodwinds (mm. 13–17; example 4.1). The dualist-union structural principle is
continuously seen in the last movement in which many repeated notes in
glockenspiel, trumpet, and piccolo are interwoven in a constant flow of active thematic figures in woodwinds, marimba, and piano (example 4.2). In

Example 4.2. *Metaphors* movement 4, mm. 5–8

composing *Metaphors*, Chou first experimented with the integration of *I-Ching*'s dualistic-union principle in harmonic, thematic, textural, and rhythmic structures of the piece; such an experimentation laid the cornerstone for developing a series of Chinese philosophy–inspired compositions during the 1960s.

Cursive (1963)

While teaching at Hunter College in New York, Chou composed *Cursive* for flute and piano. The work, written for the flutist Harvey Sollberger and the pianist and composer Charles Wuorienon, premiered with these artists on January 13, 1964, at the McMillan Theater, New York.[8] This work extends the principle of dualistic union of two polar forces, combining it with the aesthetic tenets of Chinese calligraphy.

The title of the piece suggests that the fluidity of the formal, rhythmic, and textural designs are modeled after a type of Chinese ink brush calligraphic style, *caoshu*, which requires supreme discipline and spontaneous creative power. The basic idea of this work is the interaction between movement and energy and between density and texture. In terms of instrumentation and certain intervallic material, the piece bears resemblance to Varèse's *Density 21.5* (1936), written for solo flute, and is meant to explore the timbre of the instrument through a fluid formal design. Varèse's concern of using timbral variations to delineate acoustic zones as sections in a composition is revealed in his writing. He believes that acoustical arrangements could be used to establish "zones of intensities," and "these zones would be differentiated by various timbres or colors and different loudness," and the role of color would become "an agent of delineation, like the different colors on a map separating different areas, and an integral part."[9] In embracing the Varèsean emphasis on the role of color in delineating forms and sound as a moving mass, Chou translated these concepts into Chinese terms. In this work, the composer explores a set of dualities, that is, "specified but indefinite pitches and duration and the use of regulated but variable tempo and intensity," and wants to bring forth a condensation of experiences."[10]

What this means is that the coordinated control of inflections in pitch, timbre, intensity, duration, and the exploration of all articulatory and vibratory characteristics of the instruments demand that performers achieve a state of mind for the execution of each detail.

Among several concepts mentioned in this passage such as "individual sound as living matter," "spontaneous but controlled flow of ink," and "an interplay of movement and energy, of density and texture," a central idea can be detected: the directive force in the continuous flow of a sound mass. At a conceptual level, Chou has been able to merge Varèsean views of the nature of musical sound with the tenet of Chinese calligraphy and the *I-Ching* concept of germinating power of dualistic-union, or in a Chinese *I-Ching* scholar Jin Jing Fang's term, "two aspects of an entity."[11]

In 1970, Chou published his article, "Single Tones as Musical Entities: An Approach to Structural Deviations in Tonal Characteristics," in which Chou explains the Chinese view of the innate expressive power in each individual tone and compares this view with that of Western tradition. In retrospect, by extending Varèsean views on music as a living and evolving substance, also espoused by the Franco-American composer Dane Rudhyar in the 1920s,[12] the article represents a stage during which Chou drew some conclusions from his experiments.

Though the parallel between Chou's *Cursive* (1963) and Varèse's solo flute piece, *Density 21.5* (1936) seems to be superficial, the interest in the exploration of the timbral intensity and the range of registral and durational aspects of the music on the flute is obvious. While *Density 21.5* involves only a single voice and is initially conceived to probe the timbre of the platinum, Chou's *Cursive* involves two instruments and is conceived, besides the timbral range of the flute, as interplay between the flute and the piano. The primary intervals in *Cursive* are major seventh and minor seventh or their inversions of major second and minor second in different registral ranges, and minor third (example 4.3). These intervals also appear abundantly in *Density 21.5* as they have been documented in Jonathan Bernard's analysis, that is, [3] [10] or a minor seventh interlocked with a major seventh, that is, B♭–G♯–B.[13] Both *Density 21.5* and *Cursive* explore the timbral capacity of the flute. This includes the use of some unusual playing techniques such as slapping the keys, fast vibratos, trill

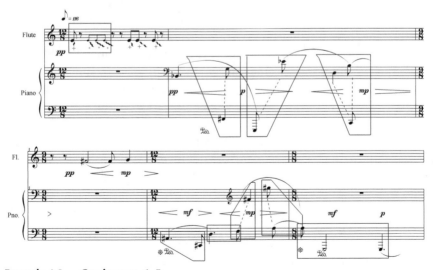

Example 4.3. *Cursive* mm. 1–5

1. Flute,

2. Piano,

Example 4.4. *Cursive* p. 3

with harmonics, and production of microtones. In addition to these, *Cursive* also calls for various materials such as wooden slabs, metal slabs, and metal chains to be placed on the piano strings, and specifies the different sounds at certain places. Piano strings are plucked and so play a role in extending flute pitches into lower register. While sudden and sharp contrasts in dynamics with register and timbral changes, that is the attack, and the intensity change on each note, for example, the sudden piano on a low range note after a loud high-pitched note, stands out prominently in *Density 21.5*; intensity change is more gradual and systematized in *Cursive*. In *Cursive*, Chou devised a scale and symbols for the change of intensity (example 4.4). The purpose of this is to create an impression in which an uninterrupted motion is maintained, like the constant flow of ink so important to Chinese calligraphers. The idea of ebb and flow of ink in a controlled and constant motion is reflected in the flexibility of tempo. In *Cursive*, Chou allows the piano and flute to move at different rates. Each could accelerate or slow down and the two would eventually come together or coincide with each other at three places: (1) in mm. 56–57, the fifth note of the flute is designed to overlap with the sixth quarter note of the piano, (2) in mm. 68–69, the sixth quarter note of the flute and the fifth quarter note of the piano should overlap, and (3) in mm. 98–99, the fifth quarter note of the flute and the sixth note of the piano should coincide.

Counterpoint

Texturally, there is a contrapuntal section between mm. 26 and 45 in which the flute's rhythmic figures are imitated in inversion 1 1/2 beats later by the piano; the tempo here is rather strict and held steady at eighth note=126 (example 4.5). Two instruments moving at different rates and then coinciding at certain points is seen in Indian music, especially that of solo instrument and the drum meeting at *sam*. In his notes on the work, Chou indicates that the Indian practice of *tala* in which the first beat of both soloist and drummer overlap on *sam* after improvisatory passages, has served as a model for the fugal section, mm. 26–45, in *Cursive*.

Example 4.5. *Cursive* mm. 24–34

Form

The form of the piece features alternation between fugal and rubato sections, where variable tempi are marked and very gradual accelerando and rallentando are specified by ♪=100, to ♪=116, to ♪=132, to ♪=116, and to ♪=100, and so on. This again emulates the Chinese calligraphic idea, which emphasizes controlled and continuous flow of ink. This structural fluidity is a direct result of the change of texture. The thin texture flows and the thick texture ebbs. Chou's concept of translating Chinese calligraphy into composition in *Cursive* has played an indispensable role in his stylistic development.

In his lecture, "The Liberation of Sound," given at Mary Austin House, Santa Fe, in 1936, Varèse already used "the river-flow" analogy to describe his ideal timbral, textural, and formal nature of a composition. Varèse speaks of "melodic totality," which has discarded traditional conception of melodies as fragmented units in a composition, that "there will no longer be the old conception of melody or interplay of melodies," but "the entire work will be a melodic totality," and "the entire work will flow as a river flows."[14]

In a talk given in Taiwan in 1981, Chou explained the concept of inter-play between textural density, motion, and rhythm in his *Cursive*.[15] That Chou's almost measure-by-measure alternation between duple and triple me-ters in *Cursive* and other works of the 1960s has structural significance can be seen as the marriage between the Varèsean concept in which rhythm is the "element of stability" and "generator of form" and the aesthetics of Chi-nese calligraphy that require the motion of the brush to be continuous yet varied. Accordingly, the rhythm of the motion directly affects the overall form of the resultant character.

The fluid and continuous form of *Cursive* reveals Varèse's belief that form should not be a limiting factor but rather the consequence of the interaction between various forces, or as Varèse calls it, "crystallization." Here, the crys-tal is considered the result of the interaction between various attractive and repulsive elements; thus, it is used as an analogue by Varèse to explain how the form of a piece is determined. Varèse claims: "Form is a result of a process. Each of my works discovers its own form. I could never have fitted them into any of the historical containers."[16]

The Dark and the Light (1964)

The principles just outlined above are seen in Chou's next two works, *The Dark and the Light* for piano, percussion, and strings and *Riding the Wind* for wind ensemble, both composed in 1964. With 150 completed measures on February 26, 1964, *The Dark and the Light* was performed on March 8, 1964, with Arthur Bloom conducting and Yi-An Chang on piano. Chou intended to complete the rest of this work after the performance but was unable to do so and subsequently withdrew the score from the publisher. Therefore, ulti-mately this work was not published, nor was it performed afterwards. *Riding the Wind* was again commissioned by the American Wind Symphony Or-chestra and premiered in Pittsburgh on June 14, 1964, with AWSO under the direction of Robert Austin Boudreau. Chou received this commission after the American Wind Symphony Orchestra performed *Soliloquy of a Bhiksuni* (1958) in Pittsburgh on July 10, 1960. Of these two commissions from AWSO, the one preceding *Riding the Wind* was *Metaphors*, which premiered on June 25, 1960, in Pittsburgh.

The intervallic structure in *The Dark and the Light* is shown in the first chord of the piano, that is, a combination of interlocking major seventh, mi-nor seventh, and minor third (example 4.6). This sonority is the result of ver-ticalization of the melody whose basic contour is a descending minor third

Example 4.6. *The Dark and the Light* mm. 1–5

and minor seventh plus an ascending major seventh or vice versa. The same is also true in *Riding the Wind*.

The alternation between duple and triple meters in the piece is even more pronounced than in *Cursive*; interplay exists between three distinctive timbral strata: (1) strings, (2) percussions, and (3) piano and various rhythmic motives. This illustrates the basic concept of contrast upon which the piece was conceived. *The Dark and the Light* (1964) represents an intermediate stage between *Cursive* (1963) and *Pien* (1966).

Riding the Wind (1964)

The title of *Riding the Wind* is from a quotation from the Chinese philosopher Lie Zi (ca. fifth century BC) found in the frontispiece of the score that reads, "I am borne hither and thither like a dry leaf torn from a tree. I know not whether the wind is riding on me or I the wind."

There is a *qin* piece, "Lie Zi Yufeng" or "Lie Zi Riding the Wind," that bears the same title as *Riding the Wind* by thirteenth-century Chinese poet-musician Mao Min-Zhong, but the musical link between these two works cannot be established.

While *The Dark and the Light* is written for strings, piano, and percussion and features contrast between these three timbral strata, in *Riding the Wind*, such variety and contrasts of timbre are combined with the homogeneous sound of a large wind ensemble. In contrast to the active motivic activities in *The Dark and the Light* and, linearly, the wind ensemble in *Riding the Wind*, this piece appears to be static—almost every pitch is drawn out as soon as it sounds (example 4.7). Thus, attention is focused on a single sonority, one at a time, and the swell of each sonority, for example, pp < mf > pp at very close intervals, and constant overlapping shows that Chou is more concerned about the spatial arrangement of a sound mass as a whole than individual lines. Used in this way, the winds as a group or a particular layer of sound mass form a contrast to the active role of the percussions and piano in rhythmic and motivic aspects of the piece. This kind of writing, which focuses on a single sonority, that is, a chord or a stack of pitches, can be observed clearly in the third movement of *Metaphors*.

Yu ko (1965)

Yu ko, a work scored for nine instruments (violin, alto flute, English horn, bass clarinet, two trombones, piano, and two percussion instruments) premiered on April 19, 1965, in New York by the Group for Contemporary

Example 4.7.   *Riding the Wind* mm. 68–73

Example 4.8. *Yu ko* mm. 23–28

Music at Columbia University directed by Harvey Sollberger. According to Chou, Sollberger's chamber ensemble had a tradition that the group would perform an ancient piece before performing contemporary ones, and *Yu ko* was written for this purpose.[17] Like *Willows Are New* (1957), this work is a parody of a *qin* piece by Mao Min-Zhong (ca. 1280). But instead of a single instrument like the piano, the varied timbre of a chamber ensemble provides a wide range of possibilities for emulating various *qin* timbres, variable tone inflections, or microtones on Western instruments (example 4.8 and 4.9). Chou's adaptation of Mao's work includes thematic material, basic rhythmic profile, and pitch content. For specific timbral effects in imitating the *qin*, the sound of the instrument is altered, for example, the pi-

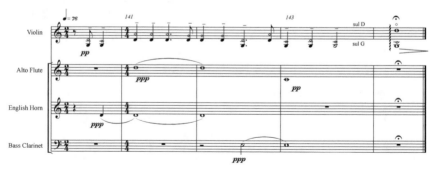

Example 4.9. *Yu ko* mm. 140–144

ano player wears a thimble to tap the string and while stopping the strings near the bridges, trombone and bass trombone are muted with stone-lined cups, English horn's slow and wide vibrato imitating *qin*'s tone inflection, and violin's gliss-pizzicato, and so on. The two groups of percussions help to set the mood of the piece. The piece begins and ends in *shang* mode in F. The piece is structured in the form of theme and variation. There is a recurring cadential phrase in *shang* mode attached to sections 3, 6, 10, and 12. As Chou indicated, the dissonant timbre of the *qin*'s silk strings is approximated by dissonant harmony, and in this piece, the use of dissonant major second in chords stands out prominently.

It must be pointed out, however, that the imitation of the sound of *qin* is only the means for creating an atmosphere in which a solitary fisherman is in harmony with his surroundings, the lake, and the sky. What Chou tries to achieve in this work, besides the novel concept that Western instruments are capable of imitating the sound of *qin*, is to evoke the solitary mood.

Originally, Mao's version appeared during the Ming period (1368–1644) in a *qin* book, *Xilutang Qintong* (1549), and later, it was reprinted in *Ziyuantang Qinpu* (1802), which has been widely used after the eighteenth and nineteenth centuries. Mao was a scholar and *qin* player of the late Song period. According to Xu Jian, he composed this piece to express his resentment of the rule of Yuan invaders in his native south and his desire for his friends not to cooperate with the conqueror.[18] Unlike *Willows Are New*, *Yu ko* is not associated with a poem and has no text. Thus, it is not a *qinge* or a text song played on the *qin*.[19] The expressive content of the piece, namely, its solitary mood, has been interpreted in the *Wuzhizhai Qinpu* (1721), a *qin* book.[20] Chou's explanation for the program content of the piece reads, "'Yu ko' means 'song of the fisherman.' The fisherman here is a symbol of the man who is in harmony with nature."[21]

Speaking of specific means for his adaptation of Mao's piece, Chou commented on orchestration, which was aimed at amplifying pitch inflections, articulations, timbre, dynamics, and rhythm according to capacities of each Western instrument; he also pointed out that the subtle temporal fluctuation is "in accordance with the tradition of the *da qu* of the T'ang dynasty."[22] *Da qu* was the performance formula; it is also a multisectional musical composition for dance, song, and instrumental ensemble developed from the Han (25–220 AD) through Song (960–1279 AD) periods, reaching its peak during the T'ang (618–960 AD) period. Descriptions of the T'ang *da qu* have been preserved in chronicles of the T'ang and Song periods.[23] The composition is typically in three sections, and the following is Yang Yin-Liu's description of the three-part structure of the *da qu*:

I. Introduction:
    Instrumentation: solos or ensemble (not specified)
    Rhythmic character: rubato, free rhythm with ritardando.
II. Second Introduction (features voice):
    Instrumentation: not specified but with singing
    Rhythmic character: regular beats, slow tempo later
    Accelerando (dance: optional)
III. Entering the Proper (features dancing):
    Instrumentation: not specified
    Rhythmic character: from free rhythm to regular beats, tempo from slow to fast then slow again (voice: optional)
    Seven Subsections:
    1. free rhythm
    2. free rhythm—regular pulse
    3. moderately fast
    4. accelerando
    5. presto
    6. ritardando
    7. finale[24]

In Mao's version,[25] there are nineteen sections separated by thematic material as well as rhythmic and temporal changes. The tempo accelerates gradually with each section reaching section 11 about quarter note=80, and then slows down to about quarter note=72 for sections 12, 13, and 14, and then accelerates back to about quarter note=80 for sections 15, 16, and 17. Section 18 slows down to about quarter note=60, and the coda corresponds to the opening, which is about quarter note=30. Similarly, Chou's version has fourteen tempo markings instead of maintaining a steady tempo for two or three sections. Like Mao's, Chou's tempo change is frequent. In the course of tempo change, there are no two successive sections sharing a tempo marking. Chou's temporal fluctuation is an interpretation of the *da qu* principle in a personal way, and it creates a sense of ebb and flow of a fluid moving mass.

Most reviews of the work have concentrated on how Chou makes his imitation close to the original while the reason Chou was interested in doing so has been neglected.[26] Ultimately, the significance in the degree of likeness in parodying the sound of an instrument cross culturally is superseded by the outcome for the composer's expression conveyed in his work. Chou felt strongly about introducing Chinese high art forms such as *qin* music to the West and experimented with different techniques for expressing his sentiments toward Chinese arts.

Pien (1966)

Chou's interest in defining the Chinese calligraphic concept in music in terms of Varèsean sound as a moving mass continued to dominate his compositional style of the early and mid-1960s. Yet, spurred by his genuine interest in the *I-Ching* and by his desire to compose a work of substantial duration,[27] Chou continued to refine his compositional theory after the completion of *Metaphors*; the direct result was the composition of *Pien* (1966) for wind, piano, and percussion. During and after completing *Pien*, Chou felt that he had come to a new understanding of Chinese philosophy espoused in *I-Ching* and the *I* principle. *Pien* in Chinese means transformation. In *Pien*, Chou devised six variable modes following *I-Ching's* fundamental concept of *pien*. Modes I and II are shown below (example 4.10). The words *pien* and *I* of the *I-Ching* mean the same thing, namely, that things are evolved from simplicity to complexity, complexity to phenomena, phenomena to their conglomeration and dispersion, and finally arriving at invariability. Here, the most essential substances in the universe are *yin* (signifies "negative" in the sense of physics) and *yang* (opposite of *yin*), represented by a broken line "– –" for *yin* and unbroken line "__" for *yang*. The combination of either two broken or unbroken lines with one of their opposite line forms the basic generating power unit called the trigram. The combination of two trigrams becomes a hexagram, which is represented by cosmologically significant characters such as *da guo*, or "overdone." The six strokes (*yao*) are numbered from the bottom to the top, and the interaction between broken *yin* lines and unbroken *yang* lines is that of constant permutation, generating different hexagrams. Each hexagram is paired with a complimentary one that is the inversion of the one in the pair, for example, *Kan* is paired with *Li*. Chou's term "variable modes" is defined as consisting of modes whose microstructures are variable but whose macrostructure remains the same. For example, at macrolevel, mode I (*chen*) and II (*sun*) share the same intervallic pattern, that is, minor third–minor third–minor third, or m3–m3–m3, while at the microlevel, there are two pitches inserted in the second and third m3, between the root and the third in the interval of minor third, for example, m3–m3–(M2–m2)/m3. This construction reflects the worldview of the *I-Ching* that we live in a world behind whose seemingly unchanging facade, myriad changes are constantly taking place.

Example 4.10. *Pien* mm. 1–7

Each mode contains three groups of minor thirds, for example, F–A♭, A–C, C♯–E, in an octave. Within any one of the minor thirds, an extra pitch can be interpolated, for example, pitch B can be interpolated between pitches A and C, and thus A–B–C will consist of a major second (A–B), minor second (B–C), and a minor third (A–C). If the ascending order contains one uninserted third and two inserted pitches in two thirds, the descending order will negate it by putting two uninserted thirds in front of one inserted third. In ascending order, the major second goes under the minor second, and in descending, it stays above the minor second.

Two modes are related in terms of mirroring: ascending mode I relates to descending mode II and vice versa:

Mode I (*chen*) (☳)
Ascending: F–A♭   A–B–C   C♯–D♯–E
             (_)   (– –)   (– –)

Mode II (*sun*) (☴)
Descending: F–D   C♯–A♯   A–G–F♯
              (_)   (_)   (– –)

Mode II (*sun*) (☴)
Ascending: F♯–G–A   A♯–C♯   D–F
             (– –)   (_)   (_)

Mode I (*chen*) (☳)
Descending: E–D♯–C♯   C–B–A   A♭–F
              (– –)   (– –)   (_)

The central idea of this design is to symbolically apply complementary mutational and directional principles of *I-Ching*. The complementary principle is seen in the relationship between ascending and descending orders of the modes and the positioning of the m2 in accordance with these orders. In terms of structure, the uninserted or unbroken third is somewhat like the long unbroken line (__) in a trigram, and the inserted third, a broken line (– –). Each hexagram in *I-Ching* has a metaphoric name that symbolically represents the worldview of its creator.

The names for these six modes are taken from the 64 hexagrams of the *I-Ching*: chen, sun, ken, tui, kan, and li (figure 4.1). In these, *chen* and *sun*, *ken* and *tui*, and *kan* and *li* are complementary pairs. Each negates its counterpart in terms of the rotating order of uninterpolated and interpolated thirds in an octave:

Pair I. Modes I and II in mm. 1–6.
Mode I (*chen*, thunder)
Ascending: m3–M2+m2–M2+m2
           (–) (– –)   (– –)

Mode II (*sun*, lake)
descending: m3–m3–M2+m2
            (–) (–) (– –)

Mode II
Ascending: m3–m3–M2+m2
           (–) (–) (– –)

Mode I
descending: m3–M2+m2–M2+m2
            (–) (– –)   (– –)

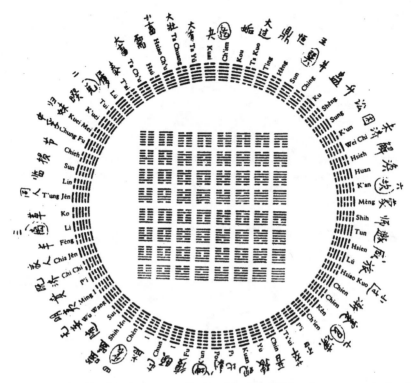

Figure 4.1. The sixty-four hexagrams displayed in the traditional arrangement of a circle and a square

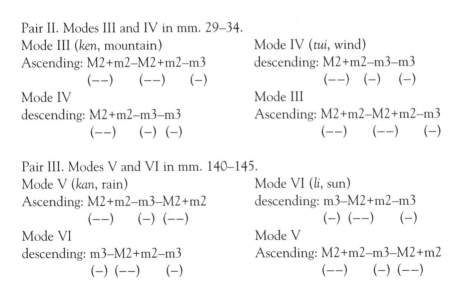

Pair II. Modes III and IV in mm. 29–34.

Mode III (*ken*, mountain)
Ascending: M2+m2–M2+m2–m3
    (––)   (––)   (–)
Mode IV
descending: M2+m2–m3–m3
    (––)   (–) (–)

Mode IV (*tui*, wind)
descending: M2+m2–m3–m3
    (––) (–) (–)
Mode III
Ascending: M2+m2–M2+m2–m3
    (––)   (––)   (–)

Pair III. Modes V and VI in mm. 140–145.

Mode V (*kan*, rain)
Ascending: M2+m2–m3–M2+m2
    (––)   (–) (––)
Mode VI
descending: m3–M2+m2–m3
    (–) (––)   (–)

Mode VI (*li*, sun)
descending: m3–M2+m2–m3
    (–) (––)   (–)
Mode V
Ascending: M2+m2–m3–M2+m2
    (––)   (–) (––)

The complete statements of the modes are outlined above. However, in most places, these modes are used in fragmentary fashion or, in other words, in the forms of two basic intervallic cells, that is, major second and minor second. There is a parallel to this kind bi- and trinumeric combination. A well-known example is Schoenberg's *Three Piano Pieces* op. 11 in which minor third/major third and minor second serve as basic harmonic, scalar, and melodic material. The isolation of the fragments of the modes, that is, minor third or major second with a minor second plus minor second, reflects Schoenberg's idiosyncratic ways of making trichords, which are especially prominent in his *Three Piano Pieces* op. 11: mm. 1–4, G–G♯–B, F–F♯–A, D♭–E–F, A–B♭–D♭, C–D♭–E, G–B♭–B, G–G♯–B.

In terms of dynamics, the six graded levels outlined in the preface of the score are not in actual use and are not organized in a serial manner. The way intervallic cells are used in *Pien* shows Chou's first consistent and systematic exploration of intervallic cells, and the meaning of harmonic structure in relation to line mirroring two generating elements in the *bagua* of *I-Ching*.

Yun (1969)

Yun was Chou's last work composed in the 1960s. The pitch organization, orchestration, and rhythmic structure in *Yun* are much less complex in comparison to *Pien*. The texture in *Yun* is much thinner and the length of the piece, 166 measures, is only half of *Pien*. This was because the work was intended for college orchestras, commissioned by Wisconsin State University at River Falls in 1968, and premiered there on February 6, 1969, under the direction of Donald Nitz. In comparison to *Pien*, the seemingly less complex material and treatment in *Yun* is quite undemanding. The interpretation of the work from spiritual and intellectual points of view requires imagination. Specifically, one needs to relate the concept of *xieyi* or expression of idea through simple means, which was developed by Chinese painters during the thirteenth century to the compositional process. Chou explains in his "Notes on *Yun*,"

> The title *Yun* is taken from the expression *Ch'iyun*, the foremost principle in Chinese art, which means "reverberating of the vitalizing force in nature (ch'i). . . ." This is perhaps best illustrated by the concept of *hsieh i* in Chinese ink painting: the open space untouched by the brush is where the ideas are.[28]

Having developed a system to accommodate pitch and structural organization between the concept of Western atonal music and structural models

Example 4.11. *Yun* mm. 6–10

based on *I-Ching*, Chou was again able to experiment with the application of his variable modes in *Yun* (example 4.11). Example 4.11 shows the ascending order of a variable mode in *Yun*, that is,

C–E♭   E–F♯–G   A♭–B♭–B.
(–)   (– –)   (– –)

The piece is organized in five sections divided by temporal, motivic, and rhythmic characters and textures:

Section 1: 1–40—features sustained long notes
Section 2: 41–79—pointillist single notes with inflection
Section 3: 80–93—counterpoint between piano and percussion rhythmic mode in percussion
Section 4: 94–107—contrast between two rhythmic motives
Section 5: 108–166—combination of the above

Chou's ideas about the harmonic organization of the work is that he combined his variable modes with added pitches.[29] Like *Pien*, the variable modes in *Yun* are stated in complete form in certain sections. In other sections, they are broken down into fragments in the form of intervallic cells. In these two works, Chou again extended the structural principle of contrast or reflection within several strata of a moving sound mass. Here, influences of serial and Varèsean concepts are readily recognizable.

From *Pien* and *Yun* one sees that the use of the variable modes or in Chou's words, "mutually complemented intervals but exclusive pitches,"[30] instead of always being recognizable orders in certain sections, is often in a fragmentary fashion that eventually compromises the composer's initial plan. The emphasis on registral, temporal, timbral, and textural contrasts between sections and the contrast between single tones shows the prominence of the concept of musical calligraphy, which was developed in the 1950s and 1960s, first in *And the Fallen Petals* and *Willows Are New*, and then in subsequent works up to *Yun*.

The formal aspect of the piece reminds one of the Webernian way of focusing on the microaspect of musical activity, that is, on the inflections of each isolated individual tones, and Webern's brevity in constructing musical forms.[31] In fact, what appears to be fragments or isolated tones are only points of a continuing line, representing the trigram (example 4.12).

Because there is no concrete Chinese musical reference to be detected, the direct link between *Yun* and Chinese music is rather tenuous. In this respect, Chou has abandoned traditional aural ways of determining the identity of a composition. He suggests in *Yun*'s program note, "a fair definition for the nature of the piece would be: this is a piece, which is composed by a Chinese composer who was inspired by Chinese ways of perceiving music."[32]

For seventeen years, between completing *Yun* in 1969 and his first work of the 1980s, Chou devoted his energy to administration at Columbia University and elsewhere. In comparison with his works of the 1950s, Chou's works of the 1960s show sensitivity to his musical environment in the United States and tendencies in contemporary American compositions. In line with

Example 4.12. *Yun* mm. 60–63

his European and American colleagues, his own study in Chinese philosophy, such as *I-Ching*, has become an inspirational source for composition.

Except for *Yu ko* (1965), the descriptive nature of his works of the 1950s has given way to the abstraction of Chinese musical interpretation of philosophical and aesthetic ideas. In addition to the marriage between Chinese calligraphic idea of the flow of ink and the Varèsean view of the fluidity of sound as a moving mass, Chou added yet another dimension. This was the application of his "variable modes."

The intervallic patterns of these modes, that is, basically minor third with two pitches and minor third with three pitches, seems to bear some similarities with the works of Webern. Yet, Chou was able to find a structural model in the basic structure of the trigram in the *bagua* of the *I-Ching* for organizing these intervallic cells into a mode. The constructive forces applied and the sentiments expressed in these works are clearly Chinese. In doing so, Chou successfully avoided a simplistic approach to combining Chinese musical material with Western harmony. In his two works of the 1980s and two works of the 1990s, the *I-Ching*-inspired structural principle to tonal organization was extended to rhythmic organization especially seen in his percussion piece *Echoes from the Gorge* (1989).

Notes

1. *I-Ching* (*Yi Jing*) or book of changes is one of the five oldest Confucian classics or the so-called five *jings*. The other four are: *Shu Jing, Shi Jing, Li Ji,* and *Chuenqiu.* John Cage tapped the philosophical principles of the *I-Ching* for his compositions as early as 1951.

2. The eight basic trigrams in *I-Ching* are not to be viewed as merely a device for predicting future outcome for a set of given conditions but as a vehicle to express a set of complete philosophical ideas.

3. Wen-Chung Chou, "Asian Music and Western Composition," in *Dictionary of Contemporary Music* (New York: Dutton, 1974), 26.

4. Joseph Needham, *Science and Civilization in China,* vol. 2 (Cambridge: Cambridge University Press, 1954), 304–5.

5. Wen-Chung Chou, program notes in the score of *Metaphors,* published by C. F. Peters Edition, 1961.

6. Eric Lai has studied these modes or the "variable modes" from a theorist's point of view. See "The Evolution of Chou Wen-Chung's Variable Modes," in *Locating East Asia in Western Art Music,* ed. Yayoi Uno Everett and Frederick Lau (Middletown, Conn.: Wesleyan University Press, 2004), 146–67.

7. Chou, program notes in *Metaphors.*

8. Announcement, *American Composers Alliance Bulletin* 12, no. 1 (September 1964): 17.

9. Edgard Varèse, "New Instruments and New Music" (1936), from "The Liberation of Sound," ed. and ann. Chou Wen-Chung, *Perspectives of New Music* 1 (Fall-Winter 1966): 11–19.

10. Wen-Chung Chou, "Toward a Re-Merger in Music," in *Contemporary Composers on Contemporary Music,* ed. Elliot Schwartz and Barney Childs (New York: Da Capo Press, 1978), 314.

11. Jin Jing-Fang and Lu Shao-Gang, *Zhou Yi Quanjie* [*A Full Exposition of the I-Ching*], 2nd ed. (Changchuen: Jilin University Press, 1991), 3.

12. Edgard Varèse, "The Liberation of Sound," in *Contemporary Composers on Contemporary Music,* ed. Elliot Schwartz and Barney Childs (New York: Da Capo Press, 1978), 199.

13. Jonathan Bernard, *The Music of Edgard Varèse* (New Haven, Conn.: Yale University Press, 1987), 81.

14. Varèse, "The Liberation of Sound," 197.

15. Wen-Chung Chou, "Wode Zuoqu Guannian Yu Jingyan [My compositional Concepts and experiences]," *Xin Xiang Yixun [New Trends in the Arts]* (January 10–16, 1982): 8.

16. Edgard Varèse, "Rhythm, Form, and Content" (from a lecture given at Princeton University in 1959), reprinted in *Contemporary Composers on Contemporary Music*, ed. Elliot Schwartz and Barney Childs (New York: Da Capo, 1978), 203.

17. Gang Chen, "Zaochuen Eryue Liuse Xin [New Willows of the Early February]," *People's Music* 11, no. 12 (1979): 69.

18. There has been debate among Chinese historians on Mao's attitude toward the Yuan occupation. See Jian Xu's *Qinshi Chubian [A History of the Qin: A Preliminary Study]*, 2nd ed. (Beijing: People's Music Publications, 1987), 90–91, 104–5.

19. Not to be confused with Zong-Yuan Liu's poem "Fisherman," which was set to a *qin* piece called *ai nai*. See Jian Xu.

20. This anthology of *qin* music contains thirty-three *qin* pieces with annotations of origins of the pieces as well as performing directions. The printed Qing edition was edited by Lu-Feng Zhou. See *Zhongguo Yinyue Cidian [Dictionary of Chinese Music]* (Beijing: People's Music Publications, 1984), 413.

21. Wen-Chung Chou, *Yu ko* (New York: C. F. Peters Edition, 1968), 1.

22. Chou, *Yu ko*, 1.

23. See *Jou Tang Shu—Yinyue Zhi*; *Tang Hui yao*, chapter 33; Mi Zhou, *Qi Dong Ye Yu*; Xiu Ouyang, *Tangshu—Li Yue Zhi*; Ju-Yi Bai, "Nishang Yuyi Wu Ge"; and *Yang Tai-Zhen Waizhuan*; all cited in Yin-Liu Yang, *Zhongguo Gudai Yinyue Shigao [Drafts of History of Chinese Music in Antiquity]*, 2nd ed. in Chinese, vol. 1 (Beijing: People's Music Publications, 1981), 222–23.

24. Yin-Liu Yang, *Zhongguo Gudai Yinyue Shigao [Drafts of History of Chinese Music in Antiquity]*, 2nd ed. in Chinese, vol. 1 (Beijing: People's Music Publications, 1981), 221. My translation.

25. This is based on Hong Wu's *Zi Yuan Tang Qinpu [Anthology of the Qin Pieces by the Zi Yuan Tang Printing House]*, 12 vols. (1802) in *Zhongguo Yueqi Jieshao [An Introduction to Chinese Instruments]*, trans. Fu-Xi Zha and ed. Jian Xu (Beijing: Music Research Institute, Chinese Academy of Arts, 1985).

26. See Gang Chen, "Zaochuen Eryue Liuse Xin [New Willows of the Early February]," *People's Music* 11, no. 12 (1979): 69; Alfred Frankenstein, "The Sound World of Chou Wen-Chung," *High Fidelity/Musical America* 20 (July–Nov. 1970), 84; David Tsang's program note for the performance of *Yu ko* together with other works on April 27, 1989, at Lila Acheson Wallare Auditorium, New York; Bruce Archibald's record review of four of Chou's works in *The Musical Quarterly* 58 (1972): 333; and A. Cohn's "Very Special: The Music of Chou Wen-Chung," *The American Record Guide* 36 (September–August 1969–1970): 886.

27. This refers to a comment made in the late 1950s by Franco Autory, Chou's friend and Toscanini's associate conductor, who admired Chou's *And the Fallen Petals* and asked him if his techniques would allow him to compose large works. Chou Wen-Chung, correspondence with Peter Chang, May 7, 2004, 5.

28. Wen-Chung Chou, "Notes on *Yun*," unpublished. In this program note the date of the composition was erroneously referred to as 1968, which was the year the work was commissioned. The work was completed in January 1969 as indicated in the score by Chou.

29. Wen-Chung Chou, letter to Tim Wilson dated September 26, 1988.

30. Chou, correspondence, 4.

31. Chou believes that Webern's concerns over timbre, texture, duration, register, and articulation in constructing musical forms echoes those structural and aesthetic concepts seen in the Chinese *qin* in his 1971 article "Asian Concepts and Twentieth-Century Western Composers," *The Musical Quarterly* 57, no. 2: 214.

32. Chou, "Notes on *Yun*."

CHAPTER FIVE

~

Chou's Works of the
1980s and 1990s

Chou's works of the 1980s and 1990s show increased abstraction, much greater than his works of the 1960s. During the 1960s, Chou was translating his newly discovered hexagram configuration of the *ba gua* from the *I-Ching* into a concrete way of organizing pitches, which corresponds to the trigram of the *ba gua*. However, Chou was not satisfied with the simplistic alternating three segments within an octave and had refined his concept of variable modes by adding a minor second in each trigram according to the ascending or descending orders that appeared in *Cursive* (1963) and *Pien* (1966). To make his modal concept more inclusive and flexible, Chou further modified it by adding additional pitches in the interval within a given segment, like auxiliary ones were added to principal ones in the mode to preserve the identity of modes. For example, pitches for the minor third C–E♭ are principal ones and the filler pitches C♯ and D are auxiliary ones. Chou acknowledges this as a conceptual union between the Chinese calligraphic concept of *Tian Bai* (fill the space, opposite of *Liu Bai* or leaving out white space) and Bartokian idea of filling out a larger interval with additional pitches.[1] He worked out these ideas in *Windswept Peaks* (1989–1990), the Cello Concerto (1990), and the string quartet "Clouds" (1996). Instead, using symbolic labels of the trigram of *ba gua* such as "mountain," "lake," and "wind," and the associated reflective principle are used only for changing a collection of major second and minor third dyads according to either ascending or descending orders. The elaborate modal structure of minor third (__) plus minor third (__) and the combination of minor second and major second (_ _) as unbroken-unbroken-broken segments has been replaced with two kinds of dyads: major second and minor third and their inversions. The idea of two against three[2] is viewed as the interaction between two fundamental forces, the *yin* and the *yang*, the interaction presumed responsible for the evolution of the universe. Therefore, each of Chou's work of the 1990s is a philosophical statement that concerns the relationship between man and nature.

All three works of the 1980s and 1990s, excluding *Beijing in the Mist*, emphasize working out the basic germinal material and counterpoint, which controls the fluidity of the texture. Also, the emphasis on the process of composition and on the aesthetic experience of listening already seen in *Yun* (1969)—which explores different vibratos corresponding to the symbolic meaning of the title suggesting vibration in nature—is continued in *Echoes from the Gorge*, which explores not the sound itself, but different types of echoes.

As the first work Chou completed in the 1980s, *Beijing in the Mist* signifies a transitional stage leading to three consequent compositions. Differing sharply from the three later works, *Beijing in the Mist* is a "Chinese-flavored" work that employs Chinese melody.

Beijing in the Mist (1986)

The composition of this work is Chou's second venture in associating his music with dance choreography after *Poems of White Stone* (1959), which was choreographed by Merce Cunningham. For working out the details of the production, Chou and Jacques D'Amboise, a dance choreographer, worked together from 1985 to 1986. The work was completed on February 24, 1986, and presented on June 2, 1986, at an international event, "China Dig," National Dance Institute's Event of the Year in the Felt Forum in New York City with Lee Norris conducting. The event involved more than fifteen hundred American children and fifty-six children from the People's Republic of China.[3]

"Beijing Dust" was the original title for these groups of dances, and it was D'Ambrosie who named each dance with Chinese gastronomic terms such as "dumplings," "phoenix nest," and "Beijing dust." "Beijing dust" is a sweet made from mashed chestnuts with a dusty appearance. Chou changed this title to "Beijing in the Mist" to evoke the impression that Beijing is seen as an ancient city with sharply etched contours.

In this work, rather than using abstract concepts as principles for guiding the composition process, Chou turned to the suggestive approach of using

Chinese melodies to trigger the listener's imaginations. Here, the variation principle in the traditional *lao baban* or eight instrumental pieces serves as the basis for various treatment of the thematic material such as filtering, distortion, amplification, and enrichment. One good example of melodic treatment is seen in the use of upper-neighbor grace notes developed in Chou's works of the 1950s (example 5.1). As a personal trait, the appearance of this upper-neighbor figure, which has been used in many of Chou's works of the 1950s, clearly shows Chou's conception of Chinese melody.

Example 5.1. *Beijing in the Mist* **mm. 52–54**

In terms of timbre, the work employs electronically amplified instrumental sound, such as electric guitar, bass, and piano. Besides two groups of sizable percussion ensembles, saxophones are also used. Despite the incidental nature of the piece and its odd instrumentation (the only available ensemble at the time), it has been performed several times in various concerts.

Echoes from the Gorge (1989)

Chou worked out the general structural plan of this percussion quartet when he was the composer-in-residence with Koussevisky Composer's Studio at Tanglewood during the summers of 1970 and 1971.[4] After 1972, his works on this piece were interrupted by his administrative activities; in 1988, he was finally able to return to it, completing it in 1989. The New Music Consort premiered the work in New York on April 27, 1989, at the Lila Acheson Wallace Auditorium with the Asia Society.

General Observations

On the surface, the work seems to have descended from Varèse's *Ionization* (1930), since both are written for indefinite-pitched percussion ensemble. At a closer look, however, the sophistication of the union between the Varèsean concept of musical timbre, texture, and germinating rhythmic cells, the Chinese concept of percussive sound of music and the *I-Ching* principle of trigram in organizing rhythmic modes is readily recognizable. In fact, without references to *Ionization*, the line between Varèsean and Chinese concepts is difficult to draw.

The fact that this piece responded to Varèse's call for timbral exploration in indefinite-pitched percussion ensembles is evident. However, Chou's work has never been a mere imitation of Varèse. Instead, Chou searched for parallels in Chinese traditions and tried to rethink Varèsean ideas in Chinese terms in which percussion ensemble has been an indispensable part of the sound ideal in traditional Chinese music. In line with his conceptualized Chinese aesthetic ideals, such as emphasis on timbral changes in a single tone and calligraphic conception of textural fluidity, Chou found a new territory in pure percussion ensembles where he could experiment with these ideals. For Chou, *Ionization* served *Echoes from the Gorge* only as a point of departure.

Besides the emphases on timbre, fluidity of texture, and form shared by Varèse and Chou, Chou's approach in this work represents a continuation of his efforts to experiment with organizational principle for pitches but now also with rhythm and counterpoint. The principles of the musical elements' evolution from a single source, the union of the *yin* and *yang* in the *I-Ching*, that have been formulated as early as in the 1960s underscores the basic structural principle of the piece.

In *Ionization*, the rhythmic structure is based on the idiomatic use of certain rhythmic figures associated with a particular instrument; however, the rhythmic design in *Echoes from the Gorge* is based on permutation, namely, the rotations of rhythmic cells and the use of certain orders of these cells to relate four contrapuntal voice parts. Varèse's idea of exploring great varieties of a single germinal rhythmic cell in *Ionization* has been reinterpreted as the *I-Ching* principle of evolution in *Echoes from the Gorge*. In terms of voice leading, the influence of the retrograde principle in eighteen-century counterpoint is noticeably strong; however, Chou has reinterpreted this influence through the principle of dualistic union in generating a variety of rhythmic profiles.

Structure

The work consists of twelve sections. Each has a programmatic title that evokes typical images often portrayed in classical Chinese paintings, and each features a particular kind of instrumental timbre. The titles of the twelve sections and prominent timbres in each of them are listed below:

1. "Prelude: Exploring the Rhythmic Modes" (mm. 1–7)
   Prominent sonority: clave and woodblock
   Other sonorities: tam-tam, gongs, cymbal, tenor/bass drums
2. "Raindrop on Bamboo Leaves" (mm. 8–145)
   Prominent sonority: drum
   Other sonorities: in m. 42, claves, cowbells, and finger bell; in m. 69, gongs and cymbals; in m. 113, drums, wood blocks, tam-tams, and claves
3. "Autumn Pond" (mm. 146–171)
   Prominent sonority: snare drum drone with embellishing castanets and wood blocks, cowbells, and tom-toms
4. "Clear Moon" (mm. 172–197)
   Prominent sonority: cymbals
5. "Shadows in the Ravine" (mm. 198–214)
   Prominent sonority: drums and cymbals
6. "Old Tree by the Cold Spring" (mm. 215–234)
   Prominent sonority: wood blocks
   Other sonorities: snare drums, cowbells, and cymbals
7. "Sonorous Stones" (mm. 235–243)
   Prominent sonority: cowbells
   Other sonorities: cymbals and tom-toms

8. "Droplets Down the Rocks" (mm. 244–262)
    Prominent sonority: claves
    Other sonorities: in mm. 250–261, bongos, congas, woodblocks, temple blocks, timbales, and high bass drum
9. "Drifting Clouds" (mm. 263–271)
    Prominent sonority: drums
    Prominent use of hairpin-type dynamics
10. "Rolling Pearls" (mm. 272–291)
    Prominent sonority: snare drums
    Other sonorities: tom-toms, timbales, tenor/bass and parade drums
11. "Peaks and Cascades" (mm. 292–320)
    Prominent sonority: drums
    Other sonorities: cymbals
12. "Falling Rocks and Flying Spray" (mm. 321–334)
    Prominent sonority: snare drums
    Other sonorities: bongos, congas, gongs, tenor/bass and parade drums, and cymbals; metal sheet used at m. 334, the cadential point.

Section 1, the Prelude, is designed to explore basic rhythmic, timbral, and registral procedures. In Chinese *qin* pieces, this section is called *diao yi*; although no content is specified, it is often used to explore a mode and test tuning of the strings before the player starts the piece. The six basic rhythmic patterns in this section are outlined in figure 5.1.

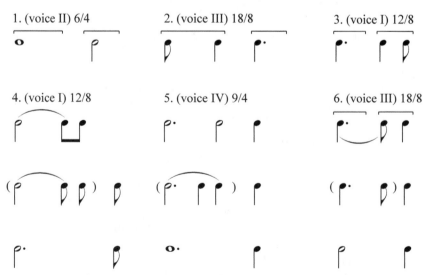

Figure 5.1.   Outline of the six rhythmic modes in _Echoes from the Gorge_ section 1

Autumn Pond

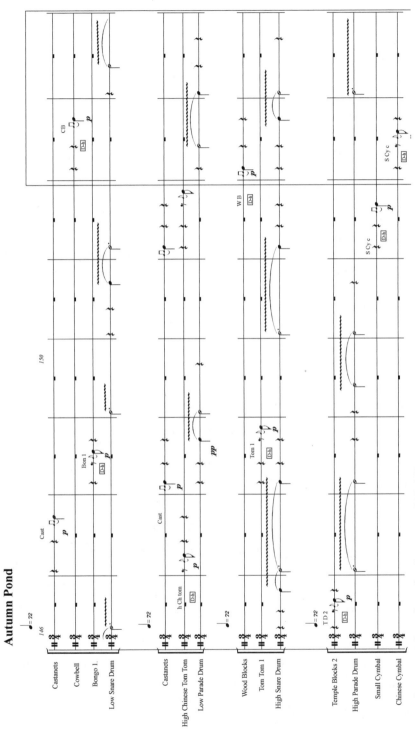

Example 5.2. *Echoes from the Gorge mm. 146–153*

The above figure also illustrates that the ratio of the tempi between voices I and II and between III and IV is 2:1, that is, 12/8 : 6/4 between voices I and II and 18/8 : 9/4 between voices III and IV. The basic contrapuntal principle of augmentation, diminution, inversion, retrograde, and rotation are discernible with ample illustrations. Example 5.2 shows how the rhythmic figure in section 3, "Autumn Pond," relates to one of the germinal rhythmic figures, mode II in augmentation.

Structural Principles

One of the organizational ideas of the piece is that all rhythmic patterns can be referred to sources of a whole note and a half note, which generate different rhythmic patterns by dividing the beats according to the ratio of 1:2. Therefore, the whole note plus the half note becomes a half note plus a quarter note, which, in turn, generates a quarter note plus an eighth note, and so forth. The rotation or permutation of a rhythmic pattern or the combination of several patterns provides even greater rhythmic variety. This is often seen as regrouping of these patterns in accordance with a ratio of 3:2:1. Example 5.3 reveals the surface level of the grouping ratio of 3:2, that is, 9/4 : 6/4, and

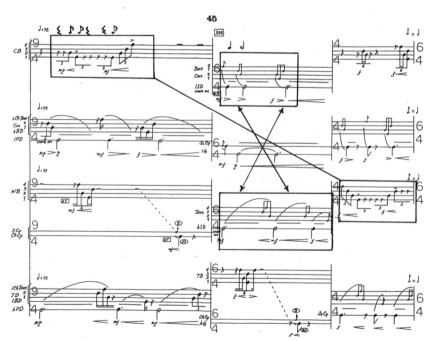

Example 5.3. *Echoes from the Gorge* mm. 324–326

at the microlevel, notational ratio of 2:1, that is, a quarter note and a half note in m. 325 in contrast to an eighth note and a quarter rest in m. 324.

Counterpoint

The contrapuntal treatment for the four parts shows them as one unit as well as the independence of each individual part at certain points, where the combination of either top and bottom two voices, of two inner and outer voices, or of voice I and III and voice II and IV is called for. Example 5.4 shows the association between timbre and rhythmic characters, that is, drum, gong, and cymbal group versus blocks group. Imitations can also be seen between two top and bottom voices. There are many instances in which the imitation of the first voice appears to be the reversal of it. Examples 5.5 and 5.6 illustrate two occurrences.

Timbre

Several distinct rhythmic figures distributed in different sections are the result of their compatible timbral characteristics. For example, the bongos' eighth-note figure (mm. 148–152) relates to high Chinese tom-tom and

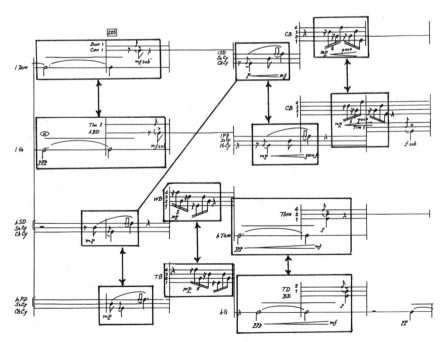

Example 5.4. *Echoes from the Gorge* mm. 224–229

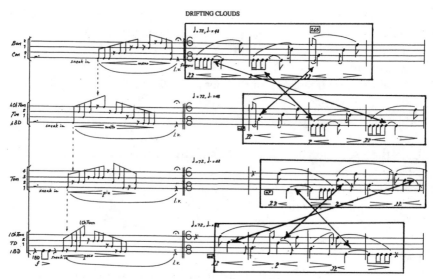

Example 5.5. *Echoes from the Gorge* mm. 262–266

Chinese cymbal in section 3, Autumn Pond, because all of them are struck by the heavy end of the drumstick, marked as "D-h." This figure can be found in sections 2, 5, 11, and 12. In section 12, the timbral tie between these figures is that either sizzle cymbals are played at the normal location, marked "N," for maximum sonority, or the Chinese cymbals are played near the cup, marked "B."

Chou's selection of several Chinese percussion instruments such as the Chinese cymbal, high and low tom-tom or *xiao gu*, and finger bells or *ling/peng zhong* for the piece may convey a false impression that this piece should sound Chinese to fit his program titles. This is not the case. Imitating Chinese sound on Western instruments was experimented with in the late 1950s and early 1960s and is no longer a novelty. By now, Chou has already applied some of the *I-Ching* principles in two of his works of the late 1960s, and this work can be seen as the continuation of that effort.

The fact that Chou specifies his preference for the Chinese or Asian instruments such as claves, wood blocks, temple bells, and tenor drum, even though they can be substituted by their Western counterparts, only shows the need for that particular kind of timbre at a particular place. However, at a conceptual level, Chou's elaborate specification of contact or playing locations on the instrument does parallel the Chinese percussion tradition in which different ways of striking the same instrument can produce a set of corresponding syllables to be notated in the score and to be recited and memo-

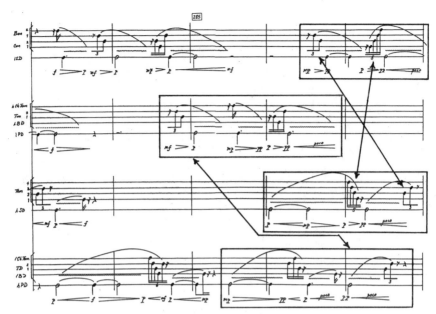

Example 5.6. *Echoes from the Gorge* mm. 283–287

rized by the performer.[5] Such a timbre-specific tradition can be seen prominently in *shi fan luo gu*, or ten rounds of gongs and drums, and also in some
theatrical genres such as Peking opera and *li yuan xi*, or drama of the pear
garden.[6]

Compatible Elements between Chinese and Western Traditions

The piece ultimately illustrates Chou's technical facility in Western counterpoint and his imaginative power both in expressing his Chinese sentiment
by using imageries for setting the mood and applying Chinese aesthetic values, such as treating the four groups of instruments as one line of continuous
flow of ink. Except for the clave's gradual *accelerando*, similar to that of Chinese *bangu's si bian* rhythm,[7] at the closing of the first movement, there are
no concrete Chinese rhythmic patterns to be found in the piece.

According to David Tsang and Chou himself, Chou's use of the programmatic title was to invoke a particular timbre of the *qin*.[8] Although characteristic use of a type of instrument in a particular section, for example, the
exclusive use of four types of drums up to m. 41 in the "Rain Drop on Bamboo Leaves" section can be observed to correlate mallet timbre with the
sound of raindrops; however, the link between this timbre and a specific *qin*
timbre such as *cui* or crisp cannot be concretely demonstrated.[9] What Chou

intended to explore in this piece is the feeling of hearing different types of echoes from different sound sources.[10]

The *I-Ching* idea of the interaction between *yin* and *yang*, seen in this piece as the ratio between the whole note and the half note, as a means of generating the maximum rhythmic variety in this work, is evident. The concept of verticalizing linear material for generating a specific timbre and texture that Chou often speaks about can be observed here as well.[11] In this piece, the direct borrowing of Chinese percussion rhythms is absent. Instead, Chou borrowed only the general concepts of the *I-Ching* and employed them to reinterpret what he had learned from Varèse's *Ionization* at certain stages of his compositional process.

Windswept Peaks (1989–1990)

Unlike *Echoes from the Gorge* (1989) and *Concerto for Violoncello and Orchestra* (1992), both of which were planned in the early 1970s and completed in the 1980s and 1990s, *Windswept Peaks* was composed in the late 1980s on a commission proffered by the Aeolian Chamber Players,[12] a professional performing group and resident ensemble at the Bowdoin Summer Music Festival. The six-week concert series of the "MusicFest '90" began July 11, 1990, at Bowdoin College and several other venues in Brunswick, Maine. Chou's piece premiered in the First Parish Church on July 13, 1990, by the commissioning group under the artistic director and the violinist Lewis Kaplan.[13]

Chou began to work on the piece in May 1989 and completed it in June 1990, concurrent with a series of political events in China leading to the Tiananmen incident on June 4, 1989. Chou was disturbed by these events and decided to dedicate the piece to his compatriots to show his sympathy and support. These sentiments are expressed in his program notes:

> The image of windswept peaks suggests the unadorned beauty of inner strength, as symbolized by the gnarled pines and craggy rocks. This stark imagery began to permeate my musical thinking when the tragic event of June fourth, 1989, at *Tianan men* took place soon after I started composing this piece.[14]

Although the work bears a program title and is intended to express sentiment toward the aesthetic ideal of Chinese calligraphy, it sounds neither oriental nor Chinese. The central idea of the work is to translate the composer's emotions into musical movements represented by the interactions of the four in-

Chou Wen-Chung's father, Chou Miao or Chou Zhong-Jie (1891–1987), and mother, Fu Shou-Xian (1895–1986)

High school graduation portrait. Shanghai, spring 1941.

Tung Shao-Yuan, a new cello student at the New England Conservatory. Boston, 1947.

Varèse, one month before his death, discussing the percussion score for Poem Electronique. *The score was copied by Chou Wen-Chung. New York, 1965.*

Boulez discussing Varèse's revised manuscript of Ameriques. *Late 1960s. Photograph by Maryette Charlton.*

Tanglewood, with Bernstein. Chou was composer-in-residence. Summer, 1970 or 1971. Photograph by Whitestone Photo.

Isaac Stern with faculty and students at Central Conservatory of Music. The trip to China was arranged by Chou. Beijing, 1979. Photograph by Chou Wen-Chung.

Arthur Miller and Yu Cao (far right), eminent Chinese playwright, in conjunction with performances of Death of a Salesman. *The trip and meeting were arranged by Chou. Beijing, 1981.*

Chou Wen-Chung on his first trip to minority villages. Yunnan, 1990.

Portrait, finishing the Second String Quartet. Rhinebeck, 2003. Photograph by Luyen Chou.

struments or, in Chou's own words, "coordinated flow of the four parts." The *I-Ching* concept in this piece is not seen as the division of the octave into three segments in accordance with the organizing principle of the trigram, that is, as the combination of one broken line and two unbroken lines (___) or vice versa (_ _) but as a philosophical view that the universe is evolved from the interaction of two essential forces, *yin* and *yang*. The embodiment of *yin* and *yang* in this piece can be seen in the intervals of major second and minor third and in their inversions. From these two intervals, all harmonic and melodic elements evolve.

Pitch Organization

The pitch organization of the work is based on dyads of major second and minor third or minor seventh and major sixth and the aggregates of these. Two sets of distinct pitch-invariable collections can be identified: (1) a set of four hexachord collections, which opens and concludes the piece and ushers in the rhapsodic middle section and (2) six hexachord collections, each containing four different orderings, arranged in pairs, and preceded or followed by a set of pitch-variable tetrachords. The longest rhapsodic middle section is based on various combinations of dyads of major second and minor third in forms of trichords or tetrachords. The first set of pitch-invariable hexachord is outlined below:

1. E♭–F G–A B–D
2. C♯–E F♯–G♯ A♯–C
3. E♭–F G♭–A♭ B♭–D♭
4. C–D E–G A♭–B

This set appears in mm. 1–12, 76–88, 89–96, and 359–367 (examples 5.7–5.11). Each of the six collections of pitch-invariant hexachords (totaling twenty-four sets) contains two pairs, each pair two sets, and each set has two orderings, ascending and descending, all of which are listed as follows:

Collection I			
Pair I		Ascending	Descending
1.		D–E F♯–G♯ A♯–C♯	E♭–C B–A G–F
2.		B–A G–F E♭–C	B♭–D♭ D–E F♯–G♯
Pair II			
3.		G–E E♭–C B–A	F♯–G♯ A♯–C♯ D–F
4.		B♭–D♭ D–F G♭–A♭	B–A G–E E♭–C

Example 5.7. *Windswept Peaks* mm. 1–12

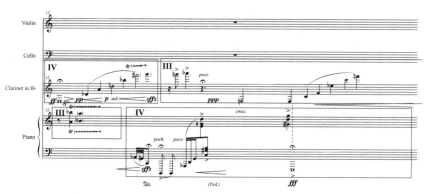

Example 5.8.   *Windswept Peaks* mm. 12

Collection II
 Pair I   Ascending   Descending
 1.   F♯–A B♭–C D–F   G–E D♯–C♯ B–G♯
 2.   G–E D♯–C♯ B–G♯   F♯–A B♭–C D–F
 Pair II
 3.   D–E F♯–A B♭–C   E♭–D♭ C♭–A♭ G–F
 4.   D♯–C♯ B–G♯ G–F   D–E F♯–A B♭–C

Collection III
 Pair I   Ascending   Descending
 1.   A♯–C♯ D–E F♯–G♯   B–A G–F E♭–C
 2.   E♭–C B–A G–F   D–E F♯–G♯ A♯–C♯
 Pair II
 3.   G♭–A♭ B♭–D♭ D–F   G–E E♭–C B–A
 4.   B–A G–E E♭–C   B♭–D♭ D–F F♯–G♯

Collection IV
 Pair I   Ascending   Descending
 1.   D–F F♯–A B♭–C   D♯–C♯ B–G♯ G–E
 2.   B–G♯ G–E D♯–C♯   B♭–C D–F F♯–A
 Pair II
 3.   B♭–C D–E F♯–A   B–G♯ G–F E♭–D♭
 4.   G–F E♭–D♭ B–G♯   F♯–A B♭–C D–E

Collection V
 Pair I   Ascending   Descending
 1.   F♯–G♯ A♯–C♯ D–E   G–F E♭–C B–A
 2.   G–F E♭–C B–A   F♯–G♯ A♯–C♯ D–E

Example 5.9. *Windswept Peaks* mm. 76–88

Example 5.10. *Windswept Peaks* mm. 89–96

Pair II
3.   D–F G♭–A♭, B♭–D♭,   E♭–C B–A G–E
4.   E♭–C B–A G–E   D–F G♭–A♭, B♭–D♭,
Collection VI
Pair I   Ascending   Descending
1.   B♭–C D–F F♯–A   B–G♯ G–E D♯–C♯
2.   D♯–C♯ B–G♯ G–E   D–F F♯–A B♭–C
Pair II
3.   F♯–A B♭–C D–E   G–F E♭–D♭, C♭–A♭,
4.   B–G♯ G–F E♭–D♭,   B♭–C D–E F♯–A

From this list, we notice that the pitch content within each pair is identical, for all these collections are generated from the dyads of major second and minor third. Further, two pairs of collections are related by sharing four

Example 5.11. *Windswept Peaks* mm. 359–367

dyads. Yet, four other dyads make the distinction between these pairs. For example, in collection VI, pair I and II share dyads B♭–C, G♯–B, E♭–D♭, and
F♯–A. Dyads D–F and G–E in pair I distinguish this pair from the second pair,
which does not share its dyads D–E and G–F with the first pair.

In working out these collections, Chou used labels derived from the *ba gua*
or the arrangement of sixty-four hexagrams of the *I-Ching* such as mountain,
lake, wind, rain, and sun as reminders for the ordering of these hexachords.
Again, in collection VI, we see that pair I, number 1 ascending is rotated to
become pair I, number 2 descending in which the dyad B♭–C is permuted
from left to right in its new location. Similarly, pair I, number 1 descending

is permuted to become pair I, number 2 ascending by rotating the dyad D♯–C♯ from left to right in its new location. Chou's reason for using metaphoric labels, besides serving as a reminder for permutation, is to apply *I-Ching*'s reflective principle in a general sense. Here the reflection between each pair, as in pair I, number 1 ascending reflected by pair I, number 2 descending, and vice versa, is not difficult to discern.

Counterpoint

The piece is written for a double duet (violin/cello and clarinet/piano), and the guiding principle in handling contrapuntal relations between four parts is that of controlled or coordinated flow of ink and the flow of sound mass found respectively in Chinese calligraphy and in the Varèsean view of the nature of sound. Like designing the six pairs of hexapitch collections, Chou deals with four parts also in pairs: violin and cello, and clarinet and piano. Thin texture is created through widely spaced alternation between two instruments at a time. Conversely, thick texture is maintained by juxtaposition of all four

Example 5.12. *Windswept Peaks* mm. 1–9

Example 5.13. *Windswept Peaks* mm. 33–45

instruments. The thin texture at the opening is gradually thickened in mm. 5–11 by strettolike close imitation between the violin and cello (example 5.12) From measures 39 to 80, the simultaneous presentation of all six pairs of hexachord collections thickens the texture considerably. Example 5.13 illustrates only the manifestation of collection II, pairs I and II in mm. 33–45. The moderately thin texture returns when the rhapsodic middle section is ushered by the opening material sets in at m. 60 where the alternation of voices occurs between all four instruments. A rhythmic and intervallic counterpoint can be seen in m. 358, where all four parts are in quarter notes and each entrance is proportionally spaced at eighth, dotted eighth, and sixteenth apart. The intervallic counterpoint that occurs between each pair of instruments is seen vertically as major second against minor third (example 5.14).

Example 5.14. *Windswept Peaks* mm. 358

Rhythm

Except for the middle rhapsodic and the rhythmic counterpoint sections near the end, the essential rhythmic conception is based on three kinds of motivic cells in triple meter: (1) dotted half note plus a half and a quarter notes, (2) dotted quarter note plus a quarter and an eighth note, (3) an eighth note plus a quarter and an eighth note as syncopation. Example 5.15 shows these cells (marked as numbers 1–3) and the prevalent triple metric division. In example 5.15, the prominent placement of an eighth rest on an unaccented beat suggests the effect of syncopation, which has been used customarily in almost all of Chou's works. Syncopation, as a means of temporal control, enables the composer to maintain rhythmic flexibility by destroying the regular pulsation on the first beat of each measure. The use of syncopation for generating

Example 5.15. ***Windswept Peaks*** **mm. 1–9**

excitement can be observed at the climatic point: mm. 192–207 (example 5.16). Measure 358 forms a sharp contrast with example 5.16 in that this measure is not only lengthened with a gradual tempo change but also eliminates accent (example 5.17). Conventionally accented 2/4 and 4/4 measures are found in the piano part in mm. 285–287 (example 5.18). These rhythmic and temporal contrasts together with textural and registral changes give one an impression of ebb and flow of a sound body, which ebbs when the use of syncopation is combined with dense texture and flows when the conventional accent pattern returns with a thin texture. The short range, hairpin-shaped dynamic markings create an impression that the piece sounds pointillistic in the style of Webern. Focusing on the growth and decay of small melodic gestures suggests an emphasis on the single tone as living matter in the compositional process.

Formal Structure

The formal structural principle of the piece exhibits some degree of symmetry, that is, the closing section corresponds to the opening of the piece with

Example 5.16. *Windswept Peaks* mm. 200–209

a cadenzalike section in the middle. The structural plan of the piece is illustrated below:

Section 1
Refrain
mm. 1–12: set of four hexachordal pitch invariable collections
Presentation of a set of four tetrachords (compound dyads):
m. 12: tow invariable tetrachords in the pf. and their variable counterparts in the cl. All are compound dyads.
Presentation of all six invariable hexachordal pitch collections:
mm. 13–80: the order of the presentation: (vln. I, v.c. I); (cl. I, pf. I); (vln. II, v.c. II); (cl. II, pf. II); (vln. III, v.c. III); (cl. III, pf. III); (vln. IV, v.c. IV); (cl. IV, pf. IV); (vln., V, v.c. V); (cl. V, pf. V); (vln. VI, v.c. VI); (cl. VI, pf. VI)

Example 5.17. *Windswept Peaks* **mm. 358**

Refrain
mm. 81–96: set of four hexachordal pitch invariable collections, with modifications of the previous collections III and IV in the new collections III and IV

Section 2
Rhapsodic section
mm. 97–326: dyads and compound dyads, and trichords

Example 5.18. *Windswept Peaks* **mm. 285–287**

Section 3
Presentation of part of six invariable hexachordal pitch collections:
mm. 327–357: the order of the presentation: (vln. III, v.c. VI); (cl. V, pf. IV);
(vln. III, v.c. IV); (cl. V, pf. V); (vln. V, v.c. II); (cl. IV, pf. VI)
Presentation of a set of four tetrachords (compound dyads):
mm. 358: dyads of M2 against m3
Refrain
mm. 359–367: set of four hexachordal pitch invariable collections

The rhapsodic middle section is the longest, 230 measures, in comparison with 41 measures of part III and 97 measures of part I. This out-of-proportion design suggests that Chou pays greater attention to the movement and direction of sound mass than to a perfectly balanced structure, or in his words, "as in calligraphy, the goal is to internalize momentous events and emotions into a distilled artistic expression through coordinated flow of the four parts."[15]

In terms of compatible elements between Western and Chinese traditions in this piece, one sees the influence of the conceptual fusion between the Varèsean concept of sound as living matter and moving mass and the Chinese calligraphic ideal of controlled flow of ink. The Schoenbergian pretwelve-tone idea of composing with intervallic cells, which are generated from a single source, and the I-Ching principle of myriad things evolving from the interaction of yin and yang are also synthesized here. Webern's isolation of pitches and exploitation of timbre in each individual tone are interpreted in terms of Chinese qin tradition in that each tone is a living matter with an identity tag, and the execution of a particular timbre on a single tone is an important accomplishment.

The 1980s saw an increased relief of Chou's administrative responsibilities, and in the later part of the decade, Chou was to become productive again. The next work following Windswept Peaks is his Concerto for Violoncello and Orchestra, the work that had been long overdue since the beginning of the 1970s.

Concerto for Violoncello and Orchestra (1990)

In 1970, Chou received a commission from the New York State Art Council to write a cello concerto for a young cellist, Paul Tibias. By this time Chou had just finished Yun and felt that he could apply his newly formulated compositional procedures, based on what he had learned from Varèse and the I-Ching, to a wider range of genres. He was looking forward to composing new works.

However, Chou hesitated before beginning to write this concerto because writing a serious traditional concerto was a challenge that many composers of his generation had not even attempted.[16] But as a string player, Chou had never written a piece for a solo stringed instrument and orchestra. His doubts eventually gave way to the idea that it would provide him an opportunity to explore formal design in which the cello would be treated as a voice (representing man), which interacts with orchestra (representing nature). This idea sprang from his study of Chinese landscape painting in which man's interaction with nature is an indispensable and perennial subject.

It took Chou several summers to work out the pitch organization. However, not until the late 1980s was Chou able to devote more time to it, completing it in 1992, and having it premiered by the cellist Janos Starker and Dennis Russell Davis's American Composers Orchestra on January 10, 1993, in New York.

Alex Ross, a music critic for the New York Times made the following comments about the premiere:

> His three-movement concerto echoes the hieratic, ultra-dissonant gestures of Varèse's revolutionary works, although the intermediary texture is softened by precise, painterly detail. The initial motif on open strings was arresting, but the three movements each lacked a sense of forward motion, and the instrumentation did not flow as richly as the composer might have intended. Toward the end, Mr. Starker's energy and intonation flagged; a tighter performance might prove more revealing.[17]

Ross's criticism of Chou's work seems to be colored by his impression of Roger Reynolds's four-movement orchestral piece Dreaming, a work that fantasizes on Wallace Stevens's poem "The Men That Are Falling" and that challenges listeners' imagination. The other works presented at the concert included Chinary Ung's Inner Voices, the winning composition of the 1989 University of Louisville Grawemeyer Award, and Cindy McTee's Circuits. Overall, the interest in dealing with nature and landscapes and the use of the orchestra to provoke mood in these recent works suggests a new impressionistic tendency.

Chou's Cello Concerto differs from Windswept Peaks in several ways. Unlike Windswept Peaks, which was built mainly on hexachordal pitch-class sets, the harmonic organization in the Cello Concerto is more flexible to include not only hexachordal pitch-class sets but also pitch-variant dyads and trichordal collections that act as distinct motivic material. Certain rhythmic, melodic, and harmonic elements characteristically used in Chou's early works, like *Soliloquy of a Bhiksuni* (1958), are brought back in the Cello Concerto but not found in *Windswept Peaks*. The formal construction of the Cello Concerto is modeled largely after *Soliloquy of a Bhiksuni* in that both deal with the relationship between the solo instruments and the ensemble. Finally, the overall dissonant sounding of the Cello Concerto is less poignant than that of *Windswept Peaks*. The overt use of the dyads of minor third, particularly in the second section of the third movement of the concerto, has resulted from the playing technique of the cello's "broken-thirds."

Despite these differences, the two share some basic concepts such as the application of the Chinese calligraphic ideals in the contrapuntal treatment of the parts, using the dyads of minor third and major second as the germinal material to generate various pitch aggregates, the consideration of symmetry, detailed attention paid to localized events such as the timbral, dynamic, and durational change of a single tone or a chord, and the reuse of the material in subsequent movements or in the same movement.

The synthesis between Chou's symbolic view of the solo cello's interaction with the orchestra as a man with nature and the baroque concerto's emphasis on contrast and alternation between solo and instrumental groups takes place in designing the formal structure of the concerto. The piece prominently features alternations between the soloist and the orchestra.

Formal Structure

The piece is in three movements. In order to maintain coherence, the opening material and other sections of the first movement are reused in the concluding section of the third movement. This is true also in the first movement in which the material in mm. 18–21 are reused in mm. 173–176, and mm. 32–35 are reused to conclude the movement. The formal structure of the piece is outlined as follows:

Movement I
Section A (piece sets 1, 2, and 3 introduced)

Orchestra	mm. 1–4	based on set 1, I and II:
		I: C–E♭, E–G♭, A♭–B
		II: C♯–D F–G A–B♭
Solo cello	mm. 5–9	based mainly on string's open fifth; the second upper neighbor and its fifth doubling in mm. 6–7 anticipates the subsequent four-note motive

Orchestra	mm. 10–16	set 2, I and II in mm. 15–18
Solo cello	m. 17	alternating dyads of M2/m3
Orchestra	mm. 18–21	set 3, I and II in mm. 19–22
Solo cello	m. 22	
Solo cello	m. 23	accompanied by two harps
Solo cello	m. 24	
Orchestra/solo cello	m. 25	
Solo cello	m. 26	
Orchestra/solo cello	m. 27	

Section B (the four-note motive and set 5, I and II for the solo cello)

Orchestra/solo cello	mm. 28–32	m. 28 motive: E♭–D E–F
Orchestra	mm. 33–35	
Orchestra/solo cello	mm. 36–58	mm. 36–44, set 5, I and II: I: C–D E–G G♯–A♯ II: B–C♯ E♭–F F♯–A followed by a series of dyads: M2 and m3
Orchestra	mm. 59–62	
Orchestra/solo cello	mm. 63–132	Orchestra/solo cello share 2 pc sets, each presented in turn by one of the 2 harps; 4-note motive D–C E♭–E in m.120
Orchestra	mm. 133–135	
Solo cello	mm. 136–138	
Orchestra/solo cello	m. 139	
Orchestra	mm. 141–147	
Orchestra/solo cello	mm. 148–172	

Section A (reuse of material previously introduced)

Orchestra	mm. 173–176	reuse of material in mm. 18–21
Orchestra/solo cello	mm. 177–179	
Orchestra	mm. 180–186	
Orchestra/solo cello	mm. 187–194	2 sets of dyads in mm. 36–44 restated in mm. 187–192
Orchestra/solo cello	mm. 195–199	reuse of material in mm. 27–31
Solo cello	mm. 200–201	
Orchestra	mm. 202–205	reuse of material in mm. 32–35 as ending for the movement
Orchestra	m. 206	end

Movement II (with a program title "Musings on the Mountain")
Section A" (alternating piece set 11, I and II)

Orchestra	mm. 1–5	based on pc set 11, I and II:
		I: C–D E–G♭, A–B♭
		II: C♯–D♯ F–G A♭–B
Orchestra/solo cello	mm. 6–8	solo *ad libitum*
Orchestra/solo cello	mm. 9–27	alternating set 11, I and II
Orchestra	mm. 28–32	alternating set 11, I and II

Section B" (mixing of two-piece sets)

| Orchestra/solo cello | mm. 33–73 | mixing set 11, I and II |

Section A" (alternating two-piece sets)

| Orchestra | mm. 74–79 | return of mm. 1–5 with modifications |
| Orchestra/solo cello | mm. 80–93 | alternating set 11, I and II |

Movement III
Section A''' (piece set 12, I and II introduced)

Orchestra	mm. 1–4	set 12, I and II mixed
		I: C–D♭, E♭–F G♯–A
		II: D–E F♯–G A♯–B
Solo cello	mm. 5–8	alternating set 12, I and II, no mixing
Orchestra	mm. 9–12	alternating set 12, I and II
Solo cello	mm. 13–16	alternating set 12, I and II
Orchestra	m. 17	
Solo cello	mm. 18–19	set 12, I and II mixed

Section B''' (new combination of dyads: m3–m3–m3–m2)

Orchestra/Solo cello	mm. 21–31	
Orchestra	mm. 32–38	
Orchestra/solo cello	mm. 39–77	
Solo cello	mm. 78–82	
Orchestra	mm. 83–87	
Orchestra/solo cello	mm. 88–135	reuse of material from the same movement: mm. 89–91 similar to mm. 67–70; mm. 100–101= mm. 51–52; mm. 102–113=

mm. 53–64; mm. 114–124=
mm. 39–49; mm. 125–142=
mm. 21–38

Orchestra   mm. 136–142
Solo cadenza
Orchestra/solo cello   mm. 143–148   optional ending, if no cadenza; with
                                            cadenza, skip mm. 143–148

Section A (reuse of material from the first movement)
Orchestra   mm. 149–152   material from mm. 1–4 of
                                            movement 1
Solo cello   mm. 153–156   mm. 5–8 of movement 1, modified
Orchestra/solo cello   mm. 156–159   mm. 63–66 of movement 1
Orchestra/solo cello   mm. 160–196   mm. 67–68 of movement 1
Orchestra   mm. 197–200   mm. 141–144 of movement 1
Orchestra/solo cello   mm. 202–207   mm. 161–166 of movement 1
Orchestra/solo cello   mm. 208–209   mm. 177–178 of movement 1,
                                            modified
Orchestra/solo cello   mm. 210–213   mm. 187–192 of movement 1,
                                            modified
Orchestra/solo cello   mm. 214–217   mm. 196–199 of movement 1
Solo cello   m. 218   m. 200 of movement 1
Orchestra/solo cello   mm. 219–223   new material; solo last notes on
                                            B♭–A, emphasizing m2

The criteria used here for delineating sections within each movement is based primarily on harmonic and thematic content. Further, the recycling of the previous material in subsequent sections also suggests that these materials are treated iconically for maintaining coherence as in the use of ritornello in baroque concertos, if not in the same way.

Thematic Material

In comparison with *Windswept Peaks*, the thematic material in this concerto appears to be rather diverse. There are three different kinds of material: (1) the pitch-class sets or pitch-invariable collection, which are built on the aggregate of three dyads of either M2–m3–M2 or m3–m3–M2 or other combination (example 5.19), (2) a distinctive four-note theme (example 5.20), which contains an interval of minor second resulting from the minor second, upper-neighbor grace note of a theme, used in *Soliloquy of a Bhiksuni* (1958) and other works of the 1950s (examples 5.21 and 5.22), and (3) a pair of

Example 5.19.   Concerto for Violoncello and Orchestra movement 1, mm. 34–48

Example 5.20.   Concerto for Violoncello and Orchestra movement 1, mm. 34–41

Example 5.21.   Concerto for Violoncello and Orchestra movement 1, mm. 5–8

dyads of minor third or major second in ascending and descending order and its variants (examples 5.23 and 5.24). Examples 5.21 and 5.22 illustrate thematic relationship between *Soliloquy of a Bhiksuni* and the Cello Concerto not only in intervals but also in rhythmic patterns. Examples 5.23 and 5.24 show alternatives of major second for minor third of the theme and its extensions. In general, different orderings and combinations of the major second and minor third dyads constitute the fundamental building material for the entire piece.

Example 5.22. *Soliloquy of a Bhiksuni* mm. 1–11

Example 5.23. Concerto for Violoncello and Orchestra movement 3, mm. 20–22

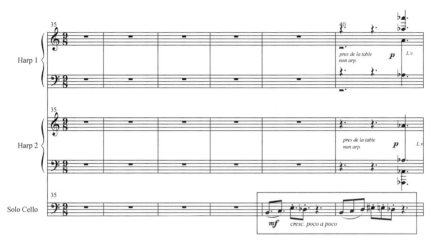

Example 5.24. Concerto for Violoncello and Orchestra movement 3, mm. 35–40

Harmonic Organization

Like *Windswept Peaks*, the harmonic construction of the piece is based on the verticalization of the pitch-class sets. This means that pitch-class sets have functioned both as thematic and harmonic material. The two harps used here are assigned a task to present the sets chordally. Each harp will have to follow its specially assigned set so that the alternation of the sets can be realized by alternating harps. Thus, the identity of a set in the solo part can be verified by harp chords (example 5.25). In example 5.25, the set C♯–E F–G A–B is found both in harp 2 and the solo cello, and the set C–D E♭–G♭, A♭–B♭, and its fragments are found both in harp 1 and the solo cello. The method of generating the second set in this pair of sets involves the inclusion of all twelve chromatic tones, and the two sets are related by sharing half of the chromatic gamut.

Throughout the first movement, ten pairs of sets for two harps and a pair of sets for the solo cello (marked svc) can be identified:

1. mm. 1–4   I. C–E♭ E–G♭ A♭–B   II. C♯–D F–G A–B♭
2. mm. 15–18   I. C–D E–G A♭–B   II. C♯–D♯ F–G A–B♭

Example 5.25. Concerto for Violoncello and Orchestra movement 1, mm. 63–66

3. mm. 19–22	I. C–D♯ E–G A♭–B♭	II. (same as I)
4. mm. 23–24	I. C–E♭–F G♭–A♭ B♭–D♭	II. C–D E–G F♯–A–B
5. mm. 36–44 (svc)	I. C–D E–G G♯–A♯	II. B–C♯ E♭–F F♯–A
6. mm. 63–69	I. C–D E♭–G♭ A♭–B♭	II. C♯–E F–G A–B
7. mm. 71–83	I. E–F♯ G–A♯ B–D	II. C♯–E F–G♯ A–C
8. mm. 84–89	I. C–D♯ E–G A♭–B♭	II. D–F F♯–A B–C♯
9. mm. 153–158	I. C–D E–G♭ A♭–B	II. C♯–D♯ F–G A–B♭
10. mm. 161–166	I. C–D E–F♯ G–B♭	II. D♭–E♭ F–G♯ A–B
11. mm. 167–173	I. E♭–F♯ G♯–A♯ B–D	II. C♯–E F–G A–C

Two pairs of piece sets used in movement 2, especially the second pair, which is also used in movement 3, are listed as follows:

Movement II

11. mm. 1–6	I. C–D E–G♭ A–B♭	II. C♯–D♯ F–G A♭–B
12. mm. 74–79	I. C–D♭ E♭–F G♯–A	II. D–E F♯–G A♯–B

Movement III

12. mm. 1–13	I. C–D♭ E♭–F G♯–A	II. D–E F♯–G A♯–B

This piece, unlike *Windswept Peaks*, which is based primarily on labeled ordering of dyads, consists of a substantial number of dyads that do not follow an ordering formula. The above list only recognizes those sets of dyads that appear more than once in the piece, thus acquiring certain identity.[18]

Generally, the harmonic structure of the piece is more flexible than that of *Windswept Peaks*. Chou is not content with the way of organizing his harmonic materials in *Windswept Peaks*; he is trying to incorporate a particular kind of thematic material such as the minor second, upper–neighbor, grace-note figure in the piece that resulted in the problem of incongruous interval of minor second, which is not compatible with the basic intervals of major second and minor third.

In Chou's works of the 1980s and early 1990s, one sees an effort to rethink and redefine harmony, melody, rhythm, counterpoint, timbre, and texture in broad and abstract terms. It is true that the more abstract a composition is, the easier it is to reinterpret Western concepts in Chinese terms and have fewer traces of Chinese sound. These works are witnesses of a trend in which postwar composers such as Chou with a non-Western background have moved away from asserting their cultural heritages by reminding the audience of these traditions through a particular kind of sound; they have come to realize that rethinking and reusing Western musical terms and concepts and finding cross-cultural conceptual parallels in aesthetic values is perhaps the surest way to avoid superficiality.

String Quartet *Clouds* (1996)

Chou received a commission to compose his first string quartet *Clouds* from Brigham Young University's Barlow Endowment for Music Composition in 1992 and completed the work in 1996. The quartet bears the dedication to Yi-An, both the pen name of Li Qing-Zhao (1084–?), one of the best-known Chinese poets, and the given name of his wife. The premiere took place on Sunday afternoon, December 1, 1996, with the Brentano String Quartet at the Alice Tully Hall of Lincoln Center, New York. In addition to Chou's quartet, the concert also included Schubert's G-minor Quartet and Schumann's Piano Quintet. Chou gave a preconcert lecture about his inspirations for the work. Chou acknowledged that the flow of ink in Chinese brush calligraphy and the continuous flow of sound of a string quartet were the major compatible ingredients for this work. Concerning the subtitle, Chou explains:

> The subtitle, *Clouds*, is neither programmatic nor extramusical. It refers to the quality shared by cloud formation and calligraphy: the continual *process* of

change. The phenomenon of "mingling and melting clouds"—in transformation, aggregation and dispersion—is the aesthetic impetus for the musical events and progressions in the quartet.[19]

As with *Windswept Peaks* and the Cello Concerto, which became more abstract than Chou's earlier works, Chou continues to follow the calling of the *I-Ching* for expanding his variable modes with added pitches to allow the central ideas of growth and the process of change to be articulated. However, he did make use of suggestive sounds of Asian instruments in this quartet, observable in his works of the 1960s. This is due, perhaps, to the opportunity for composing his first string quartet, the most suitable medium for realizing these ideas. To be sure, at a deeper level, Chou was more interested in exploring a process than an end product.

In searching for more germinal ideas, Varèse's influence is recognizable. Once again, Chou made a synthesis of the Varèsian concept of musical fluidity, the tenets of Chinese calligraphy and *qin* music allowing his main thematic material to undergo constant transformation in the given space. The deliberate exploration of timbral effects such as forceful and snapping pizzicato and *saltando* in reference to Chinese instruments, most prominent in the second movement, is also reminiscent of Chou's earlier works such as *Yu ko* (1965) and *Willows Are New* (1957), though according to Chou that was not the case. These effects were the result of stacking up ascending and descending orders of each segment of his variable modes rather than intentional imitation of performance style of the instruments.[20]

The quartet is conceived in Western tradition as a five-movement work with breaks between movements. However, one can interpret this movement plan as sections or *duan* of a *qin* piece that features cyclic poetic program contents, and sometimes thematic transformation, according to the formal tradition of the Chinese *qin*. The most expansive and elaborate is the first movement, which can stand alone as a separate quartet. After some digression in the three middle movements, the primary material (measures 41–113) is repeated in the last movement between measures 1 and 73 only with minute registral modifications in the fourth measure and the first three notes of measure 5. Chou did this to establish a sense of finality after an elaborate course of growth and continual change, and he found the solution again in the *I-Ching* in which ideas of changing and unchanging are seen as two opposing yet complementary forces in the universe.

The middle three movements, however, exhibit some of the most daring timbral effects and individualistic characters, such as the use of guitar picks for pizzicato in movement 2, exaggerated portamento, an ethereal sound and the use of variable and indefinite meter in movement 3, and the shortest and animated movement 4, which shows a clever use of additive rhythm. The Chinese calligraphic concept that Chou has spoken about is most discernible in movement 5 in which the four voices are divided in two pairs, first violin and viola as a pair and second violin and cello as another, move nearly in parallel motion, though not throughout the movement. Each pair of instruments resembles the two outer edges of the Chinese ink brush pen (example 5.26).

The tonal organization is primarily trichordal or, in other words, a collection of three pitches in a cell, which can be used both harmonically and melodically. The intervallic patterns in these cells are variable, sometimes in the forms of a minor second and a major second, and other times, a minor second and a minor third or major sixth. Such a structural construct has spawned timbral and contrapuntal materials of the piece (example 5.27). According to Chou, the nuclear theme or variable modes are derived from the *ba gua* of the permutations of *I-Ching*.[21] The basic idea for this piece, however, is the process in which the interval of minor second is variably combined with another interval in a continuous transformation almost like the exchangeability of the *yin* and *yang* and, perhaps, as the title suggests, the clouds. There is also a fair amount of intuitiveness at work in this piece showing Chou's discerning ears and refined taste. Overall, this piece sounds triadic

Example 5.26.   String Quartet *Clouds* movement 5, mm. 5–16

Example 5.27.   String Quartet *Clouds* movement 1, mm. 1–12

with a tinge of chromaticism and shows a high degree of sophistication and procedural facility, and it is consistent with Chou's stylistic development of the 1990s.

Notes

1. Wen-Chung Chou, correspondence with Peter Chang, May 11, 2004, 1.

2. In a general sense, this is also true in the fundamental unit of musical meters in the West.

3. Chou brought these Chinese children over personally under the auspices of the U.S.-China Arts Exchange and its Chinese partner for the project.

4. Chou was inspired to compose this piece by two very old Chinese gongs with a deep rim and sonorous tone that he obtained at the time.

5. This parallels the spoken drum syllables (*bol*) in northern and (*Solkattu*) in southern Indian music.

6. Zhongguo Yinyue Cidian Editorial Committee, *Zhongguo Yinyue Cidian* [Dictionary of Chinese Music] (Beijing: People's Music Publisher, 1984), 250–52.

7. Editorial Committee, *Zhongguo Yinyue Cidian*, 364.

8. See David Tsang's program note for *Echoes from the Gorge*, April 27, 1989, Lila Acheson Wallace Auditorium, New York. Tsang states that eight kinds of *qin* timbre

have been parodied in the twelve movements of the work. Also see Robert Kyr, "Between the Mind and the Ear: Finding Perfect Balance: An Interview with Chou Wen-Chung" in *League-ISCM* (Boston: League of Composers-International Society for Contemporary Music, 1990), 23.

9. In Chinese tradition, such an unexplainable situation is called *zhike yihui, buke yanchuan* or only to be understood by reticent agreement without verbal communication.

10. *Zhike yihui, buke yanchuan.*

11. Wen-Chung Chou, "*Ionization*: The Function of Timbre in Its Formal and Temporal Organization," in *The New Worlds of Edgard Varèse: A Symposium*, ed. Sherman Van Solkema (New York: ISAM Department of Music, Brooklyn College, CUNY, 1979), 29, 32–33, 43–45, 73–74.

12. The members of Aeolian Chamber Players include Lewis Kaplan, violin; Andre Emelianoff, cello; Charles Neidich, clarinet; and Peter Basquin, piano. The group was founded by Lewis Kaplan in 1964; it has commissioned and premiered at least 100 compositions since then.

13. See "Bowdoin Summer Music Festival Concert Features a World Premiere," *Coastal Journal* 24/28, Zone University (July 11, 1990); and "Piece to Premiere at Festival Concert," *The Times Record*, Brunswick, Maine, Thursday, July 12, 1990, p. 13. Other works presented at this concert include Brahms' Quintet for Clarinet and Strings, Poncielli's "Il Convigno," and Bohuslav Martinu's Sonata No. 8 for Cello and Piano.

14. Wen-Chung Chou, "Program Notes on *Windswept Peaks*," page 2 of the score that was published by C. F. Peters, 1991 (P67359).

15. Chou, "Program Notes on *Windswept Peaks*."

16. There have been precedents of the revival of concerto grosso in the twentieth century especially in the works of Ernest Bloch (two concerti grossi), Paul Hindemith (Concerto for Orchestra, op. 38), Samuel Barber (Capricorn Concerto), and Stravinsky (*Dumbarton Oaks*).

17. Alex Ross, "Composers Orchestra Paints Sonic Landscapes," *New York Times*, January 13, 1993.

18. According to Chou, this was the result of "filling out the pitch space," Chou, correspondence, 2. The question of maintaining the identity of these modes in a nonfragmentary manner, as in *Pien* and *Yun*, for the general listeners remains nonetheless.

19. Wen-Chung Chou, notes to String Quartet *Clouds* (New York: C. F. Peters, 1997).

20. Chou, notes to String Quartet *Clouds*.

21. Chou, notes to String Quartet *Clouds*.

CHAPTER SIX

~

The Reception of Chou's Works

Chou's composition approach has been positively recognized in the United States, Europe, Japan, China, Taiwan, and Hong Kong; however, certain pieces are received more enthusiastically than others. In keeping with Chinese tradition, pieces that evoke specified poetic images such as *Landscapes* (1949), *Willows Are New* (1957), and *Yu ko* (1963) are more in demand among both Chinese and Western audiences. The performance of Chou's first mature work, *And the Fallen Petals* (1954), which had been performed extensively in the West, and to a certain extent in China, induced only mild response in China. Other than the association with poetry and a fragmented Chinese melody, the Chinese imagery in this work is rather difficult for the Chinese to conceive. On the other hand, Western audiences paid more attention to texture, sonority, structure, the Oriental flavor, and innovative ideas. This is seen from the concert reviews of Chou's works both in Chinese and Western press.

In concert and record reviews of Chou's works, it is evident that most Western audiences thought that the attractiveness of Chou's works was partly due to the composer's ability to evoke oriental mysticism and mood by employing traditional Chinese aesthetic principles, such as the emphasis on timbre from the *qin* music, the emphasis on control of the flow of ink from calligraphy, and the emphasis on characterization by simplest means from painting, and a Western fascination with oriental painting, poetry, and Debussyan orientalism. Most Western listeners naturally make these associations. For example, many Western critics have pointed out that there are

"Webernian pointillistic" and "oriental impressionistic" traits in Chou's works. On the other hand, the Chinese listeners are more concerned with degrees in which Chou's works resemble the sound tradition of Chinese instruments, particularly the *qin*, and the degree in which a traditional Chinese melody is recognizable. Even though some Chinese reviewers have tried to describe certain techniques in specific terms such as structure melody range, timbre, tempo, and dissonance, they do not associate Chou's works with Western idealized notions of oriental mysticism and contemporary music styles and techniques such as Debussy's impressionism, Webern's pointillistic *klangfarbenmelodie*, or Varèse's percussive sound and concept of sound as a moving mass. The cause of this critical difference in perception is the long period of isolation of China from the West, and the Chinese composers', musicians', listeners', and music critics' lack of awareness of how much Western contemporary music developed since the end of World War II. However, Chinese listeners do value innovations based on familiar material or recreation based on traditional material. Chinese intellectuals are also fascinated with Western ideas. Chou understood these values and knew how to represent them in his synthesis. Thus, his music can be attractive to Western listeners for its mystic quality and can also be attractive to Chinese listeners for bringing new ideas to revive indigenous traditions.

During the 1920s and 1930s, many Western-trained Chinese composers tried to create a synthetic style by combining Western harmony and Chinese melody; even though most were recognized in China, they were largely ignored in the West. This failure to gain recognition in the West was perhaps due to their failure to discover fundamental principles that connect musical, visual, and literary arts. Merely following the nineteenth-century, Western art songs, especially those of Mahler's *Das Lied von der Erde*, had narrowed these composers' avenues to explore the variety of Chinese indigenous instrumental and theatrical musical forms. These Chinese composers' interrupted involvement in Western musical activities also contributed to their anonymity in the West. Except for improvements in better setting of the Chinese words to music and better fitting of Western harmony to Chinese melody, fundamental Chinese aesthetic issues have never been brought out in their works, and except for employing Western harmony of the common practice period in their compositions, exploration of contemporary Western concepts of sound, structure, and motion were left unattended.

Chou's success rests primarily on his understanding of the values of both Chinese and Western cultures and his ability to select compatible ingredients for synthesis. In other words, he has the idea and knows exactly how to communicate his ideas. Chou is musically and culturally bilingual, which affords him much larger musical and cultural resources to work with. In making cross-cultural musical synthesis, the ability to communicate with both Western and Chinese audiences and the literacy in two cultures are indispensable.

The Stokowski-Varèse Circle and the Promotion of Chou's Early Works

When Chou first made his debut in the West in 1953 and was recognized as a promising composer, he was still a graduate student at Columbia University. The American premiere of his first work *Landscapes* (1949) took place in that year. It was Colin McPhee's idea for Chou to contact Stokowski and to submit the work to him. Stokowski later responded by sending a telegram to Chou indicating that he would like to perform the work in San Francisco with the San Francisco Symphony on November 19, 1953.[1] The premiere took place as planned, and the program was repeated on November 21 in the opera house. In addition to Chou's *Landscapes*, the concert also featured Walter Piston's *Toccata*, which was the first piece on the program, and Morton Gould's *Dance Variations*. The second half of the concert was concluded by Dvořák's *New World* Symphony. Compared to Piston and Gould, Chou was less experienced. However, his imagination and simplistic style won the San Francisco audience as indicated in Alfred Frankenstein's concert review, which also revealed the sophistication of the San Francisco audience.[2]

Chou's choice of Stokowski was natural because Stokowski was a friend of Varèse and was involved with the International Composers' Guild in the 1920s and, later, the contemporary Music Society and Ford Foundation in New York. Another justification was that Stokowski was a champion for promoting contemporary music. For example, in order to perform Varèse's *Ameriques*, Stokowski fought with his orchestra committee for over three years before obtaining approval.[3] Stokowski's interest in exotics was also shown in promoting McPhee's *Tabuh-Tahuhan* by performing it in 1953, and in the performance of Jacab Avshalomov's *The Talking of Tung Kuan* in 1952.[4] Stokowski was geared very much to stretching contemporary audience's listening repertoire by changing it from "sticking to the familiar only."[5]

In the 1920s Stokowski and Varèse became friends. Stokowski admired Varèse; he performed several of Varèse's works and tried to help Varèse financially by letting Varèse take over his conducting class at the Curtise Institute, and even gave Varèse a gift of $2,000 before Varèse left New York for Paris on October 4, 1928.[6] Stokowski was associated with and helped Varèse's International Composers' Guild by conducting for concerts that boosted new concert subscriptions.[7] The two remained lifelong friends.

Slonimsky's friendship with Varèse was also long standing, going back to 1927, when Slonimsky founded the Chamber Orchestra of Boston, which promoted ultramodern music, the music by Varèse, Ives, Cowell, and others. In 1931, Slonimsky embarked on a European tour to conduct and present avant-garde works such as Varèse's *Intègrales*, Ives's *Three Places in New England*, Chavez's *Energia*, Carl Ruggles's *Men and Mountain*, Roldàn's *Ballet Suite*, and Caturla's *Bembé*.[8] Charles Ives volunteered to finance the tour and contributed $1,500 through the Paris branch of Chase Manhattan Bank. Varèse was then in Paris and helped Slonimsky hire the prestigious Orchstre Straram, arranged interviews and publicity, and introduced him to influential Parisians.[9] After his return from Europe on March 6, 1933, Slonimsky conducted the world premiere of Varèse's *Ionization* (1930–1931) in New York.[10] Also in 1933, as the executive officer of the International Composers' Guild, Varèse appointed both Slonimsky and Stokowski as his conductors.[11]

With his music historian's insight, Slonimsky saw the potential of Western interest in Chinese literary and visual arts that had intrigued the imaginations of Mahler and attracted several fin-de-siècle Viennese visual artists. He also saw the opportunity for Chou to further cultivate such an interest in the West and to succeed. He actively promoted Chou through publications and personal connections with Varèse and Stokowski.

Background of Western Interest in Chinese Arts

The fascination on the part of Western literary figures with oriental philosophy, and literary and visual arts was evident in several translations of Chinese poems during the mid-nineteenth century and fashionable brocade patterns of Gustav Klimt's paintings and Adolf Loos's Bauhaus-style architectural designs.[12] Glenn Watkins pointed out that in 1830, Goethe, in his writing *Chinesische Jahres—und Tagezeiten*, expounded the concept of *Weltliterature*, which extends the ideal of man's fraternity by promoting respect for world literature through translation and criticism of literary works of other cultures. The work also reveals Goethe's interest in the cult of Nature and in man's mysterious relationship with nature as seen in his *Die Metamorphose der Pflanzen* (1790). The work was above all an important attempt to increase the sensibilities of the artists both in the East and West.[13] In his analysis in Western fascination with orientalism, Watkins further points out that the reason for the specific appeal of the Chinese elements in the West was due to the late nineteenth-century artistic movements, such as *nouveau* in France and especially *Jugendstil* in Vienna, which rebelled "against conservative and academic taste of the city."[14] It was also the prevalent sentiment at the closing of the nineteenth century that man had become more interested in his relationship with mysterious nature than with reality. Watkins observes that "the lyrics of the Chinese and Japanese, as well as the patterns of their prints, enjoyed an overwhelming vogue in fin-de-siècle Vienna and served the new cult of Nature admirably."[15]

The U.S. Listening Public

Chou came to the contemporary musical scene at a favorable time. Because of World War II, which thwarted the musical development in Europe for six years, America was finally able to catch up with European music development during the early 1950s. The 1950s was a period in which a great diversity of composition styles, besides Schoenberg and Stravinsky, began to surface. After several years of silence, Varèse became active again, completing three of his electronically manipulated works, *Deserts* (1950–1954), *Procession de Vergès* (1955), and *Poèm Électronique* (1958). There was more innovative music available for the curious audience than ever before. Coupled with its postwar economic power, America had attracted many European composers and thus actually superseded Europe's role in nurturing modern artistic development. Except for Darmstadt, there was very little going on in Europe at the time.

Also during this period, the interest in Eastern philosophy and music was represented by Cowell, Cage, McPhee, Harrison, and others. Slonimsky was insightful in recognizing the potential of Chou's cultural heritage and the need for this kind of music in the West; he knew that the legacy of Mahler's orientalism in composition had no heir in America, yet he saw that audiences' interests were there. Therefore, he believed the continuation of the Mahler tradition in America would be the ideal way for Chou to succeed as a late-start composer.

As Chou gradually moved away from direct or indirect use of Chinese musical materials in his later works, his own program notes or preconcert lectures for each of his new works became outlets for educating his audience to get "the point."[16]

Background of the Chinese Audience

Before Chou brought his own and other contemporary Western composers' works to China, there had been political ripples caused by a series of concerts by visiting Western orchestras, such as the London Philharmonic, the Philadelphia Orchestra, the Vienna Philharmonic, and later, the Boston

Symphony and the Berlin Philharmonic in the 1970s. Madam Mao was reluctant to allow these foreign orchestras to perform in Beijing in the midst of her music and art reforms.

The Beijing audience's passion for the music of Johann Strauss, Brahms, Beethoven, and Berlioz was unbridled, for the concert hall was packed and many had to slip into the hall through transoms. As a part of the political campaign against the moderate faction in the Communist Party, Madam Mao launched an attack on advocates of performing the music of Mozart and Beethoven immediately after Beijing audiences voiced their need for more performances of Western classical music. The campaign was called "the criticism of nonprogram music," as if it was aimed at the music itself.

To the public, performing Western classical music was strictly forbidden. Yet, it was acceptable for diplomatic occasions at special venues. The Chinese intellectual's predilection for eighteenth- and nineteenth-century Western music was largely suppressed before the downfall of Madam Mao and her retinues in 1976. It was under such circumstances that Chou returned to China after thirty years of absence from his native land. Five years after the announcement of the Sino-U.S. Communiqué in 1972, Chou organized the visit of a delegate from the Committee for U.S.-China Relations,[17] consisting of directors from important American foundations, to China in fall 1977 and initiated the music and arts exchange between the two countries through sponsorship of these people and their organizations.[18]

Chou's music was first heard in China in November 1977 as he gave the Central Conservatory of Music recordings of his music. Chen Gang, a composer, reported in his 1979 article "Zao Chuen Er Yue Liu Se Xin" [New Willows of Early Spring] that the introduction and performance of two of Chou's works "*Yu ko* (1965) and *Willows Are New* (1957) have made a deep impression on the audience."[19] As modern Chinese compositions, Chou's masterpieces such as *And the Fallen Petals* (1954) have been included in the Central Philharmonic Orchestra's repertoire.[20]

In a review by Ma Dong Feng and Sun Hai Ming, Chou's *Landscapes* was described as having "folk flavor and capable of evoking traditional Chinese way of life and overseas Chinese's nostalgic thoughts."[21] Ma and Sun went on to comment on various characteristics of the piece: well-thought-out structure, quick registral range and shift, disjunctive and fluid melody, varied tempo, and poetic expression. The general impression is that these music critics perceived the work as a piece of delicate art craft, which is built on impressionist orchestration and harmony, and pentatonic modes (either complete or incomplete) rather than as an artistic experience. In the eyes of Ma and Sun, the piece expresses Chou's nostalgic feelings and his hopes for

China's future.[22] This article praises Chou's approach to composition as successful by fusing Chinese poetry, painting, and calligraphy together with Western techniques. Ye Jin and Yiao Pin Fang in their article "Xuan Ge Sheng Sheng Zu Jiao Liu" briefly note of *Landscapes* that "looking at the title, one will know that the work is poetic and imbued with the spirit of traditional Chinese culture."[23]

Due to their lack of understanding of contemporary music, most Taiwanese writers relied on U.S. reviews, comments, and Chou's own explanations of his own works. Some became interested in finding out how Chou's works were received in mainland China. For example, the long article by Zhou Fan Fu about Chou largely relied on Chou's comments and recollections of the receptions of his works on the mainland. Chou told him that both traditional and Western-trained musicians on the mainland had shown interest in *Yu ko* and *Willows Are New* and that *Yu ko* had even been performed by Shanghai Ballet Company's orchestra. Chou also told him about a serious discussion over his approach as a model for contemporary Chinese music at a national musical convention, and about Fu Cong, highly acclaimed pianist, who seemed to have performed *Willows Are New* at the Central Conservatory in Beijing.[24]

Reporting on Chou's second visit to Taiwan in March 1988, Lin Shu Mei tells that the result of the visit was a preparatory step for initiating a dialogue between the mainland Chinese and Taiwanese composers. The visit was sponsored by the Music Department of the National College of Arts for a concert of contemporary Chinese composers' works. Chou's *Yu ko* was performed at the concert. In her article, Lin calls for an in-depth study of Chinese culture and the need for "thoughtful artists."[25]

Reception of Chou's Works in Taiwan

Not surprisingly, Chou's works were introduced to Taiwan relatively earlier than to the mainland. In 1958, an American conductor, Thor Johnson, was sent by the U.S. government to help Taiwan with training their orchestras. Johnson brought recordings containing Chou's works with him to Taiwan.[26] But as Chou had not firmly established himself during the 1950s, his works were circulated only in small circles. Ku Hisen Liang was another person who promoted Chou among the Taiwanese intellectual circles. Ku was a scholar with profound knowledge of Chinese history and culture. He returned from the United States to Taiwan in the late 1950s and was very supportive of Chou for his in-depth study of the Chinese culture and music. In 1960, Deng Chang Guo, prominent Taiwanese music educator, conductor, and administrator, was conducting a survey on the educational system in the United States. He met Chou and again brought recordings of Chou's works to Taiwan.

Because of Deng's influence, Taiwanese radios began to broadcast Chou's three works, *Landscapes* (1949), *All in the Spring Wind* (1952–1953), and *And the Fallen Petals* (1954). By 1968, five articles introducing Chou and his music had appeared.[27]

With all this as a prelude, Chou made his first visit to Taiwan in December 1981.[28] After this trip, his life story as a successful Chinese composer in America and his works began to attract wide public attention. Lin Qing Xuan in *Shi Bao Xin Zhi* [*News Gazette*] (1982), reports that Chou's *Landscapes* (1949), *Cursive* (1964), and *Yu ko* (1965) had even been used in "Meng Die," a dance scenario, and by TV and radio stations as background music.[29]

Zhao Qin, in her article "Chou Wen-Chung: A Composer in Traditional Chinese Style" (1981) comments on the large structure, colorful orchestration, and strong dynamic contrasts in *All in the Spring Wind* (1952–1953) and the variety of changing rhythm and modulation in *Soliloquy of a Bhiksuni* (1958).[30] Zhao believes that it was because of the increase of Western fascination with oriental philosophy, music and arts, and Chou's in-depth study of Chinese traditional arts and mastery of contemporary composition skills that Chou was able to synthesize two traditions successfully.[31] Zhao's analysis of Chou's works focuses on discovering sections in a piece and instruments used in each section. Wu Mu, on the other hand, is more candid about the difficulty of comprehending Chou's more abstract works, especially those of the 1960s. In his concert review of Chou's and another four Taiwan composers' works, Wu writes, "Chou's early works were mainly in Chinese style. His later works were more avant-garde–like and lost ethnic flavor. This was due to Varèse's influence. Whether this is good or bad only time will tell."[32]

The new millennium ushered in a new Taiwanese interest in Chou's works and his compositional approach. In mid-November 2003, Chou was invited to Taipei to participate in a weeklong "Chou Wen-Chung Music Festival" organized by Shyhji Pan, the artistic director of the Canada-Taiwan Music and Arts Exchange.[33] Among more than two thousand participants were sixteen young Taiwanese composers, twenty-three professional musicians, and about one hundred leading professionals and scholars.[34] Chou presented master classes and gave lectures about his works and about his views on further development of Asian compositions. His ideas will continue to reverberate on the islands' cultural and musical affairs.

Reception of Chou's Works in Hong Kong

Since World Music Day '88, which was a joint meeting of the International Society for Contemporary Music and the Asian Composers League in Hong Kong in October 1988, Chou began to attract more attention in Hong Kong. Liang Bao Er published his interview with Chou in three episodes in the *Hong Kong Economic Journal* on January 11, 12, and 16 of 1988. Liang first heard Chou's *Yu ko, And the Fallen Petals,* and *Cursive* in the early 1970s, yet he describes Chou as "famous but not well known" for his actual contribution to promoting cultural exchange between East and West,[35] suggesting that, as in mainland China and Taiwan, the performances of Chou's works in Hong Kong were also limited.

In discussing Chou's use of principles of Chinese visual arts in his compositions, Liang observes that Chou's *Yu ko* is most successful in fusing the spirit of traditional Chinese music and Western techniques. While comparing *Yu ko* with *Cursive,* Liang admits that although he likes Chou's idea of "musical calligraphy," which is the basic idea for *Cursive, Yu ko* is much easier for him to understand. Liang believes that perhaps he has not listened to *Cursive* enough to catch intricate details in the piece.[36] Another Hong Kong music critic, Bi Xi Zhou, who interviewed Chou in 1981, praises Chou as "a pioneer for the future development of Chinese music, and as a result of his influence and the consequence of this influence in helping mainland and Taiwanese composers gain international recognition, it is enough for him to be written in the history of Chinese music.[37]

The mainland *People's Daily* published an article by Wu Qi Ji, a journalist of the Hong Kong magazine *The Chinese,* which notes that "in Chou's works *Landscapes, Pien, Yu ko, Willows Are New,* and *Yun* one can sense the beauty of the oriental art in that Chinese poetry, calligraphy, and philosophy are the kernels of this art as well as of Chou's music."[38]

Reception of Chou's Works in Chinese Communities in the United States

Chou's commitment to administrative duties, which drained much of his creative energy and caused his silence for two decades, largely account for his being "overlooked" in Chinese communities in the United States. However, since the 1980s, the enthusiasm for his music in these communities has grown, especially after he became involved in initiating the culture and art exchange programs between the United States and China. Two major

Chinese newspapers, *Zhong Bao* and *Hua Qiao Ri Bao* in the United States, provided extensive coverage of Chou's lectures and introductory articles about Chou's life and works.[39] Commenting on Chou's specific works, An Chen's long article, "Between East and West," which was published in three separate issues of the newspaper, states that, "*Landscapes* was based on traditional Chinese melody and French impressionist orchestration."[40] An Chen describes Chou as a "musical calligrapher" (a term invented by Stuckensmidt in the 1960s after hearing the performance of Chou's *Landscapes* in Berlin). An Chen also describes Chou's musical evolution as following a course in which Chou first worked with popular Chinese melodies and later pursued *yun wei* or inner spirit and taste, and that Chou was able to linguistically convert Chinese terms into Western terms requires an understanding of both contexts.[41] Here An Chen is talking about classical Chinese musical taste, which values timbral and dynamic nuances that can only be understood directly from the intellect but not expressed in words. This taste values suspended pleasure, which is stronger than instant gratification of the Western ideal. In his October 29, 1987, article, An Chen made a comparison between Western and Chinese reactions to *Willows Are New* and *Yu ko*. He observes that "Westerners perceived Debussy's oriental sound and Cowell's dissonance in *Willows Are New* while the Chinese could hear the sound of the *qin* in the same work."[42]

Reception of *Landscapes* in the United States

The melancholy mood of three Chinese poems featured in *Landscapes* echoed those depicted in Mahler's *Das Lied von der Erde* for audiences; Chou was the first oriental composer to rekindle interest in oriental literary and visual arts in the West since the end of the nineteenth century and the first decade of the twentieth century and to arouse sympathy in the audience for such an art.

It seems that the reaction of audiences, though basically positive, lacked enthusiasm. Frankenstein wrote, "Thirty years ago (1923) Stokowski set the world on fire with the iconoclastic scores of Edgard Varèse; the work by Varèse's pupil, Chou Wen-Chung, which he played on Thursday night will never set anything on fire."[43] Unlike other Western critics, who lacked confidence in judging Chinese tradition in Chou's works and rely on Chou's explanations, Frankenstein's comments were indeed intuitive.

As America was at the forefront of music innovation, it is not surprising that Frankenstein's article is entitled "Symphonic Novelties Not so Daring." It seems that Frankenstein's own taste kept abreast with contemporary works.

Unlike the San Francisco performance, *Landscapes* was perceived in Chicago as an ingenuous impressionistic work in contrast to Mahler's effusive pessimism in his *Das Lied Von der Erde* and Bloch's funeral procession *Cortege Funebre*. In his view of the recording of this piece, Lester Trimble remarks that it was "pointillistic and as delicately colored as the Chinese poems."[44]

In his review of the November 19, 1953, concert, Alfred Frankenstein recognized that the piece was "pleasant, ingenious and worth the effort involved in its performance. . . . *Landscapes* [bridges] the gap between oriental and occidental with exceptional success, although the score is very slight in its pretensions and stands on the periphery of contemporary music rather than near its center."[45]

In the *Chicago Daily Tribune* Claudia Cassidy's review of the same work, which was performed on November 5, 1959, by the Chicago Symphony Orchestra under Fritz Reiner, was also an intuitive general description. However, Cassidy did point out that the work was impressionistic and the "poems were used more as orientation than as point of departure."[46] The concert opened with Chou's piece followed by Bloch's *Cortege Funebre* from three Jewish poems and Mahler's *Das Lied Von Der Erde*. At the time of this performance, Chou had already established himself with a handful of compositions, *And the Fallen Petals* (1954), *All in the Spring Wind* (1952–1953), *Soliloquy of a Bhiksuni* (1958), *Seven Poems from the T'ang Dynasty* (1951–1952), and *Suite for Harp and Wind Quintet* (1951), that had been performed, and *And the Fallen Petals* had won international acclaim. In the meantime, Chou was composer-in-residence at the University of Illinois Champaign, Urbana. The inclusion of Chou's *Landscapes* in this concert program affected the mood of the audience because Mahler's and Chou's works shared literary inspiration: melancholy, tranquil mood and pentatonicism. However, Chou's orchestration was less massive, especially the strings. Mahler's obsessive passion in portraying Chinese poetic images was much stronger than Chou's.

Performances of *And the Fallen Petals* in the United States, Europe, and Japan

Among Chou's frequently performed works, *And Fallen Petals* (1954) firmly established his reputation as a successful composer not only in creating the Chinese-Western musical fusion but also in the caliber of his compositions and his technical facilities. The work was commissioned by the Louisville Orchestra and premiered on February 9, 1955, in Louisville, Kentucky, with the Louisville Orchestra conducted by Robert Whitney.[47] Since its world premiere, the work has been performed at least two dozen times in the United States, Europe, and Asia (see a performance chronology of the work in appendix C).

Western Reviews of *And the Fallen Petals*

Most reviewers appear to be impressed with Chou's mastery of orchestration and his ability to shake off stereotypically simple, pentatonic-mode "oriental sound" by concentrating on timbral, directional, and dynamic aspects of the music rather than on melody and harmony. The constant shifting of layers of sound and decorative harmony led some critics to draw references from Debussy and Varèse.

The first two reviews by William Mootz and Harold Schoenberg appeared in Louisville's *Courier Journal* on October 8, 1955, and the *New York Times* on October 10, 1955, respectively. These reports concerned two concerts held in Louisville on October 7, 1955, as part of a musical critics' workshop, when seven commissioned works were presented by the Louisville Orchestra. In his report, Harold Schoenberg writes:

> The most unconventional work on the two programs, and perhaps the most interesting, was Chou Wen-Chung's *And the Fallen Petals*. It was a short, pointillistic study in timbres that had oriental touches but avoided the usual pentatonic "chu-chin-chow" type of phony orientals. Mr. Chou's work is a sensitive piece of scoring, and one that will be interesting to hear again.[48]

Mootz's reaction was also positive. He conveys his impression:

> But for me, the most remarkable piece on the program is Mr. Chou's *And The Fallen Petals*. I was completely won by it last February, and last night's performance only strengthened my impression that it is a daringly conceived and brilliantly executed piece.[49]

In his review of the 1959 San Francisco performance of the work, Alfred Frankenstein describes the piece this way:

> *And the Fallen Petals* begins like a typical Chinese-charm piece with simple, wistful tunes palely orchestrated. In a moment, however, the hearer is involved in some of the most flavorsome, intricate, and compelling dissonances in the literature, and some of the most brilliant virtuoso writing for the instruments. Harmonically, the piece reminds one somewhat of the style of Chou's teacher, Edgard Varèse, but is massive, epical, and violent, and Chou is everything but

that. He calls his unusual technique "melodic brushwork," and it certainly does suggest the flecks, twists, darts, and slashes of a Chinese brush man's painting. *And the Fallen Petals* is an altogether fascinating piece, and one of more than individual significance since it suggests that in music, as in the arts of the brush, East and West are making a new and important synthesis.[50]

Frankenstein also points out the significance of Chou's approach in making East-West musical synthesis by noting that "Chou is the first Chinese composer in history to make his mark in Western music."[51] This is true because although there have been several talented Western-trained Chinese composers such as Huang Zi (who studied at Oberlin), Chao Yuan-Ren (who studied at Cornell and Harvard), Tan Xiao-Lin (who studied at Yale with Hindemith), and Xian Xing-Hai (studied at the Paris Conservatory), all of whom were influential among the younger generation of Chinese composers seeking an East-West musical synthesis, no one has been so widely recognized by Western contemporary composers, musicians, critics, and audiences, as Chou.

Accompanied by program notes and short poems, the work is supposed to evoke exotic and poetic images by contrasting elements: melody versus melodic fragments, sustained tone color versus shifting tone color, traditional Chinese poetic ideas and pentatonism versus modern Western dissonance in the works of Varèse, Mahler, Debussy, Messiaen, and Webern. Although most of these critics are not versed in Chinese music, their reviews reflect their criteria for successful musical synthesis and demonstrate a guided Westerner's listening experience.

German writers seem to be more fascinated with exoticism than their American counterparts. Most of these reviews associate Chou with Debussy, Mahler, and Messiaen. About ten German reviews of the June 1, 1960, Berlin performance of the work by the Berlin Philharmonic conducted by John Bitter convey such an impression. An article in the *Berliner Morganpost* of June 3, 1960, describes the work as a short "mood poem" and "in the charm of its instrumentation, it recalls Debussy as well as Mahler's 'Das Lied von der Erde.'"[52] On the other hand, the reviewer for *Der Kurier* of June 2, 1960, calls the work "impressionistic," while cautioning the reader "this label must not evoke an association with Debussy—rather more of Massiaen."[53] The music critic for *Der Tag* (June 3, 1960) describes the work again as an "exotic 'mood poem'" and that the work "indulges in a sublime sonority by translating into various flecks and darts of sound of what might be interpreted by the nervous ear of the city dweller as the voices of the Far Eastern night."[54]

The reviewer for *Der Tagesspiegel* (June 3, 1960) perceives the work as "an impressionistically-colored orchestral prelude which evokes the impression of wind, rain, and falling blossom petals."[55] In a review in *Telegraf* (June 5, 1960), the work is viewed as "in an impressionistic style of tone painting."[56] Christian Weickert, the music critic for *Freie Presse* of Bielefeld, Germany, clearly recognized the motif of fourth and the nocturnal mood of the work.[57]

The review in *Der Abend* describes the work as "conveying the atmosphere of his homeland. Delicate as a Chinese watercolor painting, and surrounded by the lovely scent of Far Eastern poetry, his musical brushwork opens a view into a world of exotic images."[58] The first European performance of the work took place on March 25, 1958, in Hamburg by Northern German Radio Orchestra conducted by Francis Travis. The Hamburg newspaper *Die Welt* wrote, "the unraveling of the petatonic substance is charming through its use of modern analytical composition techniques."[59] However, the music critic for another Hamburg paper, the *Hamburger Echo*, published a review that links Varèse's music to that of the futurist and claims that for Chou, "the thirty years reign of futuristic methods were very virulent."[60]

On January 5, 1961, the New York audience first heard the work in Carnage Hall with the New York Philharmonic Orchestra conducted by Stanislaw Skrowaczewski; the work received favorable reviews, one by Harold Schoenberg appeared in the January 7, 1961, *New York Times* and another by Miles Kastendieck in the January 7, 1961, *New York Journal-American*. Both reviewers feel that the work is dissonant and that it transcends cultural boundaries and time constraints (style periods). Trying not to be influenced by the composer's explanation of the work, Schoenberg points out that "Chou's view points seem to be more cosmopolitan than nationalistic." Kastendieck perceives the work as "a piece of oriental impressionism as modern as it is traditional (oriental mood and atmosphere)."[61] Another review of the New York performance in *Time* magazine (January 13, 1961) reflects the fact that listeners tend to focus their attention largely on the contrasting sections in the work: the Chinese melody of the first and last sections and the percussive effects in the middle section.[62]

Comparing Western and Chinese Reviews of
And the Fallen Petals

In contrast to Western reviews of the work, the mainland Chinese reviews tended to be more descriptive than analytical, and the audience reactions to the work were not as strong as those to Chou's other pieces, *Willows Are New* and *Yu ko*, which, though dissonant, are less abstract and more easily associated with Chinese *qin* music or certain familiar tunes. To Chinese audiences, the pointillistic and dissonant middle section of the work makes the work hard to comprehend. The gap between Eastern and Western audiences' perception of the unfamiliar is reflected in Western listeners' perceptive emphasis on modern sound, structural contrasts, and the association with styles of other contemporary Western composers, and Eastern audiences' perceptive emphasis on melody, on mood, and on the recognizable timbre or sound which can be easily referred to the familiar sound of the traditional instruments, such as the *qin*. Except for retelling Chou's own words about the meaning of the work, there is no single analytical review of the work in Taiwan and Hong Kong press. This also shows that the contemporary Western sound is still foreign to Chinese ears.

For Western audiences, the oriental sound is only an impression derived from Hollywood movie music and from the works of Debussy, Ravel, Mahler, Puccini, and Russian nationalist composers of the late nineteenth century. Karl Kroeger in his 1962–1963 review of the issuance of three of Chou's scores, *Landscapes*, *And the Fallen Petals*, and *All in the Spring Wind*, by C. F. Peters, points out that Chou understood the psyche of the Western listener, and he was not only "an excellent composer, but also a good psychologist."[63] Despite these positive remarks, Kroeger's reservations about the listeners' ability to translate literary stimuli to aural perceptions are also expressed.[64]

Alfred Frankenstein's record review of four of Chou's works, *Pien*, *Yu ko*, *Willows Are New*, and *Cursive*, is also geared toward identifying Western traits of Webern, Varèse, Debussy, and Cowell.[65] Bruce Archibald's review of the same record set goes into some detail in highlighting techniques employed in these works such as the use of pentatonic modes in evoking *qin* music in *Willows Are New*, experimentation with timbre and texture in *Yu ko*, permutation of "variable modes" or intervallic cells in *Pien*, and the balance between structural sonority and line in *Cursive*.[66] Another review of the same record by A. Cohn (1969–1970) describes that the music "seems to be without climax; it seems rather to consist of a single subject being displayed as if prismatically, from all of its coloristic angles."[67] However, Cohn was negative about *Pien*. He felt that the piece lacks balance, transparency, and poetry.[68] In other words, *Pien* is most complex in terms of its source of inspiration and least concrete in its resemblance to "oriental sound" and its power to evoke oriental images.

In a review of Chou's two lesser-known works, *In the Mode of Shang* (1957) and Suite for Harp and Wind Quintet (1951), Edward Downes comments that *In the Mode of Shang* was "pleasantly exotic" and that the Suite for Harp and Wind Quintet is "rigidly bound to more primitive 5-tone scales and harmonies [that] came closer to a conventional Western notion of Eastern music and also to the pentatonic sonorities we associate with Debussy."[69]

An overt claim of exoticism in the Suite for Harp and Wind Quintet appeared in the *New York Herald Tribune* on January 25, 1954, after the 1954 New York performance of the piece at Town Hall, New York City, for the National Association for American Composers and Conductors by the National Arts Club Wind Quintet. In this review, Lester Trimble commended Chou's way of synthesizing oriental and occidental ideas.[70]

In the concert review of the Louisville Orchestra's 1960 performance of *All in the Spring Wind* (1952–1953), William Mootz compares listening to this work as to that of absorbing "exotic aroma" and cautions the listener that "old listening habits must be discarded."[71] A connection between *And the Fallen Petals* and the imagery of Chinese scroll painting was established by Harold Rogers in his review of Louisville Orchestra's recordings of *And the Fallen Petals* that appeared in the *Christian Science Monitor*.[72] However, Ross Parmenter in his concert review of Chou's *To a Wayfarer*, which was presented with Cowell's *Persian Set*, McPhee's Nocturne for Chamber Orchestra, Shukichi Mitsukuri's *Ten Haikus*, Odeon Partos's *In Memoriam*, El-Dabh's *Fantasia-Tahmeel*, Malloy Miller's *Prelude*, Alan Hovhaness's *October Mountain*, and Walter Piston's *Divertimento* for Nine Instruments by contemporary Music Society conducted by Stokowski at the Grace Rainey Rogers Auditorium of the Metropolitan Museum of Art in New York City, claims that among these eight works, which were "all concerned with delicate and exotic sonorities," Chou's work "made the deepest impression on him."[73] Parmentor also pointed out that Chou's music "was individual in expression, being neither strongly oriental nor markedly American."[74]

Lester Trimble's review of this work characterizes that Chou has an "affection for colorism and mood illustration," and "in the case of Westernized Oriental composers, the result is likely to be Impressionism."[75] Commenting on the premiere of Chou's vocal work *Poems of White Stone*, conducted by John Garvey and choreographed by Merce Cunningham for performance in March 1959 at the Lincoln Hall Theater on the Urbana campus of the University of Illinois, Lynn Ludlow echoes Parmentor by saying that "Chou's music began and ended with themes built on a pentatonic scale; it was otherwise more non-Occidental than oriental in expression."[76]

Some recent record reviews for reissuing Chou's works on CD and some concert reviews tend to be more perceptive and often deal with compositional issues at greater depth by relating Chou's ideas in his works. On the other hand, a focal point of these reviews is the discussion of Chou's use of cross-cultural musical sources, even in Chou's most non-Asian sounding works.[77] Concerning *Pien, Yu ko, Cursive, The Willows Are New,* and *Landscapes,* Art Lange wrote that Chou "has created marvelously crafted, imaginatively expressive music from contrasting Asian and Western sources."[78] To be sure, in these reviews, there are qualitative statements as well. Specifically, in his review for *Echoes from the Gorge,* Peter Burwasser praises this work as "one of the most evocative and expressive works ever written for percussion ensemble."[79] He commends Chou's ability to create a "stunningly rich composition," which extends from "gut-wrenching, explosive power to serene, quiet beauty."[80] For the same work's performance at the San Francisco Contemporary Music Players Concert Series, Allan Ulrich wrote that "this is a gorgeously arranged piece in which tension is built through texture."[81] Don Gillespie in his 1997 article "Chou Wen-Chung: A Meeting of East and West," published in *Peters Notes* (a C. F. Peters journal focusing on composers) acclaims that Chou's "more than twenty orchestral and chamber works—from *Landscapes* of 1949 to *Clouds* of 1996—have been accorded the highest respect from performers, fellow composers and a discriminating musical public."[82] Indeed, Chou's works are much better known today than they were three decades ago. It certainly has something to do with a wider dissemination of recordings and more frequent performances of his works, but more important, perhaps, is Chou's more recent active role in composing, a unique outlet that makes his voice heard.

Notes

1. Chen An, "Between East and West," in *Hua Qiao Ri Bao* [Overseas Chinese Daily], Thursday, October 29, 1987.

2. Stravinsky's *Symphony of Psalms* had won San Francisco audiences and that work had been performed there several times already. See Alfred Frankenstein, "Symphonic Novelties Not So Daring," *San Francisco Chronicle,* Saturday, November 21, 1953, 11.

3. Gilbert Chase, *America's Music, from the Pilgrims to the Present,* 3rd ed. (Urbana: University of Illinois Press, 1987), 455.

4. Oliver Daniel, *Stokowski: A Counterpoint of View* (New York: Dodd, Mead, and Co., 1982), 572.

5. Daniel, *Stokowski,* 223.

6. Fernand Ouellette, *Edgard Varèse* (New York: Orion, 1968), 97.

7. Daniel, *Stokowski,* 228.

8. Nicolas Slonimsky, *Perfect Pitch* (Oxford: Oxford University Press, 1988), 121–22.

9. Slonimsky, *Perfect Pitch,* 121–22.

10. Slonimsky, *Perfect Pitch*, 138.

11. Slonimsky, *Perfect Pitch*, 152.

12. Carl Schorske, "Gustav Klimt: Painting and Crisis of the Liberal Ego," in *Fin-de-Siècle Vienna* (New York: Knopf, 1979), chapter 5.

13. Glenn Watkins, *Soundings: Music in the Twentieth Century* (New York: Schirmer Books, 1988), 17.

14. Watkins, *Soundings*, 17.

15. Watkins, *Soundings*, 17.

16. Anthony Tommasini, "Calligraphy Is Reflected in a Premiere," *New York Times*, December 3, 1996, 16.

17. Chou was director of the committee.

18. This group includes David Rockefeller, Jr., Porter McKeever (advisor to John D. Rockefeller III Fund), Martha Wallace (president of Henry Luce Foundation), Russell Phillips, Jr. (vice president of Rockefeller Brothers Fund), and Jack Bresnan (Ford Foundation). William Cossolias of the Center for U.S.-China Arts Exchange provided this information.

19. Gang Chen, "Zao Chuen Er Yue Liu Se Xin" [New Willows of Early Spring], *Ren Min Yin Yue* [*People's Music*] 11/12 (1979): 68–70, 88.

20. In July 1991, I attended a Central Philharmonic Orchestra's weekend concert in Beijing. Chou's *And the Fallen Petals* was included as a contemporary Chinese composition (see the concert program).

21. Dong-Feng Ma and Hai-Ming Sun, "Dang Dai Zuo Qu Jia Zhou Wen-Zhong Ji Qi Zuo Pin" [Contemporary Composer Zhou Wen-Zhong and His Works], *Yin Yue Sheng Huo* [*The Musical Life*] 7 (1985): 30.

22. Ma and Sun, "Dang Dai Zuo Qu Jia Zhou Wen-Zhong," 30.

23. Jin Ye and Pin-Fang Yiao, "Xuan Ge Sheng Sheng Zu Jiao Liu" [Songs for Promoting Exchange], *People's Daily*, 1987 (from a clip, no dates given).

24. Fan-Fu Zhou, "Fang Zhou Wen Zhong" [Interviewing Chou Wen-Chung], *Music Audiophile* 81 (March 1981): 97.

25. Shu-Mei Lin, "Zhou Wen-Zhong Dai Lai De Shen Si" [Contemplating on Zhou Wen-Zhong's Ideas], *Music and Audiophile* 4 (April 1988): 38–41.

26. "Zhou Wen-Zhong" in *Jin Dai Zhong Guo Yin Yue Shi Hua* [*A Talk on Contemporary Chinese Music*] (Taipai: Chen Zhong Chubanshe), 128.

27. Writers include Chang Guo Deng, "Wo Suo Zhi Dao De Zhou Wen Zhong" [My Impression of Zhou Wen Zhong], *Gong Xue Yue Kan* [*Gong Xue Monthly*] 3 (1966); Gu Xian-Liang, "Dong Xi Yin Yue Zai He Liu Zhong De Di Zhu—Zhou Wen-Zhong" [Zhou Wen-Zhong: The Promoter of East-West Musical Confluence], *Gong Xue Monthly* 4 (1966); Si Lu, "Ming Zhen Guo Ji Yue Tan De Zhong Guo Zuo Qu Jia—Zhou Wen-Zhong" [A Famous Chinese Composer—Zhou Wen-Zhong], *Ai Yue* [Philharmonic] 4 (1966); and Guo-Huang Han, "Wu Zhou Wen-Zhong" [Meeting Wen-Zhong Zhou], *Ai Yue* [*Philharmonic*] 7 (1968). All articles are cited in "Zhou Wen-Zhong," (1970), 129.

28. For some unknown reason, Chou was on the Taiwanese government's blacklist, which prevented him to travel to Taiwan until 1981. The Taiwanese composer Hsu Tsang-Houei was forced publicly to accuse Chou as a spy for the mainland government. A possible explanation for this would be because Chou's father, who had served the nationalist government as a high official, did not flee with the nationalist government to Taiwan but remained on the mainland till his death in 1987.

29. Qing-Xuan Lin, "Zhou Wen-Zhong," *Shi Bao Xin Zhi* [*News Gazette*], no. 112, January 24, 1982, 42–45.

30. Qin Zhao, "Chou Wen-Chung: A Composer in Traditional Chinese Style," *Xin Xiang Yi Xun* [*New Trends in the Arts*] (December 20–26, 1981): 6–7.

31. Zhao, "Chou Wen-Chung," 6–7.

32. Mu Wu, "Yi Shu Ji Zhong De Guo Ren Xin Zuo" [New Works of Chinese Composers for the Art Festival] *Music and Audiophile* 39 (January 1985): 24–26.

33. Shyhji Pan-Chew, ed., *Chou Wen-Chung Music Festival Special Album, 2003* (Taipei: Canada-Taiwan Music and Arts Exchange, 2004), 149–50.

34. Shyhji Pan-Chew, *Chou Wen-Chung Music Festival Special Album*, preface.

35. Bao-Er Liang, "Zhou Wen-Zhong Zhi Li Liang Di Wen Hua Gou Tong" [Zhou Wen-Zhong's Efforts in Cultural Exchanges], *Hong Kong Economic Journal* (January 11, 1988).

36. Bao-Er Liang, "Zhou Wen-Zhong Zhi Li Liang Di Wen Hua Gou Tong" [Zhou Wen-Zhong's Efforts in Cultural Exchanges], *Hong Kong Economic Journal* (January 16, 1988).

37. Xi-Zhou Bi, "Zhou Wen-Zhong," *The Esquire* (February 1989).

38. Qi-Ji Wu, "Mei Ji Hua Ren Zuo Qu Jia Zhou Wen Zhong Tan Yin Yue" [American-Chinese Composer Professor Zhou Wen-Zhong on Music], *Hua Ren* [The Chinese] 4 (from a clip—no dates given).

39. Lan-Gu Chen, ed., trans., "Wei Lai Shi Jie Yin Yue De Zhu Liu" [The Main Stream for the Future of World Music], *Zhong Bao* [*The Chinese Journal*] (September 23, 1982); and Chen An, "Zai Dong Xi Fang Zhi Jian" [Between East and West], *Hua Qiao Ri Bao* [*Overseas Chinese Daily*], October 28, 1987.

40. Chen An, "Between East and West," *Hua Qiao Ri Bao* [*Overseas Chinese Daily*], no. 2, October 29, 1987.

41. An, "Between East and West."

42. An, "Between East and West."

43. An, "Between East and West."

44. Lester Trimble, "Records Review," *The Nation* 186, no. 21 (1958): 484.

45. Alfred Frankenstein, "Symphonic Novelties Not So Daring," *San Francisco Chronicle*, November 21, 1953, 11.

46. Claudia Cassidy, "Some Marvelous Mahler on a Night of Oriental Overtones," *Chicago Daily Tribune*, Friday, November 6, 1959, part II, 11.

47. Nicolas Slonimsky, "Chou Wen-Chung," *American Composers Alliance Bulletin* 9, no. 4 (1961): 8.

48. Harold Schoenberg, "Seven Modern Works Heard in South," *New York Times,* October 10, 1955, 31.

49. William Mootz, "Critics Hear Orchestra and Open Workshop," *The Courier-Journal,* October 8, 1955, 10.

50. Alfred Frankenstein, "Symphony Plays Work by Chinese," *San Francisco Chronicle,* December 4, 1959, 43.

51. Frankenstein, "Symphony Plays Work by Chinese," 43.

52. Quote from *Berliner Morganpost,* June 3, 1960, in *American Composers Alliance Bulletin* 9, no. 4 (1961), 20.

53. Quote from *Der Kurier,* June 2, 1960, in *American Composers Alliance Bulletin* 9, no. 4 (1961), 20.

54. Quote from *Der Tag,* June 3, 1960, in *American Composers Alliance Bulletin* 9, no. 4 (1961), 20.

55. Quote from *Der Tagesspiegel,* June 3, 1960, in *American Composers Alliance Bulletin* 9, no. 4 (1961), 20.

56. Quote from *Telegraf,* June 5, 1960, in *American Composers Alliance Bulletin* 9, no. 4 (1961), 20.

57. Christian Weickert, quote from *Freie Presse,* June 7, 1960, in *American Composers Alliance Bulletin* 9, no. 4 (1961), 20.

58. Quote from *Der Abend,* June 2, 1960, in *American Composers Alliance Bulletin* 9, no. 4 (1961), 20.

59. Quote from *Die Welt,* March 26, 1958, in *American Composers Alliance Bulletin* 8, no. 2 (1959), 22.

60. Quote from *Hamburger Echo,* March 26, 1958, in *American Composers Alliance Bulletin* 8, no. 2 (1959), 22.

61. Harold Schoenberg, "Philharmonic Concert Is an Exotic Blend," *New York Times,* January 7, 1961, 13; and the review of the same concert by Miles Kastendieck in *New York Journal-American,* January 7, 1961.

62. Concert announcement, *Time,* vol. 77, no. 3, January 13, 1961, 42.

63. Karl Kroeger's review of Chou's three scores in *Music Library Association Notes* 20, no. 2 (Winter–Fall 1962–1963), 406.

64. Kroeger, review, 406.

65. Alfred Frankenstein, "The Sound World of Chou Wen-Chung," *High Fidelity Magazine/Musical America* 20 (July–November 1970): 84.

66. Bruce Archibald, "Record Review," *Musical Quarterly* 58 (1972): 333–35.

67. A. Cohn, "Very Special: the Music of Chou Wen-Chung," *American Record Guide* 36 (September–August, 1969–1970): 886–87.

68. Cohn, "Very Special," 886–87.

69. Edward Downes, "Work by Chinese Has Its Premiere," *New York Times,* Monday, February 4, 1957, 15.

70. Lester Trimble, "Composers, Conductors," *New York Herald Tribune,* January 25, 1954, 10.

71. William Mootz, "Concertmaster Kling Stars As Soloist in Mendelssohn's Violin Concerto," *The Courier Journal*, December 8, 1960, 18.

72. Harold Rogers, "Opportunity Needed for New Works," *Christian Science Monitor* (February 7, 1956): 10.

73. Ross Parmenter, "Stokowski Conducts Contemporary Works," *New York Times*, December 4, 1958, 53.

74. Parmenter, "Stokowski Conducts Contemporary Works," 53.

75. Lester Trimble, "Records Review," *The Nation*, December 27, 1958, 483–84.

76. Lynn Ludlow, "Chinese Poetry in Dance," *The Champaign Urbana Courier*, March 16, 1959, 4.

77. Peter Burwasser, record review of *Echoes from the Gorge, Yu ko*, Suite for Harp and Wind Quintet, and *Windswept Peaks* in *Fanfare* (September/October, 1995): 177. See Don Gillespie's "Chou Wen-Chung: A Meeting of East and West," in *Peters Notes* 2, no. 1 (Winter 1997): 4. Also see Allan Ulrich, "Bang-up Performance Showcases Percussion," *San Francisco Chronicle*, December 6, 2000, E3.

78. Art Lange, record review of *Pien, Yu ko, Cursive, The Willows Are New*, and *Landscapes* in *Fanfare* (March/April, 1996): 148–49.

79. Peter Burwasser, record review, 177.

80. Peter Burwasser, record review, 177.

81. Allan Ulrich, "Bang-up Performance Showcases Percussion," *San Francisco Chronicle*, December 6, 2000, E3.

82. Don Gillespie, "Chou Wen-Chung: A Meeting of East and West," in *Peters Notes* 2, no. 1 (Winter 1997): 4.

CHAPTER SEVEN

~

Background of Chinese Approaches
To Musical Synthesis

Chou spent his youth and formative years in China, where he experienced both the traditional Chinese and the new Western ways of life as well as music from these cultures. He saw Peking opera performances at traditional teahouse-like theaters and heard street singers in market places, Buddhist chanting in temples, *Kunqu* singing at parties, *qin* music on the radio, and folk songs in his backyard and later on college campus; he was familiar with Western opera and ballet music from attending live performances in concert halls, in addition to his familiarity with the violin repertoire and his collection of recordings of Western instrumental music made in the 1920s and 1930s in Europe. He developed an interest in music as a schoolboy, and following in the footsteps of two of his older brothers, he was eager to absorb all the musical nutrients that were accessible to him. Although never enrolled in Chinese conservatories, Chou was aware of his immediate musical environment especially in Shanghai where his interest in musical studies grew more serious. He was exposed to modern Chinese compositions such as works by Huang zi (1904–1938),[1] though not impressed by it at the time because of his Western classics' bias, the style of these works would have some bearing on him only to manifest later. With such an interesting background and upbringing, Chou created a very personal music style after he left China. To put Chou Wen-Chung's musical development in its cultural and historical perspective and to provide a backdrop for later comparison, it is necessary to discuss some of the issues regarding Chinese approaches to musical synthesis.

Western Techniques as Backbone for Musical Synthesis

The establishment of the Republic of China in 1911 signified the beginning of a full-scale adaptation of Western political, social, economic, educational, and technological systems and lifestyles. These changes deeply affected Chinese views of the world.[2] This new view was the reflection of these two realities: (1) the adaptation of Western way of life among the urban populations and (2) a search for answers to China's failure to maintain its long-standing cultural, military, and economic superiority during modern times. As a result, major efforts have been focused on reevaluating Chinese tradition through "flaw" findings. It was generally believed that China's inability to deter the invasion of Western culture was due to the weakness imbedded in Chinese political, social, and technological systems. Chinese music naturally paralleled these aspects of the culture; its inability to compete with Western music was described as the lack of form and harmony, and because of the lack of precision, the inconsistency between notating and playing Chinese melody was the norm.[3] According to the late Dr. Liu Fu, Chinese melody was still shrouded in the realm of unsolved mysteries.[4] Chinese instruments were viewed as "still quite crude and simple,"[5] and Chinese singing was too nasal and throaty.[6] John Levis, the son of a missionary raised in China, compared the Chinese heterophonic tradition to that of medieval European counterpoint, which was eventually developed while the Chinese remained "primitive."[7] Benjamin Ing, a singer trained at the University of Michigan, compared the music of Chinese *Kunqu* and Wagner's music-drama, and concluded that:

> Melodically, *Kunqu* might be superior to Wagner's masterpieces; but taken as a whole, there is really no comparison between the two. For accompaniment, *Kunqu* has merely the flute and the sheng (mouth organ) which double on the melody sung, and are consequently monotonous. As to singing, vocal science in China has not been developed enough even today to afford any comparison.[8]

The reference to these "shortcomings" of traditional Chinese music were made in comparison to Western music by those Chinese intellectuals who were either trained in the West or influenced by Western music. Levis believes that the cause for such inferiority was due to the lack of a conscious system of musical composition in China, and such an impression was enforced by Western writers on Chinese music such as Soulié, Van Aalst, A. W. Faber, and Amiot.[9] This kind of faultfinding convinced a large number of Chinese composers that traditional Chinese music needed modernization, and the available catalyst was Western composition techniques.

A concept shared by these Western-trained Chinese composers was that the mastery of Western harmony of the common-practice period was a fundamental requirement for a composer.[10] They regarded the nature of Western music as scientific, and as a subject of science, its rules can be applied cross culturally.

The Chinese composers' preference for fusing Chinese melody with Western harmony, counterpoint, and orchestration was due largely to their views on the success of Russian nationalist composers to preserve national characteristics, which had won acclaim among Western musicians and audience. The Chinese composers' conviction about the compatibility between Chinese melody and Western techniques was coupled with the Western fascination with oriental modes and melody, as seen in the works of Rimsky-Korsakov, Mahler, Ravel, and Debussy. Thus, this view had become orthodox as the result of experiments, successes, and failures of two generations of Chinese composers.

The ideal for composition of the 1920s and 1930s was "seamless" fusion of Western and Chinese elements in the minds of both composers and audiences, which consisted of Chinese intellectuals educated in the Western style. However, the flaw of such an ideal was soon discovered when a concern over the lack of definite Chinese characters in Western-Chinese compositions was expressed by Alexander Tcherepnine, Russian-American composer, who was in China between 1935 and 1936, and by Chao Mei-Pa, a Western-trained singer in 1937.[11]

Using over a dozen of nineteenth- and twentieth-century Western composers' nationalistic style as examples of successful fusion of Western techniques and national character, Chao goes on to point out that, at the time of his writing, China had not produced an internationally recognized composer, and in the field of composition, China was in a state of confusion. He observed five different kinds of attitudes concerning the development of modern Chinese music: (1) laissez-faire, (2) interest in self-promotion only, (3) a sympathetic attitude to China's difficulty, (4) anti-West sentiments, while offering no constructive ideas, and (5) preservation of the best of Chinese tradition in the Chinese-Western musical fusion.[12]

Chao's idea represented the prevalent practice among Western-trained Chinese musicians and composers of using Western music as the backbone and adding Chinese elements, which were often subjugated under the Western techniques, to create musical fusions.

Although the majority of composers of Chao's generation realized that as Chinese composers, they must use Chinese material in their compositions, Western music was considered superior to that of its Chinese counterpart.

Therefore, no one would claim that Chinese music is just as scientific or as complex as Western music. Such an inferiority complex mixed with the worship of Western music was the dominant mood among the first generation of Chinese composers. Their conclusion was that traditional Chinese music, although it had a long history, could not compete with Western music.

During the 1930s, prediction of the future of Chinese musical development was a perennial topic, which appeared in almost every article on modern Chinese music. Chao Yuan-Ren, for example, believed that the evolution of Chinese music should reach a point where its national characteristics were preserved and that through employment of harmony, chromaticism in traditional Chinese pentatonicism, and Western instruments, both oriental and Western audiences can appreciate it. Thus, for creating a modern Chinese composition, it was necessary to rectify the impression given by the "national-cultural-preservation" complex of Chinese cultural purists and the "China-as-museum-of-antiquities" complex of Westerners.[13]

Tcherepnine, who organized a composition competition in China in 1934 to work out a piano study based on the pentatonic scale, points out that contemporary Western music is closer to the Chinese psyche than the Western music of the eighteenth and nineteenth centuries. Tcherepnine wrote:

> I had the opportunity of giving some young students pieces of modern music to study, and I was amazed how quickly and easily they caught on to our modern idioms; the same students found it rather difficult to feel at home with Chopin or Franck. The Chinese musical student should be treated in a special way: for a beginner, both the instrument and the music to be played on this instrument are unknown quantities. At least one of these can be eliminated by the use of familiar music, adaptations of Chinese folk songs in a modern manner. These should be followed by modern compositions, beginning with Debussy (especially congenial to the Chinese ear through the Javanese affinity in his art) and Stravinsky, and leading to the best works of the postwar musical literature.[14]

Also critical of the Chinese composers, Tcherepnine was the first to notice a lack of knowledge in the history of Western music among Chinese composers, which resulted in shallowness and an almost uniform approach to composition in their adaptations of Western music to Chinese melodies. In predicting the future of Chinese music, Tcherepnine further points out that "the more national his product, the greater will be its international value."[15]

Chao Mei-Pa questions Tcherepnine's suggestion on bypassing training in eighteenth- and nineteenth-century Western music, "Mr. Tcherepnine forgets that in working the Pentatonic Scale Study, he has Bach, and others behind him, and possesses their technique."[16] Paradoxically, when enumerating the "flaws" and incompatible elements with Western music in Chinese music, traits could be quite specific, but beyond melody, which was to be retained in the Chinese-Western fusion, no other "desirable" Chinese element for the fusion was mentioned. Other than melody, everything else was considered inferior in comparison to Western music, and the idea of entering the mainstream in the West or becoming modernized musically was urgent; the Chinese composers' eyes were fixed on approaches to the national yet widely recognized music, the music of the "Russian Five," Bartok, Debussy, Peter Benoit, De Falla, Sibelius, and early Franck.[17] Moreover, the Western fascination with oriental modes and melody, as seen in the works of Rimsky-Korsakov, Mahler, Ravel, and Debussy, provided another kind of opportunity for Chinese composers to assert the legitimacy of combining Chinese melody with Western harmonic material. For over half of a century, as the result of experiments, successes, and failures of two generations of Chinese composers, this kind of practice had become a rule. Because of this, rarely had anyone seriously searched for compatibility between Western music and other aspects of Chinese culture, nor had anyone contended that the fusion of Chinese melody, Western harmony, counterpoint, and orchestration was not the only desirable way to create contemporary Chinese music.

Under Western influence, debate over the course for contemporary Chinese music between conservative and progressive Chinese thinkers was stimulated. Because of differences in educational background, Western conservatory-trained composers tended to support the maintenance of Western composition curriculum as composers' primary training, while the conservatives were in favor of maintaining traditional Chinese musical training, that is, learning to play traditional instruments by traditional notation, tuning, and venue for performance. As a result, the Western-trained composers' experimentation with Chinese materials went barely beyond melody, and the conservatives were reluctant to incorporate Western techniques or elements in traditional Chinese music. The conservatives saw the composition curriculum in conservatories as "blind" imitation of the West that undermines Chinese tradition. On the other hand, conservatory composers felt that the conservatives' adamant refusal to adopt Western scientific ways of treating polyphony, orchestration, and construction of instruments as merely making Chinese traditional music a living fossil incapable of development.[18]

With tensions existing among various groups, only the conservatory-trained composers stood at the center in developing modern Chinese music. However, limitations on their ability to go beyond the superficial view of traditional Chinese arts and music to discover fundamental principles in these arts had much to do with constraint of Western training in composition and failure to appreciate traditional Chinese music through a systematic study. By now, Western music had acquired a permanent position in the lives of urban populations especially in that of the musical circles in China.

Chinese Materials as Backbone for Synthesis

Under the nationalist rule (1927–1949), composition was a relatively free enterprise, while under the Communists, it became much politicized and was constantly under the Communist Party's tight grip.[19] The reversal of emphasis on Western music as the backbone of a composition is evident in the Communist art policy, which encouraged composers to create works for the masses by using traditional Chinese folk materials as the basis for composition and cautiously selecting those apolitical foreign materials such as composition techniques for adding potency of Chinese material in the synthesis. The Chinese Communists understood that techniques themselves are politically neutral. Yet, techniques can serve political objectives. A composition becomes political only when a social or political group claims it. The Chinese Communists saw their comrades in France and Russia appropriate bourgeois material for revolutionary use and employ bourgeois technical personnel in various revolutionary capacities. They believed that music was no exception. The Chinese Communists believed that past achievements in the arts, whether Chinese or foreign, could be utilized for revolutionary purposes when sanctioned, shaped, and interpreted according to the new ideology.[20] Mao Ze-Dong in his 1942 "A Talk at Yan An Forum of the Fine Arts," encouraged artists to combine ideologically suitable forms of Chinese tradition and materials from the West in making fusion an effective tool for boosting revolutionary morale and indoctrinating Communist principles in the masses.[21]

Filtering out the unsuitable elements from the tradition requires reevaluation of the tradition. The Communists' reevaluation of traditional Chinese music never went beyond the notion that folk tunes were associated with the working class and therefore were politically desirable. Their work was largely confined in collecting folk songs for practical uses, albeit some newly composed tunes were also used. Their aim in reevaluating and rewriting political, sociocultural, and art history was to legitimize and justify their causes in their struggle against the Japanese and nationalists during World War II and the Civil War and subsequently against "revisionists" during the Cultural Revolution. Most of the Communists' experimentation of censoring and synthesizing Chinese and Western materials for the new kind of revolutionary music for the masses was carried out in Yan An between 1938 and 1945. Several active party member composers at the Yan An Lu Xun Arts Institute were involved in such experimentation: Lu Ji (1909–2002), Xian Xing-Hai (1905–1945), Xiang Yu (1912–1968), Zheng Lu-Cheng (1918–1976), Li Huan-Zhi (1919–2000), and Ma Ke (1918–1976).

Also during the war in 1943, the nationalist leaders, while under pressure of invading Japanese troops, sought to boost morale of the army and the masses with Confucian ethics by establishing the Institute of National Rites and Music, which was responsible for researching, compiling, and implementing Confucian ritual music as representative of Chinese national music.[22] Though from different ideological bases, these two approaches to creating a kind of Chinese national music in the process of politicizing music have one thing in common: the realization that the backbone for nationalistic Chinese compositions was in Chinese material, with grassroots in the masses. Despite their political claims, this habit of purging undesirable elements in rewriting history and particularly in using music for educating the masses goes back to the Confucian tradition and represents the Chinese dynastic style of scholarship.

Chinese leaders' regard for traditional Chinese music and its relationship to Western music after the establishment of the People's Republic was always practical. Their promotion of studying and collecting traditional music was largely focused on political education of the masses and on their newly envisioned revolutionary music for the Chinese working class.

The history and development of modern Chinese music during the People's Republic was continually characterized by the struggle involving Western music's position in relation to a Chinese context as being between the radical Maoist and conservative composers. For example, in 1964, the ideological differences between these two camps resulted in open conflict in which five professors at the Central Conservatory condemned one of their conservative colleagues for asking his students to choose Western composers as their models, instead of thinking about the Chinese working class and working to create a national style. Chen Lian, a student from the Central Conservatory, directed his complaints about the heavy emphasis on Western classical music in conservatory's curriculum to Mao Ze-Dong. In the same letter, he also suggested that China stage a festival of Asian, African, and Latin American music. Mao's response, though, was never published; apparently he supported Chen because he published an article openly attacking foreign romantic and religious songs.[23] A significant reduction in the number of Western orchestras and the "four cleanups" political campaign soon followed these events.

Under Communist control, composition students and accomplished composers alike were encouraged to go to rural and remote areas to collect indigenous musical material for political sanction. This kind of "field work," referred to by the Chinese term *caifeng* or collecting, was institutionalized in Chinese conservatories. The Chinese have a long tradition of collecting musical material from the people by court officials. The purposes of this were (1) to detect people's sentiment toward policies of the current administration, hence keeping the administration fully informed; and (2) to enlarge the repertoire of the court music. The "folk" materials were refined to suit the taste of the court. A good example is one of the earliest anthologies of songs and poems, the *Shijing*, allegedly compiled by Confucius during the sixth century BC. The original melody of the anthology was lost. However, 305 song texts were preserved and classified in three categories, that is, *Feng*, *Ya*, and *Song*, in an ascending hierarchical order: (1) *Feng*, or folk songs collected from the masses; (2) *Ya*, or elegant songs based on *Feng* but refined by court officials; and (3) *Song*, or odes for Confucian ritual ceremonies. The crude folk tunes, *Feng*, were collected and then refined to become *Ya*, and some of the *Ya* songs were further refined to become *Song*, the most important ceremonial odes.

The tradition of collecting folk songs has been handed down through the centuries. In modern times, as a response to Western influence, this tradition was brought alive in the "folk song preservation campaign" during the first two decades of this century by a group of nationalistic and culturally conscious musicians and scholars. This was also true in similar campaigns initiated by the Communist Party in the 1930s with production of the *Yellow River* Cantata and the opera *White-haired Girl*, in the 1950s and 1960s, with the resultant violin concerto *Butterfly Lovers*, and in the 1980s the rise of a group of young avant-garde Chinese composers publishing new works such as the string quartet *Feng-Ya-Song*, the symphonic poem *Li Sao*, and the voice and percussion piece *Meng Dong*.

Around the mid-1960s, the left-wing faction in the Chinese leadership gradually gained control in arts and music. In 1964, contemporary subjects began to replace traditional stories in Peking opera, and in 1968, not only were Western orchestra and staff notation introduced into this genre but also several types of its arias were used in the new fusion of Peking opera and Western cantata. The revolutionary symphony *Sha Jia Bang* was an example, and the attitude that the Chinese Communists were able to appropriate Western musical material for the revolutionary causes was clearly shown. In light of the high degree of the government's involvement in blocking information on the development of contemporary music in the West and of its total control of music production during the Cultural Revolution between 1969 and 1976, the fact that only eight "model dramas" were allowed to be performed as legitimate art forms is astonishing. Mao turned the general Chinese fascination with combining Chinese and Western musical elements by producing contemporary Chinese compositions to the politically charged doctrines, "Guwei Jinyong, Yangwei Zhongyong," or using Western techniques for the Chinese cause, and using the ancient tradition for contemporary needs.[24] Jiang Qing, Mao Ze-Dong's wife, was chiefly responsible for designing and carrying out the artistic reforms. Mao's confidence in the capability of proletariat to appropriate Western as well as traditional Chinese material for the revolutionary cause is revealed in a series of talks given by Jiang Qing between 1964 and 1968.

A New Approach to Synthesis During the Cultural Revolution 1966–1976

The effort to filter out undesirable materials and select those preferable for transcending the original materials and to create a new breed of revolutionary works is self-evident in Jiang's talks.[25] Undesirable foreign and traditional elements were never technical but ideological. Since Maoists' legitimization of appropriating Western "scientific" compositional techniques for the Chinese musical revolution, that is, the fusion of Western harmony, counterpoint, and Chinese melody, works continued to manifest in the second and third generations of Chinese composers.

In her earlier career as a movie actress, and like most Western-influenced Chinese musicians and artists, Jiang Qing's attraction to Western music came mainly from her familiarity with Western-influenced Chinese popular movie music and partly by her subsequently acquired, ideological stance that Western music was associated with science (after becoming Madam Mao in Yan An). Her palate for Western music formed a sharp contrast with her negative view of Chinese traditional instrumental music. This was not an isolated incident, but a reflection of the general attitude of the Chinese urban middle class toward traditional Chinese music and Western music.

During the Cultural Revolution (1966–1976), emphasis was on the process of class struggle. Jiang wanted very much to hide her bourgeoisie past; she wanted to be identified with the proletariat and, above all, to be recognized as the dictator in the arts, equivalent to Mao in politics. This motivation underlay a need for creating a new kind of musical synthesis, which after the appropriation would accommodate Jiang's preference for Western music. The new synthesis was also designed to transcend its original sources and acquire new meanings representing the Chinese proletariat class. As a result, the sinicized Western music, especially the music of the eight "model dramas," the product of Jiang's revolution, was to have a profound impact on Chinese views of Western instruments and harmony and the society as a whole. Because these dramas were widely disseminated through media, it is extremely rare to find someone who has not heard or cannot hum their melodies.

Ironically, during the Cultural Revolution, Western music enjoyed such an unprecedented prestige that Western-style orchestras became absolute necessities for art troupes, which mushroomed in every school, factory, barracks, and government unit nationwide. The popularity of Western instruments such as strings, woodwinds, and brass had produced a large number of Western orchestral players; also, because of the introduction of Western instruments in Peking opera, many young instrumentalists in Peking opera troupes began to get acquainted with Western orchestration and were eventually attracted to composition. Many of the so-called new-wave academic composers were direct products of the popularization of Western instruments and composition techniques.

Chou's Impact on Contemporary Chinese Music of the Post-Mao Era

The downfall of Jiang's leftist clique, and the halt for performing "model revolutionary dramas" in the mid-1970s, brought about much confusion among post–Cultural Revolution composers, who were facing problems with loss of direction so that no one knew which approach to follow in writing contemporary Chinese compositions. Not until China opened its door to the West in the late 1970s, did Chinese composers begin to realize that they were totally ignorant about musical changes in the West during the past thirty years. They also felt a need to enrich contemporary Chinese compositions with new techniques and approaches that would supersede the conventional type of Chinese melody. This resulted in Western harmony synthesis, which had been around since the first generation of Chinese composers in the first two decades of this century and culminated in the synthetic "model dramas" of the Cultural Revolution. At this time, Chou's visits to China to inform Chinese composers about the development of contemporary music in the West and to show them his personal approach to composition offered new directions to Chinese composers. Chou's historic impact on contemporary Chinese music of the post-Mao era cannot be underestimated.

Since his first visit to the Central Conservatory in Beijing in 1977, Chou's own experience in creating a new style aroused strong interest among the post–Cultural Revolution generation of composers at the conservatory, and his approach to contemporary Chinese music was widely imitated. Chou's influence on the development of contemporary Chinese music is shown through the rise of a group of post–Cultural Revolution conservatory composers known as *xinchao* or the "new wave" movement in the early 1980s in China. In the "new wave" style, the Chinese concept of brush-ink fluidity in form and the Varèsean concept of musical form as an ebbing and flowing moving mass, the Chinese elevation of timbre and wide spectrum of changes in a single tone above other aspects of music, and the discovery of timbral importance in twentieth-century Western music, the twentieth-century ideal of percussion sound was interpreted through traditional Chinese preference for percussive sound. Again, these Chinese avant-garde works met with stiff resistance from ideologically conservative composers and audiences alike, and much-heated debate over some of the basic Western creative principles such as originality and the autonomy of the arts ensued. Conditioned to hear harmonized Chinese melodies, the Chinese audience was not ready for contemporary sound.[26]

In associating aesthetic tastes with corresponding social stratas of French society, Pierre Bourdieu pointed out that pure aesthetic taste implies a break with the ordinary attitude toward the world, which, given the condition in which it is performed, is also a social separation.[27]

Bourdieu's observation is also applicable to the Chinese situation, with one important difference: in China, Mao and his followers had legitimized and reinforced popular taste (the taste of the working class). The eight revolutionary dramas had monopolized artistic production for ten years during the Cultural Revolution. The sudden removal of this monopoly in the period immediately after Mao's death caused much confusion. Accustomed to one mode of thinking, conservative composers felt insecure about other aesthetic views than their own. This is the core of argument between new wave and conservative composers.

It is clear that in combining Western and Chinese elements, most middle-aged composers and music critics preferred the tonal approach and felt that tonal music could serve the masses best. They maintained that since music had a social function, it could not be autonomous. On the other hand, new wave composers claimed that during the past years under Mao's rule, the aesthetic taste of the people had been shaped and controlled. People were not allowed to pursue Western aesthetics, even the traditional aesthetics of Chinese philosophers. The combination of revolutionary (or socialist) realism and revolutionary romanticism[28] became the only aesthetic criteria for art works.[29] As a result, people were quite unaware of new developments and trends in Western music.

The loosening of political control encouraged liberal thinking. The new wave's rebellion against Mao's views on art and their employment of Western and traditional Chinese aesthetics reflect such a change.

Curiously, a similar situation also occurred in Russia. In 1956, shortly after Stalin's death, the Twentieth Congress of the Communist Party of the Soviet Union criticized Stalin for his choking of artistic creativity. An editorial in *The Communist* proclaimed a new policy of the party to combat Stalinist artistic rigidity and conformity. For a while, new forms of creative subjectivity and experimentation were encouraged, and artistic creativity reduced to the lowest common denominator was condemned.[30] Changes of social climate in both countries sparked the long-suppressed creative urge.

Chou's Individualistic Approach to Musical Synthesis

Chou Wen-Chung's approach to the fusion of Western and Chinese elements in music differs from the first generation of modern Chinese composers in that, instead of completely restricting himself to work with musical material, Chou tried to find compatible elements in general artistic principles and in the traditional intellectual values known as *shi* or *wenren*.[31]

Chou's realization of the compatible aspects between Chinese and contemporary Western music took him almost ten years. In his early years, Chou was neither formally trained through composition programs in a conservatory nor was he an "imperceptive" imitator of Western music. An impartial view on Western and Chinese traditions had always been present in his family and his early training. Chou was versed in several fundamental Chinese intellectual traditions: knowledge in classical poetry, the Confucian classics, calligraphy, and painting. Yet, he also had a strong interest in reading Western literature. His stay in Shanghai during the 1930s enabled him to hear China's finest orchestra, the Shanghai Municipal Orchestra, which, as well as performing eighteenth- and nineteenth-century Western works, also performed works by Ravel, Stravinsky, Respighi, Malipiero, Rieti, de Falla, Bartok, Kodaly, Graener, and Hindemith.[32] As a composer-to-be, this exposure to contemporary Western music was important to Chou's later alliance with twentieth-century Western music, rather than that of the eighteenth and nineteenth centuries, as most Chinese composers did.

Although in his early works such as the "Chinese-flavored" fugue and *Landscapes* (1949) Chou experimented with Western counterpoint, orchestration, and harmony in combination with Chinese melody, he did not stop there. Unlike other Western-trained Chinese composers, Chou was able to go beyond the superficial understanding of traditional Chinese music by investing time in studying and researching traditional Chinese music. And as a result, Chou's understanding of the fundamental principles—not only in traditional Chinese music but also in Chinese art—was much deepened and by applying these basic principles in composing his works, he made strides in discovering, extracting, and fusing compatible artistic principles between contemporary Western music and traditional Chinese art and music.

Chou's presence in the United States where he experienced the developmental stages of Western contemporary music firsthand forms a sharp contrast to those mainland Chinese composers who were isolated from the West for a half a century. Chou's study with Varèse afforded him an opportunity to learn how a true Western musical innovator thinks, how he incorporates scientific concepts and principles of visual art, such as space and color, in characterizing and defining the nature and properties of music, and how he could find the Chinese equivalent of these concepts in applying what he learned from Varèse to create his style of synthesis. Chou's approach to the fusion of contemporary Western and traditional Chinese aesthetic concepts is a good example of what Herskovits, Merriam, and Waterman called "acculturation through reinterpretation" of the familiar concepts and traits.

Chou's venture in identifying compatible concepts between two seemingly incompatible cultures won critical acclaim in both cultures, and his approach to the synthesis of Western and Chinese music broke the spell of conventional constraint of Chinese melody plus Western harmony, counterpoint, and orchestration, and opened new avenues for wide possibilities in bringing about the union between eclectic musical ideas of twentieth-century Western composers and comparable concepts in Chinese tradition.

Chou's choice of Varèse's concepts, which share many aspects of artistic principles with their Chinese counterpart, illustrates that conceptual compatibility plays an indispensable role in the process of synthesis. In Chou's case, the external cause, or environment, which brought about his idea of searching for compatible elements in both Western and Chinese culture, was partly the influence of Varèse's musical style (which in many ways paralleled several important aesthetic principles of Chinese art) and partly due to the interest many contemporary U.S. composers (such as Cowell, McPhee, Cage, Harrison, and Hohvaness of the 1960s) had in oriental or exotic arts, whose philosophies again began to attract Western composers. Unlike others, however, Cage was more involved in oriental aesthetic ideals and applied these principles in structuring his compositions, rather than producing simplistic adaptations of oriental materials.

Chou realized that Varèse's concept of sound (as a moving mass and as having geometric dimensions that are simultaneous) is compatible with the principles in Chinese calligraphy, particularly the ideal of a controlled flow of ink, and the emphasis on spontaneity. Further compatible elements between Varèsean and Chinese principles are seen in the elevation of unpitched percussive sound as a basis for compositions, the emphasis on timbral exploration, and the concept of the invertability of intervallic patterns and collection of intervallic cells. These compatible elements were consciously explored, vigorously pursued, and experimented with both at a conceptual level and in technical details. In his compositional career, Chou functioned as an agent for discovering and disseminating the compatibles. Because of his early training in Chinese poetry and calligraphy, his subsequent studies in Chinese artistic principles and classical Chinese music, his enthusiasm for Western music, and his studies with Varèse, Chou was familiar with both Eastern and Western musical concepts. This familiarity with both musical cultural concepts formed the basis for articulating compatible elements in and extracting them from both musical cultures and for fusing these compatible elements.

Notes

1. Huang returned to China to teach composition at the Shanghai Conservatory after receiving his BA in psychology from Oberlin College and BM from Yale in 1929. Huang composed large orchestral and choral works and many lieder types of art songs.

2. Hu Shi, an influential Western-educated Chinese literary figure, observed, "our society is now undergoing a period in which its foundations are shaken." See John Israel's *Student Nationalism in China: 1927–1937* (Stanford: Stanford University Press, 1966), 253.

3. Yuan-Ren Chao's article on music, in *Symposium on Chinese Culture*, ed. Sophia Zen Chen (Shanghai: China Institute of Pacific Relations, 1931), 87, 94–95, 96.

4. Cited in John Levis's *Foundations of Chinese Musical Art* (Peiping: Henri Vetch, 1936), 200.

5. Benjamin Z. Ing, "Music Chronicle," *T'ien Hsia Monthly* IV, no. 1 (January 1937): 54.

6. Mei-Pa Chao, "The Trend of Modern Chinese Music," in *T'ien Hsia Monthly* IV, no. 3 (March 1937): 285.

7. John Levis, *Foundations of Chinese Musical Art* (Peiping: Henri Vetch, 1936), 198. Also, "The Musical Art of Ancient China," *T'ien Hsia Monthly* 1 (1935), 404–22.

8. Benjamin Z. Ing, "Review of *Foundations of Chinese Musical Art*," *T'ien Hsia Monthly* IV, no. 3 (March 1937): 317–18.

9. Levis, *Foundations of Chinese Musical Art*, 199.

10. See Yuan-Ren Chao's *Anthology of New Poetry and Songs* (Shanghai: Commercial Press, 1926), 10.

11. Mei-Pa Chao, "The Trend of Modern Chinese Music," in *T'ien Hsia Monthly* 4, no. 3 (March 1937): 280–81.

12. Chao, "The Trend of Modern Chinese Music," 280–81.

13. Chao, article on music, 94–96.

14. Alexander Tcherepnine, "Music in Modern China," *The Musical Quarterly* 21 (October 1935): 398.

15. Tcherepnine, "Music in Modern China," 399.

16. Chao, "The Trend of Modern Chinese Music," 283.

17. Chao, "The Trend of Modern Chinese Music," 281.

18. Chao, "The Trend of Modern Chinese Music," 280–81.

19. The Communists' rule also refers to their control of rural resurgent areas where the revolutionary government were set up by the Communist Party in opposition to the nationalist government during the 1930s and 1940s. Yan An, the Communists' headquarters in Shanxi province, is an example of a resurgent area.

20. Arnold Perris, "Music as Propaganda: Art at the Command of Doctrine in the People's Republic of China," *Ethnomusicology* (January 1983): 5.

21. See Bonnie S. McDougall, *Mao Zedong's "Talks at the Yan'an Conference on Literature and Art": A Translation of the 1943 Text with Commentary* (Ann Arbor: University of Michigan Center for Chinese Studies, 1980); Isabel K. F. Wong, "Geming Gequ: Songs for the Education of the Masses," in *Popular Chinese Literature and Performing Arts in the People's Republic of China, 1949–1979*, ed. Bonnie McDougall (Berkeley: University of California Press, 1984), 112–43; and Arnold Perris, "Music as Propaganda: Art at the Command of Doctrine in the People's Republic of China," *Ethnomusicology* (January 1983): 1–28.

22. The Institute of National Rites and Music was established in 1943 in Chungqing and was later moved to Nanjing. See its publications from October 1945 to April 1948 under three different names: *Liyue Zazhi* [Rites and Music Magazine] (October 1945), *Liyue Banyuekan* [The Rites and Music Semi-Monthly] (March 1947), and *Liyue* [Rites and Music] (April 1948).

23. Richard Kraus, *Pianos and Politics in China* (Oxford: Oxford University Press, 1989), 112. Kraus's use of terms "populist" versus "cosmopolitanist" to identify political factions in the conservatory appears to be imprecise.

24. See McDougall, *Mao Zedong's "Talks at the Yan'an Conference."*

25. Kraus, *Pianos and Politics in China*, 135–37.

26. Peter Chang, "Tan Dun's String Quartet Feng-Ya-Song: Some Ideological Issues," *Asian Music* XXII, no. 2 (Spring/Summer 1991): 127–58.

27. Pierre Bourdieu, *Distinction: A Social Critique of the Judgement of Taste* (Cambridge, Mass.: Harvard University Press, 1984), 4–5.

28. Revolutionary romanticism, proposed by Mao's wife Jiang Qing, stresses expressiveness; unlike Western romanticism, it serves as a complement to revolutionary

realism. The unity of the two was the sole measure for judging artistic quality during the Cultural Revolution.

29. Xi-An Li et al., "Xian Dai Yin Yue Si Chao Dui Hua Lu" [Conversation on contemporary musical concepts] *People's Music* 6 (1986): 13.

30. Henri Arvon, *Marxist Esthetics* (Ithaca, N.Y.: Cornell University Press, 1970), 13.

31. *Wenren* literally means men of letter. It also refers to the spirit of these learned men of the past that identify themselves with the *Tao* or the ultimate reality, and nature was the ideal. Some representatives of this line of Chinese intellectual tradition were the "Seven Scholars of the Bamboo Grove" and among them, the philosopher, music aesthetician, and *qin* master, Ji Kang (223–263 AD), was most well known.

32. Tcherepnine, "Music in Modern China," 395.

~

CHAPTER EIGHT

Epilogue

This is the time, then, when a true understanding of some refreshing concepts from another culture can be as revelatory as a miracle or Zen enlightenment. —Chou Wen-Chung

Wenren: The Essence of a Tradition

In many of his more recent talks concerning his approaches to composition, Chou has repeatedly acknowledged the Chinese concept of *wenren* as his cultural root and a source of his artistic inspiration. *Wenren*, in Chou's definition, means men of the arts and culture; not only is he an artist accomplished in a variety of artistic media but a scholar, philosopher, and statesman as well.[1] A *Wenren* is endowed with lofty ideas, which enables him to be observant and to create spontaneously. Chou clearly attributes his philosophical, psychological, and artistic disposition to his family tradition, the way he was brought up, and the way his father and grandfather functioned in the very essence of the word. Chou wishes to share such a cultural awakening or conscious search for cultural roots with others and has elevated his personal experience to a higher level where it can even transcend cultural boundaries. Chou believes that his own cultural tradition has much to offer to the development of a "global culture," and he has been urging Asian composers to find their true cultural roots to avoid trivializing their heritages. Today, Chou still reads, from time to time, the Chinese classic philosophical treatises to immerse himself in his rich tradition and to renew himself with the *wenren* spirit.

After his retirement from Columbia University in 1991, he began to spend more time composing to make up the time he spent in administration. Chou recalls that he was quite uneasy about spending most of his time in administration rather than composing, as his colleagues and friends had criticized him. His problem was that he was always compelled to accept new responsibilities, a trait he inherited from his forefathers. He remembers what his father had confided to him repeatedly: all his life, his father was "distracted so much, had to do so many things, that he was never able to devote himself to a single career."[2] Chou's family heritage has become ever clearer and sharply focused to him, and he begins to consider all of his life achievements as inextricably linked to this tradition.

As composer-in-residence, Chou participated in a weeklong composers' forum held at the Music Department of the University of California at San Diego from April 16 to April 21, 2001. The conference devoted one of its sessions named "Nonference: Blurring Borders" to explore issues concerning creative and intellectual engagement around the subject of the new music in Pacific Rim countries or, in other words, the creative process for musical synthesis. Chou delivered a keynote lecture "Music: What Is Its Future" on April 21, in addition to his lectures "Origins of My Musical Language" on April 19, "Varèse: Heritage and Vision" on April 16, and "Varèse: Free in the Sonic Space" on April 17. Again, Chou acknowledged the concept of *wenren* as a guiding spirit in his creative journey. This is in sharp contrast to the idea of composing for popularity and commercial success. As Chou could no longer afford further delays in completing new works, he has been working on two new works feverishly. In June 2003, he finished his second string quartet "Streams," which was an expansion of a fugue honoring Bach's *Art of Fugue* commissioned by the Brentano Quartet and is subtitled *Contrapunctus Variabilis* with four separate contrapuntal movements. The world premiere of this work took place in Boise, Idaho, on February 19, 2004. It was performed again in New York on April 23, 2004. Chou hopes to finish the next double quartet for strings (violin, viola, cello, and bass) and woodwinds (flute, clarinet, oboe, and bassoon) commissioned by Speculum Musicae and Musica Viva by 2005.

Interpreting Chou's Approach to Musical Fusion

From an aspiring young violin student to a successful composer, Chou Wen-Chung's musical journey provides a fascinating story for learning about the mechanism for cultural synthesis in music. In keeping Chou's experience in the context of twentieth-century musical development and musical synthe-

sis with some ethnomusicological insights, we can make the following observations.

Biographical Material and Analysis

Chou's upbringing reveals that Chinese composers who come from a family
with a tradition in Western sciences, literature, and music and have adopted
a partially Westernized lifestyle while retaining the Chinese intellectual tradition, can better understand both traditions at once and, as such, are better
equipped to produce a cultural fusion that goes beyond a mere blending of
discrete elements to become a sophisticated synthesis of aesthetics. This synthesis would allow the composer to communicate comfortably with audiences cross culturally.

However, this background alone is not sufficient. In Chou's case, the influence of Varèse, Webern, and Slonimsky served as stimuli and are discernible in his work. Slonimsky was the first to direct Chou to benefit from
the rich traditional Chinese musical resources and later helped him launch
his career by introducing him to Stokowski. Chou's study and research in traditional Chinese music and drama in the West provided him with not only
the knowledge of this tradition but also the Western interpretive approach
for reflections on his native tradition. Through his study with Varèse, Chou
discovered that many of Varèse's views on the nature and property of music
parallel the aesthetics of Chinese visual arts such as painting and calligraphy.

Although Chou remained critical of Cage's interpretation of the I-Ching
and his use of it as compositional matrix, by and large, he is seen as part of
the "neo-orientalistic movement" during the 1960s and 1970s among Western oriental composers in the West.

The analysis of Chou's works in this book is not geared toward devising an
inclusive and consistent method that explains only the structural relationship between musical facts but ignores human factors; indeed, it is unfit to
use a standard yardstick to identify and describe prominent musical features
because they do not exist in a vacuum but are rather associated with human
and cultural data. Furthermore, in an effort to achieve the ideal analytical
objectivity, it is difficult, perhaps even unwise, to ignore the composers' own
analytical notes alongside certain scores. All variables, whether technical,
intentional, or cultural, must be considered. Nevertheless, such an analysis
does not require a new set of analytical vocabulary; instead, the commonly
used musical vocabulary is sufficient, although its use needs to be contextu-
alized in a fuller discussion.

In the end, the analytical data reveals that Chou's musical development
in fusing Chinese and Western elements progressed from the impressionistic

use of Chinese modes, rhythmic figures, and percussion sound in his early works to abstract portrayal of Chinese subjects, ideals, and aesthetic principles through structural manipulation in his later works, which are compositions of generalized musical concepts. For example, *Cursive* (1965) is a piece about the concept of spontaneity, fluidity, shape, and controlled flow of the music based on the aesthetic principles of Chinese calligraphy. The compatible elements between Western and Chinese music found in this study are seen mainly at the conceptual level. In his later works, Chou has altogether avoided the use of pentatonic modes, a superficial link between Mahler, Debussy, and Chinese music.

Theoretical Considerations

In order to interpret Chou's approach to musical synthesis with an ethnomusicological perspective, the concepts of syncretism and culture broker can be applied, since both deal with the intercultural transfer of musical concepts or material. Although the concept of syncretism is rooted in studies of the contact between cultural groups or societies and is used primarily for groups, the data generated from these studies appear to be similar to those derived from my investigation of an individual.[3] Because foreign traits are often transferred first through the efforts of individuals acting as mediators between contacting cultures and, then, passed on to groups, the study of these mediators can add a new perspective to the concept of syncretism.

Since Waterman proposed his theory of syncretism in 1952, few studies have been done along this line. In his 1955 article, Merriam compared and contrasted Western influence on the music of Belgian Congo and the Flathead Indians. He concluded that only when there are similarities between Western and native culture is interchange of musical material likely to occur.[4]

In his 1959 paper, William Bascom pointed out that "innovations which are incompatible with the preexisting patterns are usually rejected."[5] If fusion is to be accepted, these observations require natives' cognition of certain traits in their own traditions that are comparable to that of the foreign traits or innovations.

Less emphatic in the study of cultural syncretism are the documented effects of music fusion such as jazz and Latin American dance music in the West, although the natives' reception of fusion have been mentioned briefly by Merriam.[6]

The concept of culture broker was developed initially in cultural anthropology in the early 1950s as a framework for studying the nature, function, and motivations of special groups that mediate between different social hierarchies in a society. Application of this concept in the study of music is fairly recent. It has been explored in a group of articles published in *Ethnomusicology and Modern Music History* (1991). Previously, the issue of the role of individuals as cultural mediators was neglected. Stephen Slawek's study of Ravi Shankar as a mediator demonstrates how Shankar, a performer of traditional Hindustani music and a creative modern musician, resolved the conflict between his need for preserving his Indian thoughts and for reaching a large number of Western listeners by finding new ways and techniques to express his creative thoughts. Slawek illustrates this by tracing Shankar's life experiences and influence of his innovative, eclectic teacher, Allaudin Khan. In contrast to Shankar's critics' views that he catered to Western desires in using a Western orchestra to accompany his sitar in his sitar concerto is, in Slawek's view, a way of showing the equality between Indian and Western traditions.[7] Slawek's study illustrates a strategy in confronting Western influence by reinterpreting and emphasizing the compatibility between the traditions of the cultural mediator and the West in order to make them compatible for survival of the native tradition. This strategy is also observable in Chou's case.

Victoria Lindsay Levine also noted such a strategy in her study of several intertribal brokers' contributions for bringing about a pantribal music practice among Indian tribes in Louisiana and eastern Texas. Levine points out that "Louisiana pantribalism developed as an accommodation to rapid changes in demographic and socioeconomic domains [and] it emerged gradually as the traditionalists among the tribes redefined themselves and reinterpreted their cultures in order to survive."[8] Carol Babiracki's study of tribe-caste interaction in Chotanagpur, northeast India, accounts for the effect of cultural brokers, the Mundas, in fusing influence from foreign culture and finding acceptance of their repertories in several linguistically distinct communities and accounts for the resilience of a musical culture in which innovations of traditional repertories does not weaken survival of tradition; instead, it strengthens survival.[9]

The concept of reinterpretation of conflicting ideas and practices serving as an active agent for change is illustrated in William Noll's study in which Polish and Ukrainian regional practices are mediated and fused with national music though the agent of musical institutions.[10]

The purpose for the study of acculturation is to reveal several factors in the process from initial contact to the final product of synthesis. Among these factors, reinterpretation constitutes an important link between natives' response to Western influence and their selection of compatible materials for synthesis. Reinterpretation is carried out by cultural mediators who are the individual carriers of their own tradition and, at the same time, "insiders" of the foreign culture. These individuals are motivated or inspired to create cultural synthesis either by conscious decision to preserve their native tradition in transformed, modern forms and to contend that their tradition is on equal terms with that of their Western counterpart, or simply by the creative urge to make something original. In Chou's case, we see both of these motivations as articulated by Chou himself in his program notes, articles, and speeches.

The idea of nationalism—which is associated with the concept of ethnicity and power relations seen in the supply and demand for musical and cultural products in a market—is also an important motivating factor for Chou's musical synthesis. Chou's success in gaining a share in the Western musical market boosts prestige of ancient Chinese musical tradition and proves that this tradition, though mixed with Western technology, cannot be weakened and is capable of serving the contemporary Chinese as well as Westerners.

Chou's ethnic pride is clearly marked by his ability to control Chinese musical resources; gaining such control was viewed as desirable by many Western composers in their attempts to incorporate non-Western material in their compositions. However, as to the definition of Chou's ethnicity, the Chinese tend to emphasize his citizenship, the environs of his major activities, and the major venue and audience of his music. On the other hand, Westerners tend to emphasize his Chinese cultural background, the Chinese material used in his works, and his Chinese compositional concepts.

Another motivating factor for Chou's reinterpreting Western concepts in Chinese terms is the dynamics between the concepts of Westernization and modernization. Both of these abstractions are seen as inspirational sources for the composer to create something new, something modern, and perhaps something Western. In contrast to the notion that these two abstractions are tinged with an unstated bias that either modern or Western is better than the native or old tradition, Chou treated tradition and modernity on equal terms. Chou does not despise his tradition, nor does he reject Western tradition. Instead, he integrates these two traditions to advance the cause for modern music. Here, modernization is viewed as the goal, and Westernization is only a transient stage in the course of modern Chinese musical development.

Through the study of Chou's musical development, we see a pattern of musical acculturation, which, as Herskovits suggested, has historical dimensions.[11] This pattern encompasses a set of dyads: contact-response, motivation-action, mediation–choices of materials, and reinterpretation-synthesis.

In an annual report to the Bureau of American Ethnology, W. J. Powell, a pioneer in the study of acculturation, put forward a hypothesis for predicting regularities in acculturation process. Powell writes, "The process of culture . . . is by invention and acculturation. The invention is at first individual, but when an invention is accepted and used by others it is accultural."[12] The adaptation of Chou's approach has been overtly observable in the post–Cultural Revolution generation of composers in China during the 1980s. Up to now, the impact of such an approach is still strongly felt, as many of these Chinese composers have come to the United States where they actively promote neotraditional Chinese composition style, that is, the fusion between Chinese ideas and contemporary Western idioms.[13]

Another applicable theoretical model is Edward Bruner's discussion of the anthropology of experience, which seems to be relevant for interpreting the process of musical synthesis. Bruner sees expression as a cultural text arising from experience, which is defined as a person's conscious reception of events or reflections of actions and feelings.[14] As the expression or reflection of an experience, a musical work might be identity in one or both cultures. This experience is usually shared with others or is interpreted through expression.[15] In Chou's case, musical composition served as an outlet to express his cross-cultural experiences.

Through investigating Chou's cross-cultural experience and his musical development, we can see some correlations: conflict-reconciliation, mediation–choices of materials, and reinterpretation-synthesis. In synthesizing two different musical cultures, the most original contribution made by Chou is the union of the two at the conceptual level. This choice was made rationally, and specific concepts on the nature and property of musical sound were discovered through reliving the cultural experience and reinterpretation of previous experiences.

Chou's musical development clearly shows his initial problem with a naive idea of mixing Chinese and Western materials, resulting in his crisis of self-identification, that is, inadequacy of knowing about Chinese culture as a Chinese person, and his efforts in subsequent years to reconcile these elements in different ways in his later works. As he gained new experiences, he grew more articulate about what he had experienced. He began to share these experiences with other Asian composers who were inspired to gain recognition both in their native countries and in the West. Here we have a good example of one person's personal experience playing a significant role in influencing changes in the musical style of his native culture.

Musical Fusion as a Process

In considering Chou's musical synthesis as a process, four areas are identified: (1) the learning process, in the form of assimilation and adaptation of foreign elements; (2) the evaluative process, in the form of reflection on one's own tradition; (3) the selection and fusion process, in the forms of synthesis of musical and ideological concepts and associated techniques; and (4) the educating, propagating, and influencing process, in the form of dissemination of the synthesis.

Assimilation and Adaptation

As a youth, Chou was exposed to Chinese classical literature as well as to the Western way of living (having a family car and a collection of Western musical phonodisks, observing Western holidays such as Christmas, and so forth). Chou studied violin, Western sciences, and literature before coming to the United States. The idea of traveling to the West to seek the best teacher for advancing his education in Western music was firmly rooted in his mind when he was only a teenager.

On Chou's part, his curiosity and interest in learning more about Western culture and his wish to become a Western musician appears to be a major motivating factor for his assimilation in Western culture. His decision to give up a career in architecture and turn to the field of music—although seemingly impractical—was not made irrationally. Once Chou arrived in the United States and discovered that he was able to make a decision for himself, he chose music, a subject that was attractive to him all along.

Chou's assimilation into Western culture, especially music, did not happen suddenly, or happened only after he arrived in the United States. The nineteenth-century romantic notion of becoming an artist was part of Chou's education before his arrival in the United States. His interest and willingness to accept ideals from reading original English versions of Western literary works, especially those of Goethe, aligned him with the West. The assimilation process can be traced to Chou's family since Chou's father and grandfather were exponents of Western medical technology and economic theory, and the effect of such an influence on Chou emerged during his formative years. Unlike most Chinese who usually experience "culture shock" when arriving in the United States, Chou had no problem in settling in the melting pot.

Reflections on Chinese Tradition

Chou's first experience in thinking seriously about questions of what is real Chinese music and how to create a style that reflects true Chinese cultural legacy occurred when his teacher Slonimsky asked him about his knowledge of traditional Chinese music and suggested that he get away from the trite styles associated with Chinese melody plus Western harmony by creating his own personal style. Not knowing much about Chinese music, he was compelled to delve into the study of tradition and music.

Chou spent a great deal of time in research of traditional Chinese music and drama and so was able to contemplate and grasp the underlying aesthetics of this music. Chou's earlier training in and familiarity with Chinese calligraphy and poetry helped him to discover the general aesthetic ideal for the Chinese literati. Chou pursued this ideal in his creative career as a composer and eventually aligned himself with the Chinese Taoist philosophy espoused in the I-Ching. This discovery profoundly influenced his views on the nature of musical organization with a metaphysical basis.

Synthesis of Concepts and Associated Techniques
From trying to write a "Chinese-flavored" fugue for Martinue at Mannes School of Music in New York to evoking the "oriental mood" through imageries in his works of the 1950s and to the interest in discovering a theory based on Chinese views of the universe as a guide for composing, Chou's experimentation with Chinese and Western musical fusion encompass a wide range of elements.

Among these elements, instead of borrowing Chinese melody, the basic tenets, perceptions, and attitude toward artistic creation were Chou's points of departure. The compatible Chinese and Western elements are observable in Chou's early works as the impressionistic uses of images in painting to evoke poetic moods in both Chinese and Western listeners.

In his works of the late 1950s and 1960s, Chou combined Varèse's concept of sound as moving mass, which, like a river, ebbs and flows, with the aesthetic ideal of achieving spontaneous control of ink flow in Chinese calligraphy.[16]

Besides the analogies of sound as river and flowing ink, for Varèse and Chou, musical form is seen as the result of registral range, timbral contrasts, and rhythmic activities—in other words, the result of process. The elevation of the importance of musical timbre in Chou's works was adopted from the aesthetic ideal of the Chinese *qin* music and parallels Varèse's concern for timbral contrast in the flowing sound masses and, even more, for sonority for its own sake. Varèse's ideas of sound as living matter and of musical space as unbounded were reinterpreted by Chou through his study and understanding of the Chinese *qin* music for which subtle timbral changes are the basic requirement for achieving aesthetic and sound ideals by the performer.[17]

In his formative years in Paris, Varèse showed an interest in aesthetics of the visual and literary arts, which, in terms of redefining the nature and the purpose of art, were more progressive than their musical counterparts. From his association with cubist painters (especially Picasso), Varèse became acquainted with cubist principles, such as spatial thinking, the avoidance of repetition, recognizing color contrast as an important structural element, simultaneous juxtaposition of different elements, and geometrical and multiple views of an object, and successfully applied these principles in his musical compositions.

Varèse was not uncritical of cubism. While avoiding the cubist motionless objectified and dispassionate style, Varèse absorbed and synthesized into his aesthetic views on music as a whole the futurist concern for motion and Kandinsky's concept that rules must give way to internal expressive needs.[18]

As old rules were rejected, Varèse had to think hard to find reasoned and conscious solutions. Varèse's experience in finding solutions for compositional problems resulting from his eclectic aesthetic principles was passed on to Chou, who took Varèse's advice and found parallels between Varèse's and his perception in Chinese aesthetics. Chou's study with Varèse was beneficial in that Chou did not imitate his teacher technically. Instead, he was forced to think and find solutions for himself and the different type of material he was working with. Through Varèse, Chou discovered parallels between Varèse's alliance with the aesthetics of visual arts and his subsequent alliance with the principles of Chinese visual arts.

With Varèse as his role model, Chou was able to selectively adopt aesthetic principles from Chinese visual arts, literary arts, and classical writings, such as the I-Ching, in his compositions. Chou's analogy of music as a painter's canvass on which a composer creates images with tonal brushwork echoes the Varèsean concept of fluidity and spatial and timbral aspects of music.

In his later works, beginning with his works of the late 1960s, Chou became more interested in solving philosophical issues such as organizational principles for pitch and rhythmic materials. His interpretation of the I-Ching challenges Cage's use of the same work for formulating the theory of indeterminacy, and it was from the I-Ching that Chou developed his so-called variable modes, that is, dividing an octave into three segments of minor thirds with a moveable minor second within each minor third. "Reflective principle" was another of Chou's I-Ching derivatives; it refers to the reflection between ascending and descending and between forward and backward rotations of intervals in a selected series of pitches or modes and, as such, parallels but reinterprets the structural principles in Western serial music. The compatibility between Chinese and Western concepts on different compositional issues is established by the selection process and by reinterpretation.[19] Chou's understanding of the aesthetics of both cultures was needed to create the musical fusion and also his realization of these aesthetic views in his composition process (acting as a cultural broker) make the fusion accessible to both Chinese and Western audiences.

Dissemination of the Synthesis
In 1977, Chou set Beijing Central Conservatory on fire by openly challenging for the first time the stereotypical Chinese-melody-plus-Western-nineteenth-century-harmony approach, which had been promoted by the Communist Party since the establishment of the People's Republic in 1949. The fact that mainland "new wave" composers responded to contemporary Western music much more positively and quickly than their colleagues in Taiwan and Hong Kong is the natural result of thirty years of repression and isolation from the West. A culture, which had previous contact with the West, is likely to respond to new influences from the West more positively and quickly after a period of isolation than its counterparts who maintained such contact without interruption.

Some Issues for Further Research and Discussion
In his works of the 1960s, Chou abandoned the direct use of Chinese melody and the experimentation of Chinese musical sound ideal with Western instruments and replaced them with his interpretation of the Varèsean concept of sound with aesthetic principles of Chinese visual, literary, and musical arts. The difficulty in judging how the actual sound of these abstract compositions relates to the aesthetic ideals behind them poses the question of cross-cultural perception and of taste associated with certain social strata. Without program notes a work is judged only by its sound; therefore, it would be hard for any Western listener to perceive it as being Chinese. Similarly, a Chinese person would also find this sound incomprehensible. After his early experimentation with Chinese materials in his works such as *Landscapes* (1949) through *Yu ko* (1965), Chou moved away from recreating oriental sound. Perhaps avoiding neo-orientalism is a way for Chou to go beyond the quagmire of being entangled in conflict between a composer's ethnicity and the perception of his compositions. Chou himself stated in the program notes for *Windswept Peaks* (1989–1990) that "despite these influences [Chinese aesthetics], there is no intention to make the music 'appear' to be 'oriental' or Chinese."[20]

The next problem is the aptness for comparing Chou and Ravi Shankar as culture brokers. Unlike Shankar, who trained at an early age with traditional Hindustani music in his native land, Chou acquired the knowledge of traditional Chinese music mainly through study and research as a university student in the West. Viewing Shankar as a carrier of his native musical tradition is unquestionable. However, because Chou neither trained in traditional Chinese music nor used Chinese musical material in his later works, his ethnic and musical identity became difficult to define without the aid of program notes. The fact that Chou is considered an outsider by both the Chinese and

Westerners shows the disparity between Chou's effort in musical bilingual communication and the difficulty to reach these audiences. This questions the validity of interpreting Chou's musical synthesis as the synthesis of conceptions, since the gap between our perception of actual sound and of the idea behind it can hardly be bridged. Further, unlike Shankar, Chou sees his approach in making conceptual fusions as the answer to the call for confluence of world music.[21] Perhaps, the differences between Chou's and Shankar's synthesis is the degree of sophistication.

Receptions of the Fusion
For Western audiences, the serene mood and vivid shimmering colors in Chou's works, in contrast with their powerfully dissonant contemporary works, offer an exotic escape, and in fact, most Western music critics have perceived Chou's works as exotic objects, such as Chinese silk paintings and porcelains. Although Chou's influence on Western composers remains largely in academic institutions and its long-term effects still remain to be seen, his approach to the synthesis of Western and Chinese music has stimulated creative thinking in a generation of young Chinese composers, known as the "new wave" composers. Chou's approach has been widely imitated in China; it has consequently stirred up debates between conservatives and new wave composers over various sociocultural and political issues arising from abandonment of the familiar Chinese-melody-plus-Western-harmony style. Despite split opinions, Chou's works have been favorably received in mainland China, Taiwan, and Hong Kong. Chou's works were introduced in China when the country was trying to reopen its door to the West, after a period of isolation, and to become a modernized nation. Through the nationalistic drive for modernization, the Chinese found that Chou's techniques were modern and the thought behind his composition was archetypically Chinese. Thus, Chou's works acquired new symbolic meaning in his native land. This reintroduction of native values in their place of origin (after being discovered in foreign countries) and then expressed by foreign instruments and techniques, parallels the introduction of African-American music in Africa.[22]

As a culture broker, Chou's motivation to make fusions possible, in addition to artistic and creative needs, suggests a desire to preserve the tradition in a new guise that would be communicable for members of both donor and receiving cultures. A musical fusion is a two-way street in which members of both cultures are motivated to make fusion with materials from the other culture. Musical fusions can also generate interest in a cultural group to create new fusions. In fact, Chou's experience indicates that the Western impact on other musical cultures caused repercussions on Western music itself.

In conclusion, Chou's musical development reflects social and artistic changes and general attitudes in the West and, in the meantime, shows how these changes affected Chou's choices in selecting conceptual material for his cultural musical synthesis. Western composers' interests in non-Western music and philosophy played an important role in attracting audiences to the music by contemporary Western composers with non-Western backgrounds. There was also an interest in the development of contemporary music in the West among Asian composers with training in Western music and among a younger generation of intellectuals in Asia, especially in post–Cultural Revolution China. Chou's style channeled mutual interests. By promoting exchange of ideas between two cultures, Chou functions as a cultural broker, whose own experience in making musical fusion has political and ideological implications so that many young Asian composers are inspired in an effort to gain recognition both in their native countries and in the West.

Chou's original and personal approach to composition and his writings advocating musical confluence between East and West have increased awareness of the possible ways to explore new resources and avenues in contemporary compositions among Western composers in the West and have rekindled the interest in oriental mysticism in Western audiences of contemporary music. A pioneer in initiating and advocating conceptual fusion, Chou witnessed the fruition of his own cultural musical synthesis and will continue to see transformation or even new growth of traditional Chinese music for years to come.

Notes

1. Wen-Chung Chou, "*Wenren* and Culture," in *Locating East Asia in Western Art Music* (Middletown, Conn.: Wesleyan University Press), 213–4.

2. Wen-Chung Chou, "Sights and Sounds," www.chouwenchung.org, 3.

3. For the concept of cultural process, which deals with the transfer of foreign traits from individuals to the receiving groups or societies, see W. J. Powell, "Report of the Director," 19th Annual Report for 1897–1898 (Washington, D.C.: Bureau of American Ethnology, 1900), xxi.

4. Alan Merriam, "The Use of Music in the Study of a Problem of Acculturation," *American Anthropologist* 57 (1955): 28–34.

5. William Bascom, "The Main Problems of Stability and Change in Tradition," *JIFMC* 11 (1959): 11.

6. Merriam, "The Use of Music," 32.

7. Stephen Slawek, "Ravi Shankar as Mediator between a Traditional Music and Modernity," in *Ethnomusicology and Modern Music History*, ed. Stephen Blum, Philip Bohlman, and Daniel Neuman (Urbana: University of Illinois Press, 1991), 178.

8. Victoria Lindsay Levine, "Arzelie Langley and a Lost Pantribal Tradition," in *Ethnomusicology and Modern History*, ed. Stephen Blum, Philip Bohlman, and Daniel Neuman (Urbana: University of Illinois Press, 1991), 194.

9. Carol Babiracki, "Music and the History of Tribe-Caste Interaction in Chotanagpur," in *Ethnomusicology and Modern History*, ed. Stephen Blum, Philip Bohlman, and Daniel Neuman (Urbana: University of Illinois Press, 1991), 227.

10. William Noll, "Music Institutions and National Consciousness among Polish and Ukrainian Peasants," in *Ethnomusicology and Modern Music History*, ed. Stephen Blum, Philip Bohlman, and Daniel Neuman (Urbana: University of Illinois Press,1991), 155–56.

11. Melville Herskovits, *Acculturation: The Study of Cultural Contact*, reprint of 1938 edition (Gloucester, Mass.: Peters Smith, 1958), 15.

12. Powell, "Report of the Director," xxi.

13. These Chinese composers, together with several conservatory-trained, young Chinese musicians of traditional music, have formed an organization, Music from China, in New York. New works are often premiered at Merkin Concert Hall in New York, and Chinese composers from Taiwan and Hong Kong have had their works performed there.

14. Edward Bruner, "Experience and Its Expressions," in *The Anthropology of Experience*, ed. Victor Turner and Edward Bruner (Urbana: University of Illinois Press, 1986): 4–5.

15. Peter Chang, "Chou Wen-Chung's Cross-Cultural Experience and His Musical Synthesis: The Concept of Syncretism Revisited," *Asian Music* 32, no. 2 (Spring/Summer 2001), 94.

16. Edgard Varèse, "The Liberation of Sound," in *Contemporary Composers on Contemporary Music*, ed. Elliot Schwartz and Barney Childs (New York: Da Capo Press, 1978), 197.

17. Wen-Chung Chou, "Single Tones as Musical Entities: An Approach to Structured Deviations in Tonal Characteristics," *American Society of University Composers Proceedings* III (August 1968): 88–89.

18. Wassily Kandinsky, "Reminiscences," in *Modern Artists on Modern Art: Ten Unabridged Essays*, ed. Robert Herbert (Englewood Cliffs, N.J.: Prentice-Hall, 1964), 35.

19. Wen-Chung Chou, "East and West, Old and New," *Asian Music* 1 (1968–1969): 19.

20. Wen-Chung Chou, program notes on *Windswept Peaks*.

21. Wen-Chung Chou, "Asian and Western Music: Influence or Confluence?" *Asian Culture Quarterly* (Winter 1977): 60–66; also his "Asian Concepts and Twentieth-Century Western Composers," *The Musical Quarterly* 57, no. 2 (April 1971): 211–29.

22. Bruno Nettl, *The Study of Ethnomusicology: Twenty-nine Issues and Concepts* (Urbana: University of Illinois Press, 1983), 352.

~

List of Chou Wen-Chung's Works

Date of Composition	Title	Publisher	Date of Premiere
1. 1949	*Landscapes* (orchestra) 2 flutes, piccolo, 2 oboes, English horn, 2-0-2-0, timpani, percussion, harp, and strings	CFP	11/19/53 San Francisco San Francisco Symphony orchestra, Stokowski conductor (7'30")
2. 1950	*Three Folk Songs* (Harp/Flute)	CFP	1/19/52 New York Lucile Lawrence, harp Thomas Piacenza Benton, flute (4')
3. 1950	*Two Chinese Folk Songs* (harp solo, arrangement from *Three Folk Songs*)	CFP	
4. 1951	*Suite for Harp and Wind Quintet* (Harp/wind quintet)	CFP	2/22/52 New York Marietta Bitter, harp Metropolitan Wind Quintet (7')
5. 1951/1952	*Seven Poems of Tang Dynasty* (high voice/instrumental ensemble) Solo high voice, 2 tenors, flute, oboe, clarinet, bassoon, horn, trumpet, trombone 2 percussion, piano	TP	3/16/52 New York Int'l Society for Contemporary Music, John Clark, conductor (11')
6. 1952/1953	*All in the Spring Wind* (orchestra) 2 flutes, piccolo, 2 oboes, English horn, 2 B-flat clarinets, bass clarinet, bassoon, double bassoon, 2-2-2-1, timpani, 3 percussion, celesta (piano), harp, and strings	CFP	12/7/61 Louisville, KY Louisville Orchestra, Robert Whitney conductor (8')

No.	Year	Title	Publisher	Premiere
7.	1954	*And the Fallen Petals* (orchestra) 2 flutes/piccolos, 2 oboes, English horn, 2 B-flat clarinets, bass clarinet, 2 bassoons, 4-2-3-1, timpani, percussion, celesta, harp, and strings	CFP	2/9/55 Louisville, KY Louisville Orchestra Robert Whitney conductor (10')
8.	1956	*In the Mode of Shang* (orchestra) piccolo, flute, oboe, English horn, clarinet in B, bass clarinet, bassoon, horn, tuba, percussion, celesta, harp, and strings	unpublished	2/2/57 New York Composers Forum, Carlos Surinach, conductor (9')
9.	1957	*Two Miniatures from T'ang Dynasty* (chamber ensemble) 2 flutes, clarinet in B, horn, percussion, harp, piano, violin, viola, and cello	ACA	4/30/57 New York Sarah Lawrence College Orchestra, Meyer Kupferman, conductor (5')
10.	1957	*The Willows Are New* (piano)	CFP	2/2/58 New York Don Shapiro Piano (7')
11.	1958	*To A Wayfarer* (clarinet, strings, harp, percussion)	ACA	12/3/58 New York The Contemporary Society, Stokowski, conductor (9')
12.	1958	*Soliloquy of a Bhiksuni* (trumpet with brass/percussion)	CFP	12/18/58 Urbana, IL University of Illinois Wind Ensemble, Richard Tolley, trumpet, Robert Gray, conductor (5')

(continued)

Date of Composition	Title	Publisher	Date of Premiere
13. 1958/1959	*Poems of White Stone* (mixed chorus/chamber ensemble)	ACA	3/14/59 Urbana, IL Merce Cunningham and Dance Company, John Garvey, conductor (16')
14. 1960/1961	*Metaphors* (wind orchestra)	CFP	6/25/61 Pittsburgh, PA American Wind Symphony Orchestra Robert Austin Boudreau, conductor (16')
15. 1963	*Cursive* (flute/piano)	CFP	1/13/64 New York Harvey Sollberger, flutist, Charles Wuorinen, pianist (13')
16. 1964	*The Dark and the Light* (piano/3 percussion/strings)	unpublished	3/8/64 New York Yi-An Chang, piano, Arthur Bloom, conductor (8')
17. 1964	*Riding the Wind* (wind orchestra) 2 piccolos, 4 flutes, 4 oboes, E-flat clarinet, 3 B-flat clarinets, bass clarinet, 4 bassoons, contra bassoon, 4 horns, 4 trumpets, 4 trombones, tuba, 6 percussion, piano	CFP	6/14/64 Pittsburgh, PA American Wind Symphony Orchestra Robert Austin Boudreau, conductor (7')
18. 1965	*Yu ko* (9 players) violin, alto flute, English horn, bass clarinet, 2 trombones, piano, 2 percussion	CFP	4/19/65 New York Group for Contemporary Music at Columbia University Harvey Sollberger, conductor (7')

No.	Year	Title (instrumentation)		Premiere
19.	1966	*Pien* (chamber concerto for winds, percussion, and piano) flute, alto flute, English horn, bassoon, Alto clarinet, horn, D trumpet, B-flat trumpet, tenor trombone, bass trombone, 4 percussion, piano	CFP	1/9/67 New York Group for Contemporary Music at Columbia University Harvey Sollberger, conductor, Charles Wuorinen, piano (12'30")
20.	1969	*Yun* (winds, 2 pianos, percussion) flute, clarinet, bassoon, horn, trumpet, trombone, 2 percussion, 2 pianos	CFP	2/6/69 River Falls, WI Wisconsin State University, River Falls, Donald Nitz, conductor (9')
21.	1986	*Beijing in the Mist* (winds, percussion, electric guitar, bass, and piano)	CFP	6/2/86 New York National Dance Institute, Lee Norris, conductor
22.	1989	*Echoes from the Gorge* (quartet for percussion)	CFP	4/27/89 New York The New Music Consort, Brad Lubman, conductor (17')
23.	1989/1990	*Windswept Peaks* (double duet for violin, cello, B-flat clarinet, and piano)	CFP	7/13/90 Brunswick, Maine The Aeolian Chamber Players, Bowdoin College, Lewis Kaplan, artistic director (18')
24.	1992	*Concerto for Violoncello and Orchestra*	CFP	1/10/93 New York American Composers Orchestra, Janos Starker, cello, Dennis Russell Davies, conductor (31')

(continued)

Date of Composition	Title	Publisher	Date of Premiere
25. 1996	String Quartet (*Clouds*)	CFP	12/1/1996 New York The Brentano String Quartet (35')
26. 2003	String Quartet No. 2 (*Stream*)		

Incidental Works:

27. 1957	Valediction piano		
28. 1960	Hong Kong 2 flutes, piccolo, oboe, E-flat clarinet, 2-0-3-1, timpani, and 3 percussion		Music for TV program (40')
29. 1961	Tomorrow		Music for documentary film
30. 1962	White Paper of Red China		Music for documentary film
31. 1964	A Day at the Fair Chamber ensemble		Music for documentary film
32. 1966	Red China: Year of the Gun?		Music for documentary film
33. 1968	Ceremonial 3 trumpet, 3trombones		

CFP=C. F. Peters Corp., 373 Park Ave. S., NY.
ACA=Composers Facsimile Edition, American Composers Alliance, 2121 Broadway, NY.
TP=New Music Edition, c/o Theodor Presser Company, Bryn Mawr, PA.

~

Discography of Chou Wen-Chung's Works

Date of Composition	Title	Recording Company (labels) and Performers
1. 1949	*Landscapes*	Composers Recording Inc. (CRI-122) (Thor Johnson/the Peninsula Festival Orchestra). Also available on CD (CRI-691, track 5)
2. 1950	*Three Folk Songs*	On tape (Lucile Lawrence, harp, Thomas Piacenza Benton, flute)
3. 1950	*Two Chinese Folk Songs*	
4. 1951	Suite for Harp and Wind Quintet	New World Records (NW 237) (Marietta Bitter, harp, Metropolitan Wind Quintet). Also available on CDs (NW-80237, track 3; and Albany Records-155, track 15)
5. 1951/1952	*Seven Poems of T'ang Dynasty*	
6. 1952/1953	*All in the Spring Wind*	First Edition Records (LOU 614) (Robert Whitney/Louisville Orchestra)
7. 1954	*And the Fallen Petals*	First Edition Records (LOU 56-1) (Robert Whitney/Louisville Orchestra)
8. 1956	*In the Mode of Shang*	

(continued)

Date of Composition	Title	Recording Company (labels) and Performers
9. 1957	Two Miniatures from T'ang Dynasty	
10. 1957	The Willows Are New	(CRI SD 251) (Harvey Sollberger/Contemporary Music Group). Also available on CDs (CRI 691, track 4; Classico-270, track 2; and Thorofon-2034, track 12)
11. 1958	To A Wayfarer	
12. 1958	Soliloquy of a Bhiksuni	Crystal Records (S 361) (University of Illinois Wind Ensemble, Richard Tolley, trumpet, Robert Gray, conductor). Also available on CD (Crystal Records-667, track 5)
13. 1958/1959	Poems of White Stone	On tape (chorus and orchestra from the School of Music, University of Illinois, John Garvey, conductor)
14. 1960/1961	Metaphors	On tape
15. 1963	Cursive	(CRI SD 251). Also available on CD (CRI-691, track 3)
16. 1964	The Dark and the Light	
17. 1964	Riding the Wind	
18. 1965	Yu ko	(CRI SD 251). Also available on CDs (CRI-691, track 2; and Albany Records-155, track 13)
19. 1966	Pien	(CRI SD 251). Also available on CD (CRI-691, track 1)
20. 1969	Yun	CD available (Albany Records-155, track 14)
21. 1986	Beijing in the Mist	
22. 1989	Echoes from the Gorge	On tape (the New Music Consort, Brad Lubman, conductor). Also available on CD (Albany Records-155, tracks 1–12)
23. 1989/1990	Windswept Peaks	On tape (the Aeolian Chamber Players, Bowdoin College, Lewis Kaplan, artistic director). Also available on CD (Albany Records-155, track 16)

Date of Composition	Title	Recording Company (labels) and Performers
24. 1992	Concerto for Violin Cello and Orchestra	On tape by AKY (American Composers Orchestra, Janos Starker, soloist, Russell Davis, conductor)
25. 1996	String Quartet (*Clouds*)	On tape by the Chamber Music Society of Lincoln Center, N.Y. (premiere performance by the Brentano String Quartet), unpublished CD also available.
26. 2003	String Quartet No. 2 (*Streams*)	

AKY 1600 Broadway, NY, (212) 757-1401.

The Chamber Music Society of Lincoln Center, 70 Lincoln Center Plaza, New York, NY 10023.

Tapes and unpublished CD recordings of other works may be procured, subject to availability, from the Center for U.S.-China Arts Exchange, Columbia University, 423 W. 118th Sr. #1-E, New York, NY 10027

APPENDIX C

~

Performance Chronology of *And the Fallen Petals*

Date	Place	Orchestra	Conductor
1. February 9, 1955	Louisville, KY	Louisville Orchestra	Robert Whitney
2. October 8, 1955	Louisville, KY	Louisville Orchestra	Robert Whitney
3. March 25, 1958	Hamburg, Germany	North German Radio Orchestra	F. Travis
4. November 10, 1959	Tokyo, Japan	Japan Philharmonic Symphony Orchestra	Akeo Watanabe
5. December 3–4, 1959	San Francisco, CA	San Francisco Symphony Orchestra	Eugene Jorda
6. February 29, 1960	Philadelphia, PA	Philadelphia Orchestra	William Smith
7. June 1, 1960	Berlin, Germany	Berlin Philharmonic Orchestra	John Bitter
8. June 6?, 1960	Bielefeld, Germany	Berlin Philharmonic Orchestra	John Bitter
9. January 5–8, 1961	New York	New York Philharmonic Orchestra	S. Skrowaczewski
10. January 17, 1961	Chattanooga, TN	Chattanooga Symphony	Julius Hegyi
11. December 9, 1961	Minneapolis, MN	Minneapolis Symphony	S. Skrowaczewski
12. January 7, 1961	Cincinnati, OH	Cincinnati Symphony	Max Rudolph
13. March 8, 1962	Urbana, IL	Minneapolis Symphony	S. Skrowaczewski
14. November 15–18, 1962	Goeteborg, Sweden	Goeteborg Orchestra	Sten Frykberg
15. March 22, 1963	Paris, France	Orchestraestre Nationale	
16. January 17, 1982	Beijing, China	Central Philharmonic Orchestra	David Gilbert
17. February 24, 1984	Troy, NY	Albany Symphony	
18. February 25, 1984	Albany, NY	Albany Symphony	
19. July 13, 1991	Beijing, China	Central Philharmonic Orchestra	Hu Yong-Yan

Bibliography

Amnon, Shiloah, and Erik Cohen. "The Dynamics of Change in Jewish Oriental Ethnic Music in Israel." *Ethnomusicology* 27 (1983): 227–52.

An, Chen. "Between East and West." *Huaqiao Ribao* [*The Overseas Chinese Daily*], October 28, and October 29, 1987.

Anonymous. "Shih-nien-lai Wo-Kuo Yin-Yueh Shi-Yeh Te Fa-Chan [Our Country's Musical Development in the Past Ten Years 1949–1959]." *Renmin Yinyue* [*Peoples' Music*] 10/11 (1959): 32–35.

Archer, William Kay, ed. *The Presentation of Traditional Forms of the Learned and Popular Music of the Orient and the Occident.* Urbana: University of Illinois Institute of Communications Research, 1964.

Archibald, Bruce. Record review of Chou Wen-Chung's *Pien, Yu ko, Cursive,* and *The Willows Are New* issued by Composers Recordings CRI 251. *The Musical Quarterly* 58 (1972): 333–35.

Bascom, William. "The Main Problems of Stability and Change in Tradition." *JIFMC* 11 (1959): 7–12.

Baumann, Max Peter, ed. *Intercultural Music Studies Volume 2, Music in the Dialogue of Cultures: Traditional Music and Cultural Policy.* Berlin: Florian Boetzel Edition, 1990.

Bernard, Jonathan. "A Theory of Pitch and Register for the Music of Edgard Varèse." Ph.D. diss., Yale University, 1977.

———.*The Music of Edgard Varèse.* New Haven, Conn.: Yale University Press, 1987.

Bernstein, Thomas. *Up to the Mountains and Down to the Villages: The Transfer of Youth from Urban to Rural China.* New Haven, Conn.: Yale University Press, 1997.

Bi, Xi-Zhou. "Zhou Wen-Zhong." *The Esquire* (February 1989).

Blum, Stephen. "Analysis of Musical Style." In *Ethnomusicology: An Introduction*, ed. Helen Myers, 165–218. New York: Norton, 1992.

Blum, Stephen, Philip V. Bohlman, and Daniel Neuman, eds. *Ethnomusicology and Modern Music History*. Urbana: University of Illinois Press, 1991.

Boilès, Charles Lafayette. "A Paradigmatic Test of Acculturation." In *Cross-Cultural Perspectives on Music*, ed. Robert Falck and Timothy Rice, 53–78. Toronto: University of Toronto Press, 1982.

Boretz, Benjamin. "Meta-Variations: Studies in the Foundations of Musical Thought." *Perspectives of New Music* (PNM) 8, no. 1 (1969): 1–74.

Boretz, Benjamin, and Edward T. Cone, eds. *Perspectives on Contemporary Music Theory*. New York: Norton, 1972.

Brook, Tim. "The Revival of China's Musical Culture." *China Quarterly* 77 (March 1979): 113–21.

Bruner, Edward, and Victor Turner, eds. *The Anthropology of Experience*. Urbana: University of Illinois Press, 1986.

Burwasser, Peter. Record review of Chou Wen-Chung's *Echoes from the Gorge*, *Yu ko*, Suite for Harp and Wind Quintet, and *Windswept Peaks* issued on CD by Albany Troy. *Fanfare* (September/October 1995): 177.

Cage, John. "The East in the West." *Modern Music* 23, no. 2 (1946): 111–15.

———. *Silence*. Middletown, Conn.: Wesleyan University Press, 1961.

———. *A Year From Monday*. Middletown, Conn.: Wesleyan University Press, 1967.

Cassidy, Claudia. "Some Marvelous Mahler on a Night of Oriental Overtones." *Chicago Daily Tribune*, Friday, November 6, 1959, part II, 11.

Central Conservatory of Music. Meiji Yinyuejia Zhou Wen-Zhong Xiansheng Jieshao Meiguo Yin yue Xianzhuang [Chou Wen-Chung, the Musician with American Nationality, Introduces Current Musical Condition in the United States]. Beijing: Central Conservatory of Music, 1977.

Chan, Wing-Chi. "A Study of Chou Wen-Chung." MM thesis, Northern Illinois University, 1981.

Chang, Peter. "Tan Dun's String Quartet 'Feng-Ya-Song': Some Ideological Issues." *Asian Music* 22, no. 2 (Spring/Summer 1991): 127–58.

———. Interview with Chou Wen-Chung, New York (unpublished), November 8, 1991.

———. "Chou Wen-Chung and His Music: A Musical and Biographical Profile of Cultural Synthesis." Ph.D. diss., University of Illinois, Urbana, Champaign, 1995.

———. "Chou Wen-Chung's Cross-Cultural Experience and His Musical Synthesis: The Concept of Syncretism Revisited." *Asian Music* 32, no. 2 (Spring/Summer 2001): 93–118.

Chao, Mei-pa. "The Trend of Modern Chinese Music." *T'ien Hsia Monthly* 4, no. 3 (March 1937): 269–87.

Chao, Yuan-Ren, ed. *Anthology of New Poetry and Songs*. Shanghai: Commercial Press, 1926.

———. "Music." In *Symposium on Chinese Culture*, ed. Sophia Zen Chen, 82–96. Shanghai: China Institute of Pacific Relations, 1931.

———. "Tone, Intonation, Singing, Chanting, Recitation, Tonal Composition, and Atonal Composition in Chinese." In *For Roman Jakobson*, ed. Morris Halle, 52–59. The Hague: Mouton, 1956.

Chase, Gilbert. *America's Music*. 3rd ed. Urbana: University of Illinois Press, 1987.

Chen, Gang. "Zaochuen Eryue Liuse Xin [New Willows in Early February]." *Peoples Music* 11, no. 12 (1979): 68–70, 88.

Chen, Lan-Gu, ed., trans. "Weilai Shijie Yinyue De Zhuliu [The Main Stream for the Future of World Music]." *Zhong Bao* [*The Chinese Journal*] (September 23, 1982).

Chew, Seok-kwei. "An Analysis of the Selected Music of Chou Wen-Chung in Relation to Chinese Aesthetics." Ph.D. diss., New York University, 1990.

Chinese Academy of the Arts, Institute of Music Research. *Zhongguo Yinyue Qikan Bianmu Huilu: 1906–1949* [*Publications of Chinese Musical Journals: 1906–1949*]. Beijing: Publications of Arts and Culture, 1990.

Chinese Academy of Social Sciences, Institute of Chinese Classical Literature Research. *Tangshi Xuanzhu* [*Selected and Annotated T'ang Poems*]. 2 vols. Beijing: Beijing Publications, 1978.

Chou, Wen-Chung. "Varèse: A Sketch of the Man and His Music." *Musical Quarterly* 52, no. 2 (1966): 168.

———. "Single Tones as Musical Entities: An Approach to Structured Deviations in Tonal Characteristics." *American Society of University Composers Proceedings* III (August 1968): 86–97.

———. "East and West, Old and New." *Asian Music* 1 (1968–1969): 19–22.

———. "Asian Concepts and Twentieth-Century Western Composers." *The Musical Quarterly* (April 1971): 211–29.

———. "Asian Music and Western Composition." In *Dictionary of Contemporary Music*, 23–29. New York: Dutton, 1974.

———. Review of *The Lore of the Chinese Lute: An Essay in the Ideology of the Ch'in* by Robert Hans Van Gulik. *The Musical Quarterly* (April 1974): 301–5.

———. "Chinese Historiography and Music: Some Observations." *The Musical Quarterly* (April 1976): 218–40.

———. "Asian and Western Music: Influence or Confluence?" *Asian Culture Quarterly* (Winter 1977): 60–66.

———. "Toward a Re-Merger in Music." In *Contemporary Composers on Contemporary Music*, ed. Elliot Schwartz and Barney Childs, 309–15. New York: Da Capo Press, 1978.

———. "A Visit to Modern China." *The World of Music* 20, no. 2 (1978): 40–42.

———. "*Ionization*: The Function of Timbre in Its Formal and Temporal Organization." In *The New World of Edgard Varèse: A Symposium*, ed. Sherman Van Solkema, 27–74. New York: ISAM Dept of Music, Brooklyn College, Central University New York, 1979.

———. "Wode Zuoqu Guannian Yu Jingyan [My Compositional Concepts and Experiences]." *Xin Xiang Yixun* [*New Trends in the Arts*] (January 10–16, 1982): 6–8.

———. "Edgard Varèse: The Legacy of a Seminal Genius," *Symphony Magazine* 34, no. 6 (1983): 42–43.

———. "The Aesthetic Principles of Chinese Music: A Personal Quest." *Canzona* 7, no. 24 (June 1986): 74–78.

———. Letter to Tim Wilson, September 26, 1988.

———. "U.S.-China Arts Exchange: A Practice in Search of a Philosophy." In *Intercultural Music Studies Volume 2, Music in the Dialogue of Cultures: Traditional Music and Cultural Policy*, ed. Max Peter Baumann, 153–73. Berlin: Florian Boetzel Edition, 1990.

———. "Asian Aesthetics and World Music." (Originally a paper delivered at ACL Conference and Festival in Hong Kong.) In *New Music in the Orient: Essays on Composition in Asia Since World War II*, ed. Harrison Ryker. Buren, the Netherlands: Frits Knuf Publishers, 1991.

———. Interviewed by Peter Chang on November 8, 1991, New York (unpublished).

———. "Asian Music Today? What is it?" Paper delivered at the Inter-art Festival Center for the 1996 Budapest Spring Festival and Conference on the non-European Musical Traditions and Western-type Twentieth-Century Music, 1996.

———. "Sights and Sounds: Remembrances." www.chouwenchung.org, 1998.

———. "Music—What Is Its Future?" Paper delivered at the University of San Diego, April 21, 2001.

———. "Beyond Identity." Unpublished keynote speech, Asian Music Festival (Asian Composers League and Japanese Federation of Composers), Tokyo, Japan, September 18, 2003.

———. Interviewed by Richard Pittman (conductor, New England Philharmonic and the Boston Musica Viva), New York (unpublished), February 5, 2004.

———. Interviewed by Mark Steinberg (first violin, The Brentano String Quartet), New York (unpublished), February 27, 2004.

———. "Wenren and Culture." In *Locating East Asia in Western Art Music*, 208–20. Middletown, Conn.: Wesleyan University Press, 2004.

———. Correspondences with Peter Chang, April 18 and 21, May 4, 7, and 11, 2004.

Cohn, Arthur. "Very Special: The Music of Chou Wen-Chung." *The American Record Guide* 36 (September–August 1969/1970): 886–87.

Daniel, Oliver. *Stokowski: A Counterpoint of View*. New York: Dodd, Mead, and Co., 1982.

Deng, Chang-Guo. "Wo Suo Zhidao De Zhou Wen-Zhong [My Impression of Zhou Wen-Zhong]." *Gong Xue Yuekan* [*Gong Xue Monthly*] (March 1966).

Dewoskin, Kenneth. *Song for One or Two: Music and Concept of Art in Early China*. Michigan Papers in Chinese Studies, no. 42. Ann Arbor: Center for Chinese Studies, University of Michigan, 1982.

Downes, Edward. "Work by Chinese Has Its Premiere." *New York Times*, Monday, February 4, 1957, 15.

Everett, Yayoi Uno, and Frederick Lau, eds. *Locating East Asia in Western Art Music.* Middletown, Conn.: Wesleyan University Press, 2004.

Fallers, Lloyd. "The Predicament of the Modern African Chief: An Instance from Uganda." *American Anthropologist* 57 (1955): 290–305.

Feliciano, Francisco. *Four Asian Contemporary Composers: The Influence of Tradition in Their Works.* Philippines: New Day Publisher, 1983.

Fitzgerald, Charles P. *The Chinese View of Their Place in the World.* London: Oxford University Press, 1966/1967.

Frankenstein, Alfred. "Symphonic Novelties Not So Daring." *San Francisco Chronicle,* Saturday, November 21, 1953, 11.

———. "Symphony Plays Work by Chinese." *San Francisco Chronicle,* December 4, 1959, 43.

———. "The Sound World of Chou Wen-Chung." *High Fidelity/Musical America* 20 (July–November 1970): 84.

Gillespie, Don. "Chou Wen-Chung: A Meeting of East and West." *Peters Notes* 2, no. 1 (1997): 4, 7.

Gilman, Benjamin. "Hopi Songs." *Journal of American Ethnology and Archeology* 5 (1908).

———. "The Science of Exotic Music." *Science* 30 (1909): 532–35.

Goethe, Wolfgang von. *Die Metamorphose der pflanzen.* Berlin, 1924.

Graburn, Nelson. "Art and Acculturative Process." *International Social Science Journal* 21 (1969): 457–68.

Griffith, Paul. *Modern Music.* London: J. M. Dent and Sons Ltd., 1981.

Gu, Xian-Liang. "Dongxi Yinyue Zai He Liu Zhongde Dizhu—Zhou Wen-Zhong [Zhou Wen-Zhong: Important Promoter of East-West Musical Confluence]." *Gong Xue Monthly* (April 1966).

Gulik, Robert Hans Van. *The Lore of the Chinese Lute.* Tokyo: Sophia University, 1968.

Hamm, Charles. *Music in the New World.* New York: W. W. Norton, 1983.

Hampton, Barbara L. "A Revised Analytical Approach to Musical Processes in Urban Africa." *African Urban Studies* 6 (1980): 1–16.

Han, Guo-Huang. "Wu Zhou Wen-Zhong [Meeting Zhou Wen-Zhong]." *Ai Yue* [*Philharmonic*] (1968): 7.

———. "Titles and Program Notes in Chinese Musical Repertoires." *The World of Music* 27, no. 1 (1985): 68–77.

He, Jian-Jun. "Chou Wen-Chung's Cursive." DMA thesis, West Virginia University, 2000.

Herskovits, Melville. "Acculturation and the American Negro." *Southwestern Political and Social Science Quarterly* 8 (1927): 211–25.

———. "The Significance of the Study of Acculturation for Anthropology." *American Anthropologist* 39 (1937): 259–64.

———. "Problem, Method and Theory in Afroamerican Studies." *Afroamerica* I (1945): 5; also in *The New World of Negro,* 43–61. Bloomington: Indiana University Press, 1966.

——. *Man and His Works*. New York: Alfred A. Knopf, 1948.

——. *Acculturation: The Study of Culture Contact*. Reprint of 1938 edition. Gloucester, Mass.: Peter Smith, 1958.

Herskovits, Melville, and Richard Waterman. "Musica de Culto Afrobahiana." *Rvista
de Estudios Musicales* 1 (1949): 65–127.

Hitchcock, Wiley. *Music in the United States: A Historical Introduction*. 2nd ed. Englewood Cliffs, N.J.: Prentice-Hall, 1974.

Holland, Bernard. "Concert: New York City Symphony in Two Cultures." *New York
Times*, February 9, 1988.

Hornbostel, Eric M. von. "Review of Book on American Negro Songs." *International
Review of Missions* XV (1926): 748.

——. "African Negro Music." *Africa* 1 (1928): 30–62.

Huang, Zi. "Zen Yang Cai Ke Yi Chan Chu Wu Guo Min Zu Yin Yue [How to Develop
Our National Music]." *Chen Bao* [*Morning News*], Shanghai, October 21, 1934.

Hunter, Monica. "Methods of Study of Culture Contact." *Africa* 7 (1934): 335–50.

Ing, Benjamin Z. "Music Chronicle." *T'ien Hsia Monthly* IV, no. 1 (January 1937):
54–56.

——. Review of *Foundations of Chinese Musical Art* by John Hazedel Levis, *T'ien
Hsia Monthly* IV, no. 3 (March 1937): 317–18.

Israel, John. *Student Nationalism in China: 1927–1937*. Stanford: Stanford University
Press, 1966.

Jackson, George P. *White Spirituals from Southern Uplands*. Chapel Hill: University of
North Carolina Press, 1933.

——. *White and Negro Spirituals: Locust Valley*. New York: J. J. Augustin, 1943.

Jin, Jing-Fang, and Shao-Gang Lu. *Zhou Yi Quanjie* [*A Full Exposition of the I-Ching*].
2nd ed. Changchuen: Jilin University Press, 1991.

Jung, Meng-Yuan. "Lost Treasures Regained." *People's China* 2 (January 16, 1956): 9.

Kagan, Alan. "Music and the Hundred Flower Movement." *The Musical Quarterly* 49,
no. 4 (1963): 417–30.

Kandinsky, Wassily. *Concerning the Spiritual in Art, and Painting in Particular* (1912),
trans. Michael Sadler, ed. Francis Golffing, Michael Harrison, and Fernand Os-
tertag. New York: Wittenborn, Schultz, 1947.

——. "Reminiscences." In *Modern Artists on Modern Art: Ten Unabridged Essays*, ed.
Robert Herbert. Englewood Cliffs, N.J.: Prentice-Hall, 1964.

——. "Content and Form." In *Complete Writings on Art*. Vol. 1, and "Color Course
and Seminar." Vol. 2, ed. by Kenneth C. Lindsay and Peter Vergo, 501–4. Boston:
G. K. Hall and Co., 1982.

Kárpáti, János. "Non-European Influence on Occidental Music (A Historical Survey)." *The World of Music* 22, no. 2 (1990): 20–35.

Kartomi, Margret. "The Process and Results of Cultural Contact: A Discussion of
Terminology and Concepts." *Ethnomusicology* 25 (1981): 240.

Kastendick, Miles. Review of the January 6, 1961, New York Philharmonic Concert.
New York Journal-American (January 7, 1961).

Katz, Ruth. "The Singing of Baqqashot by Aleppo Jews." *ACTA Musicologica* 40 (1968): 65–85.

——. "Mannerism and Cultural Change: An Ethnomusicological Example." *Current Anthropology* 2, nos. 4–5 (1970): 465–75.

Kaufman, Robert. "Shona Urban Music and the Problem of Acculturation." *Yearbook of the IFMC* 4 (1973): 47–56.

Kerner, L. "Music: The Twain Meet." *The Village Voice* 38 (April 27, 1993): 94.

Kraft, Leo. *Gradus: An Integrated Approach to Harmony, Counterpoint, and Analysis.* New York: W. W. Norton & Co, 1976.

Kraus, Richard. *Pianos and Politics in China.* Oxford: Oxford University Press, 1989.

Kroeger, Karl. "Review of Scores." *Music Library Association Notes* 20, no. 2 (Winter–Fall 1962/1963): 406–7.

Kuckertz, J. "Reception of Classical Indian Music in Western Countries During the 20th Century." *Journal of the Indian Musicological Society* 7, no. 4 (1976): 5–14.

Kwan, Kenneth. "Chou Wen-Chung's *Echoes From the Gorge*: Chinese Wine in a Western Bottle, or What?" *Chinese Music* 18, no. 3 (1995): 56–59.

——. "Compositional Design in Recent Works by Chou Wen-Chung." Ph.D. diss., State University of New York at Buffalo, 1996.

Kyr, Robert. "Between the Mind and the Ear: Finding the Perfect Balance." *League-ISCM, Boston* (April 1990): 11–28.

Lai, Eric. "Toward A Theory of Pitch Organization: The Early Music of Chou Wen-Chung." *Asian Music* 25, nos. 1–2 (1993/1994): 177nn1–2.

——. "A Theory of Pitch Organization in the Early Music of Chou Wen-Chung." Ph.D. diss., Indiana University, 1995.

——. "Modal Formations and Transformations in the First Movement of Chou Wen-Chung's *Metaphors*." *Perspectives of New Music* 35 (Winter 1997): 153–85.

——. "The Evolution of Chou Wen-Chung's Variable Modes." In *Locating East Asia in Western Art Music*, 146–67. Middletown, Conn.: Wesleyan University Press, 2004.

Lange, Art. Record review article on the reissuing of Chou Wen-Chung's *Pien, Yu ko, Cursive, The Willows Are New*, and *Landscapes* on CD by CRI. *Fanfare* (March/April 1996): 148–49.

LaRue, Jan. "On Style Analysis." *Journal of Music Theory* VI (1962): 91.

——. *Guidelines for Style Analysis.* New York: Norton, 1970.

Lau, Frederick. "Music and Musicians of the Traditional Chinese Dizi in the People's Republic of China." DMA diss., University of Illinois, Urbana, Champaign, 1991.

——. "Fusion or Fission: The Paradox and Politics of Contemporary Chinese Avant-Garde Music." In *Locating East Asia in Western Art Music*, 22–39. Middletown, Conn.: Wesleyan University Press, 2004.

Lee, Joanna C. "Chou Wen-Chung." In *Grove Music Online*, ed. L. Macy, 2004. www.grovemusic.com (accessed March 2, 2005).

Leeuw, Ton de. "Questions, Ideas and Expectation: Premises and Aims of an East-West Experiment." *International Music Education* 7 (1980): 140–50.

Léger, Fernand. "Contemporary Achievement in Painting." In *Cubism*, ed. Edward Fry, with excerpts from documentary texts. New York: Oxford University Press, 1966.

Levis, John Hazedel. "The Musical Art of Ancient China." *T'ien Hsia Monthly* 1 (1935): 404–22.

———. *Foundations of Chinese Musical Art*. Peiping: Henri Vetch, 1936.

Liang, Bao-Er. "Zhou Wen-Zhong Zhili Liangdi Wenhua Goutong [Zhou Wen-Zhong's Efforts in Cultural Exchanges]." *Hong Kong Economic Journal* (January 11, 1988).

Lin, Qing-Xuan. "Zhou Wen-Zhong." *Shibao Xinzhi* [*News Gazette*] 112 (January 24, 1982): 42–45.

Lin, Shu-Mei. "Zhou Wen-Zhong Dailaide Shensi [Contemplating on Zhou Wen-Zhong's Ideas]." *Music and Audiophile* 4 (April 1988): 38–41.

Liu, Jing-Zhi, ed. *Zhongguo Xin Yinyueshi Lunji* [*Selected Writings on Modern Chinese Music History*]. Vol. 1. Hong Kong: The Asian Research Center, Hong Kong University, 1986.

———. *Zhongguo Xin Yinyueshi Lunji: 1920–45* [*Selected Writings on Modern Chinese Music History: 1920–45*]. Vol. 2. Hong Kong: The Asian Research Center, Hong Kong University, 1988.

———. *Zhongguo Xin Yinyueshi Lunji: 1945–76* [*Selected Writings on Modern Chinese Music History: 1945–76*]. Vol. 3. Hong Kong: The Asian Research Center, Hong Kong University, 1990.

Liu, Marjory Bong-ray. "Syncretism: An Aesthetic Approach to Chinese Arts." *Journal of Western Conference Association for Asian Studies* 2 (1976).

———. "Aesthetic Principles in Chinese Music." *The World of Music* 27, no. 1 (1985): 19–32.

Liu, Tian-Hua, ed. *Mei Lan-Fang Gequ Pu* [*Excerpts from the Favorite Arias of Peking Opera by Mei Lan-Fang*]. Peiping, 1930.

Liu, Zaisheng. "Ping Liu Jingzhi *Zhong Guo Xin Yin Yue Shi Lun*: Jian Lun Xin Yin Yue De Li Shi Guan" [Review of Liu Jingzhi's Book *A Theory of the History of New Chinese Music: Examining Its Historical View*]. *Zhongguo Yinyue Xue* [Journal of Chinese Musicology] 3 (1999): 64–76.

Lomax, Alan. *Folk Song Style and Culture*. Washington, D.C.: American Association for the Advancement of Science, 1968.

———. *Cantometrics*. Berkeley: University of California Press, 1976.

Lu, Nancy. "Asians Seek Important Place in Mainstream Music." *The China Post*, May 23, 1994, 11.

Lu, Si. "Mingzhen Guoji Yuetan De Zhongguo Zuoqujia—Zhou Wen-Zhong [A Famous Chinese Composer—Zhou Wen-Zhong]." *Aiyue* [*Philharmonic*] 4 (1966).

Ludlow, Lynn. "Chinese Poetry in Dance." *The Champaign-Urbana Courier*, March 16, 1959, 4.

Ma, Dong-Feng and Hai-Ming Sun. "Dangdai Zuoqujia Zhou Wen-Zhong Jiqi Zuopin [Contemporary Composer Zhou Wen-Zhong and His Works]." *Yinyue Shenghuo* [*The Musical Life*] 7 (1985): 30.

Malm, William P. "On the Nature and Function of Symbolism in Western and Oriental Music." *Philosophy East and West* (Honolulu) 19, no. 3 (1969): 235–46.

McBride, J. "Music Reviews" (works for clarinet and strings by Chou Wen-Chung and other composers). *Notes* 55 (June 1999): 1016–19.

McDougall, Bonnie S. *Mao Zedong's "Talks at the Yan'an Conference on Literature and Art": A Translation of the 1943 Text with Commentary.* Ann Arbor: University of Michigan Center for Chinese Studies, 1980.

Merriam, Alan. "The Use of Music in the Study of a Problem of Acculturation." *American Anthropologist* 57 (1955): 28–34.

———. *The Anthropology of Music.* Evanston: Northwestern University Press, 1964.

Metfessel, Milton. *Phonophotography in Folk Music: American Negro Songs in New Notation.* Chapel Hill: University of North Carolina Press, 1928.

Modi, Sorab. "The National Symphony's Oriental Tour-de-Force." *Symphony Magazine* (August/September 1983): 26–32.

Mootz, William. "Critics Hear Orchestra and Open Workshop." *The Courier Journal,* Louisville, Ky., October 7, 1955, section 1, 10.

———. "Concertmaster Kling Star As Soloist in Mendelssohn's Violin Concerto." *The Courier-Journal,* Louisville, Ky., December 8, 1960, 18.

Morton, Brian. "Chou Wen-Chung." In *Contemporary Composers.* Chicago: St. James Press, 1992, 181–82.

Myers, John. *The Way of the Pipa.* Kent, Ohio: Kent State University Press, 1992.

National Bureau of Rites and Music. *Li Yue Banyuekan* [*Rites and Music Bi-Weekly*] 1 (March 1947), 24 (February 1948).

———. *Li Yue* [*Rites and Music*] 1 (October 1945), new edition 1 (April 1948), new edition 3 (June 1948).

Needham, Joseph. *Science and Civilization in China.* Vol. 2. Cambridge, U.K.: Cambridge University Press, 1954.

Nettl, Bruno. "Ibo Songs from Nigeria, Native and Hybridized." *Midwest Folklore* 3 (1953): 237–42.

———. "Stylistic Change in Folk Music." *Southern Folklore Quarterly* 17 (1953): 216–29.

———. "Change in Folk and Primitive Music: A Survey of Methods and Studies." *Journal of the American Musicological Society* 8, no. 2 (1955): 101–9.

———. "Some Aspects of the History of World Music in the Twentieth Century: Questions, Problems, and Concepts." *Ethnomusicology* 22, no. 1 (1978): 133.

———, ed. *Eight Urban Musical Cultures.* Urbana: University of Illinois Press, 1978.

———. *The Study of Ethnomusicology.* Urbana: University of Illinois Press, 1983.

———. *Western Impact on World Music.* New York: Schirmer Books, 1985.

———. "World Music in the Twentieth Century: A Survey of Research on Western Influence." *ACTA Musicologica* 58, no. 2 (July–December 1986): 360–73.

———. "Recent Directions in Ethnomusicology." In *Ethnomusicology: An Introduction,* ed. Helen Myers. New York: Norton, 1992.

Nettl, Bruno, and Philip V. Bohlman, eds. *Comparative Musicology and Anthropology of Music: Essays on the History of Ethnomusicology*. Chicago: University of Chicago Press, 1991.

Oja, Carol. *Colin McPhee: A Composer in Two Worlds*. Washington, D.C.: Smithsonian Institution Press, 1990.

Ouellette, Fernand. *Edgard Varèse*. New York: Orion, 1968.

Pan-Chew, Shyhji, ed. *Chou Wen-Chung Music Festival, Special Album, 2003*, Taipei: Canada-Taiwan Music & Arts Exchange, 2004.

Parmenter, Ross. "Stokowski Conducts Contemporary Works." *New York Times*, December 4, 1958, 53.

Parsons, Elsie Clews. "Milta, Town of the Souls." In *University of Chicago Publications in Anthropology*. Chicago: University of Chicago Press, 1936.

Perloff, Nancy. "Klee and Webern: Speculations on Modernist Theories of Composition." *The Musical Quarterly* 69, no. 2 (1983): 190–91.

Perris, Arnold. "Music as Propaganda: Art at the Command of Doctrine in the People's Republic of China." *Ethnomusicology* (January 1983): 1–28.

Pian, Rulan Chao. *Sonq Dynasty Musical Sources and Their Interpretation*. Cambridge, Mass.: Harvard University Press, 1967.

Pousseur, Henri. "Stravinsky by Way of Webern: The Consistency of a Syntax." *Perspectives of New Music* 2 (1972): 13–51.

Powell, W. J. "Report of the Director." *19th Annual Report, Bureau of American Ethnology, for 1897–98*. Washington, D.C.: Bureau of American Ethnology, 1900.

Pulido, Esperanza. "Chou Wen-Chung." *Heterofonia* 9, no. 6 (1978): 10–15 (in Spanish).

Qiu, Qong-Sun. *Baishi Daoren Gequ Tongkao [A Comprehensive Investigation of Baishi Monk's Songs]*. Beijing: People's Music Publications, 1959.

Qiu, Ting. "Yinyue Chaoyue Dongxi Zhi Bian [Music Transcends East and West: An Argument]." *Minsheng Bao* (May 26, 1994): 15.

Rahn, Jay. *A Theory for All Musics: Problems and Solutions to the Analysis of Non-Western Forms*. Toronto: University of Toronto Press, 1983.

Redfield, Robert, and Melville Herskovits. "A Memorandum for the Study of Acculturation." *American Anthropologist* 38 (1935): 149–52.

Roberts, John Storm. *Black Music in Two Worlds*. New York: Praeger, 1972.

Rogers, Harold. "Opportunity Needed for New Works." *The Christian Science Monitor* (February 7, 1956): 10.

Ross, Alex. "Composers Orchestra Paints Sonic Landscapes." *New York Times*, January 13, 1993.

Salzman, Eric. *Twentieth-Century Music: An Introduction*. 2nd ed. Englewood Cliffs, N.J.: Prentice-Hall, 1974.

Saminsky, Lazare. *Music of Our Day: Essentials and Prophecies*. New York: Thomas Y. Crowell Co., 1932.

Schapera, I. "Field Methods in the Study of Modern Culture Contacts." *Africa* 8 (1935): 315–28.

Schoenberg, Harold. "Seven Modern Works Heard in South." *New York Times*, October 10, 1955, 31.

———. "Philharmonic Concert Is an Exotic Blend." *New York Times*, January 7, 1961, 13.

Schorske, Carl. *Fin-de-Siècle Vienna*. New York: Knopf, 1979.

Schrieke, B., ed. *The Effect of Western Influence on Native Civilizations of the Malay Archipelago*. Batavia, Java: Kolff, 1929.

Schwartz, Elliot, and Barney Childs, eds. *Contemporary Composers on Contemporary Music*. New York: Da Capo Press, 1978.

The Shanghai Almanac. "Zhong De Yinyuejie Juxing Zhongguo Gushi Yinyuehui [China-Germany Friendship Association and Association in Southeast Asian Research]," jointly sponsoring a concert featuring Chinese classical music and poetry. *Shanghai Almanac* (1935): 21.

Shelemay, Kay Kaufman, ed. *Cross-Cultural Musical Analysis* (the Garland Library of Readings in Ethnomusicology). Vol. 5. Reprint of articles published 1909–1980. New York: Garland, 1990.

Shen, Fu-Wei. *Zhongxi Wenhua Jiaoliu Shi* [*History of Cultural Exchanges between East and West*]. 3rd ed. Shanghai: Shanghai People's Publisher, 1988.

Signell, Karl. "The Modernization Process in Two Oriental Music Cultures: Turkish and Japanese." *Asian Music* VII, no. 2 (1976): 72–102.

Slawek, Stephen. "Ravi Shankar as Mediator between a Traditional Music and Modernity." In *Ethnomusicology and Modern Music History*, ed. Stephen Blum, Philip Bohlman, and Daniel Neuman, 161–81. Urbana: University of Illinois Press, 1992.

Slobin, Mark. "Micromusics of the West: A Comparative Approach." *Ethnomusicology* 36, no. 1 (1992): 1–88.

Slonimsky, Nicolas. "Chou Wen-Chung." *American Composers Alliance Bulletin* 9, no. 4 (1961): 2–9.

———. *Perfect Pitch*. Oxford: Oxford University Press, 1988.

Stevenson, Robert. *Music in Aztec and Inca Territory*. Berkeley: University of California Press, 1968.

Tang, Yongbao. "Chou Wen-Chung Zou Xiang 'Zai Rong He' De Chuang Zuo Li Lun Yu Shi Jian [Chou Wen-Chung's Development in His Compositional Theory of 'Musical Confluence' and Its Practice]." *Yinyue Yishu* [*The Musical Art: Journal of the Shanghai Conservatory of Music*] 3 (2003): 16–23. Based on the author's Ph.D. diss., The Central Conservatory of Music, Beijing, China.

Tcherepnine, Alexander. "Music in Modern China." *The Musical Quarterly* 21 (October 1935): 396.

Teng, Ssu-yü, and John K. Fairbank, eds. *China's Response to the West: A Documentary Survey 1839–1923*. Cambridge, Mass.: Harvard University Press, 1954.

Thomson, William. Review of *Sonic Design* by Robert Cogan. *Journal of Music Theory* 23 (1979): 125–34.

Tommasini, Anthony. "Calligraphy Is Reflected In a Premiere." *New York Times*, December 3, 1996, 16.

Treitler, Leo. "Structural and Critical Analysis." In *Musicology of the 1980s*, ed. Kern Holoman and Claude Palisca, 67–77. New York: Da Capo Press, 1982.

Trimble, Lester. "Composers, Conductors." *New York Herald Tribune*, January 25, 1954, 10.

——. "Records Review." *The Nation* 186, no. 21 (1958): 484.

Tsang, David. Program note for the performance of *Yu ko* together with other works on April 27, 1989, at Lila Acheson Wallare Auditorium, New York.

Turino, Thomas. "The History of a Peruvian Panpipe Style and the Politics of Interpretation." *Ethnomusicology and Modern Music History*. Urbana: University of Illinois Press, 1991.

Ulrich, Allan. "Bang-up Performance Showcases Percussion." *San Francisco Chronicle*, Wednesday, December 6, 2000, E1–3.

Varèse, Edgard. "'New Instruments and New Music' (1936) from 'The Liberation of Sound,'" ed. and ann. Chou Wen-Chung. *Perspectives of New Music* 1 (Fall–Winter 1966): 11–19.

——. "The Liberation of Sound." In *Contemporary Composers on Contemporary Music*, ed. Elliot Schwartz and Barney Child, 195–208. New York: Da Capo, 1978.

Varèse, Louise. *Looking Glass Diary*. New York: Norton, 1972.

Wachsmann, Klaus. "Criteria for Acculturation." Chap. 33 in *Report of the 8th Congress of the International Musicological society*, 139–49. Kassel: Bärenreiter, 1961.

Wang, P'u. *T'ang Hui Yao* [*Annals of the T'ang Dynasty*]. 2 vols. Shanghai: Shanghai Gu Ji Chubanshe, 1991.

Wang, Y. C. *Chinese Intellectuals and the West 1872–1949*. Chapel Hill: University of North Carolina Press, 1966.

Waterman, Christopher A. *Jùjú: A Social History and Ethnography of an African Popular Music*. Chicago: University of Chicago Press, 1990.

——. "Jùjú History: Toward a Theory of Sociomusical Practice." In *Ethnomusicology and Modern Music History*, 49–67. Urbana: University of Illinois Press, 1991.

Waterman, Richard. "African Influence on American Negro Music." In *Acculturation in the Americas*, 207–18. Sol Tex ed. Chicago: University of Chicago Press, 1952.

Watkins, Glenn. *Soundings: Music in the Twentieth Century*. New York: Schirmer Books, 1988.

Whately, Larry. Review of *Sonic Design* by Robert Cogan. *The American Music Teacher* 27, no. 1 (1977): 35–37.

Wolf, Edward. "Imagination in Music, Dance." *The Daily Illini*, March 17, 1959, 7.

Wolf, Eric. "Aspects of Group Relations in a Complex Society: Mexico." *American Anthropologist* 58 (1956): 1066.

Wong, Isabel K. F. "Geming Gequ: Songs for the Education of the Masses." In *Popular Chinese Literature and Performing Arts in the People's Republic of China, 1949–1979*, ed. Bonnie McDougall, 112–43. Berkeley: University of California Press, 1984.

———. "From Reaction to Synthesis: Chinese Musicology in the 20th Century." In *Comparative Musicology and Anthropology of Music*, ed. Bruno Nettl and Philip Bohlman, 37–56. Chicago: University of Chicago Press, 1991.

Wu, Hong. *Zi Yuan Tang Qinpu* [*Anthology of the Qin Pieces by the Zi Yuan Tang Printing House*]. 12 vols. Zi Yuan Tang Printing House, 1802.

Wu, Li-Pu. *Zhongguo Guohua Lun Yanjiu* [*A Study of the Chinese Classical Painting Theories*]. Beijing: Beijing University Press, 1985.

Wu, Mu. "Yishu Ji Zhongde Guoren Xinzuo [New Works of Chinese Composers for the Art Festival]." *Music and Audiophile* 39 (January 1985): 24–26.

Wu, Qi-Ji. "Meiji Huaren Zuoqujia Zhou Wen Zhong Tan Yinyue [American-Chinese Composer Professor Zhou Wen-Zhong on Music]." *Huaren* [*The Chinese*] 4 (from a clip, no dates given).

Xia, Cheng-Tao. "Baishi Daoren Gequ Kaozheng [Investigation of Baishi Monk's Songs]." *Yanjing Xuebao* [*Academic Journal of the Peking University*] (December 16, 1934).

Xu, Chang-Hui. "Chou Wen-Chung." In *Jin Dai Zhongguo Yinyue Shi Hua* [*A Talk on the History of Modern Chinese Music*], 127–39. Taipei: Chen Zhong Chubanshe, 1970.

Xu, Jian. *Qinshi Chubian* [*A History of the Qin: A Preliminary Study*]. 2nd. ed. Beijing: People's Music Publications, 1987.

Yang, Mu. "Academic Ignorance or Political Taboo? Some Issues in China's Study of Its Folk Song Culture." *Ethnomusicology* 38, no. 2 (Spring–Summer 1994): 303–20.

Yang, Schuman Chao. "Twentieth Century Chinese Solo Songs: A Historical and Analytical Study of Selected Chinese Solo Songs Composed or Arranged by Chinese Composers from the 1920s to the Present." Ph.D. diss., George Peabody College for Teachers, 1973.

Yang, Yin-Liu. "Recovering Ancient Chinese Music." *People's China* 2 (January 16, 1959): 26–30.

———. *Zhongguo Gudai Yinyue Shigao* [*Drafts of History of Chinese Music in Antiquity*]. 2 vols. Beijing: People's Music Publications, 1981.

Yang, Yin-Liu, and Fa-Lu Yin. *Song Jiang Bai-Shi Chuangzuo Gequ Yenjiu* [*A Study of Composed Songs by Jiang Bai Shi of Song Dynasty*]. Beijing: People's Music Publications, 1957.

Ye, Jin, and Pin-Fang Yao. "Xuange Shengsheng Zu Jiaoliu [Music and Songs for Promoting Exchange]." *People's Daily* (from a clip, no specific dates given), 1987.

Yuen, Godwin. "Stylistic Development in Chinese Revolutionary Song (1919–1948)." Chap. 5 in Ph.D. diss., Griffith University, Australia, 1989.

Zhang, He, ed. *Qin Xue Rumen* [*Elementary Learner's Book of Playing the Qin*], 1864.

Zhao, Qin. "Chou Wen-Chung: A Composer in Traditional Chinese Style." *Xin Xiang Yixun* [*New Trends in the Arts*] (December 20–26, 1981): 6–7.

Zhongguo Yinyue Cidian Editorial Committee. *Zhongguo Yinyue Cidian* [*Dictionary of Chinese Music*]. Beijing: People's Music Publications, 1984.

Zhou, Fan-Fu. "Fang Zhou Wen-Zhong [Interviewing Chou Wen-Chung]." *Music Audiophile* 81 (March 1981): 97.

Zhou, Jin-Min. "Timbre, Playing Technique and Structure: A Microscopic Analysis of Samples From Two Works for the Qin." *Progress Reports in Ethnomusicology* 3, no. 3 (1991): 437–88.

Zhou, Kai-Mo. "Guan Yu Kua Shi Ji De Yin Yue Tao Lun: Chou Wen-Chung Jiao Shou De Yo Lu He Qi Dai" [Forums on Twenty-first-century Music: Professor Chou Wen-Chung's Concerns and Hopes]. *Zhongguo Yinyue* [*Chinese Music*] 2 (1998): 13–15.

Newspapers containing reviews of Chou's *And the Fallen Petals*:
Berliner Morganpost, June 3, 1960.
Der Tagesspiegel, June 3, 1960.
Der Abend, June 2, 1960.
Der Kurier, June 2, 1960.
Der Tag, June 3, 1960.
Die Welt, March 26, 1958.
Hamburger Echo, March 26, 1958.
Telegraf, June 5, 1960.
Freie Presse, June 7, 1960.

The Chou Wen-Chung archive in Europe:
Paul Sacher Stiftung
Auf Burg
Münsterplatz 4
CH-4051 Basel
Switzerland
The contact person is Ms. Heidy Zimmermann, curator
Telephone: 41-61-269-66-44
Fax: 41-61-261-91-83
E-mail: heidy.zimmermann@unibas.ch

Index